SOCIAL JUSTICE
AND
THE CONSTITUTION OF INDIA
(With reference to SC's /ST's)

SOCIAL JUSTICE
AND
THE CONSTITUTION OF INDIA

(With reference to SC's /ST's)

C.B. Raju, M.A., LL.M., Ph. D.,

Reader, Faculty of Law
University of Mysore
Mysore (India)

SERIALS PUBLICATIONS
NEW DELHI

First Published 2007

ISBN: 81-8387-035-X

Published by

SERIALS PUBLICATIONS
4830/24, Prahlad Street, Ansari Road
Darya Ganj, New Delhi-110002 (India)
Phone : 23245225
Fax : 91-11-23272135
E-mail: serials@satyam.net.in

Dedicated
To My
Son Shashank
Daughter Priyanka

CONTENTS

PREFACE

This book is an attempt to highlight the plight of the members of Scheduled Castes and Scheduled Tribes in the rural areas of three Taluks in Mysore District. It provides an insight to the actual conditions of the people living in the condition of utter poverty, exploitation, degradation, humiliation, insecurity and ignorance of their rights. The approach adopted in this book is multi-disciplinary. The safeguards provided to the Scheduled Castes and Scheduled Tribes in the Constitution of India, various statutes and Government Regulations are dealt with in this book. The issues which are focused in this book are Constitutional and Statutory benefits and safeguards given to the members of SC/ST, their socio-economic conditions, State's concern towards these sections of the people, the judicial approach towards the Constitutional Provisions which provide rights and freedoms to these people. The book also focuses on how in Vedas and Upanishads, these sections of the society were treated with contempt. The enforcement and implementation of Constitutional rights and benefits of the Scheduled Castes and Scheduled Tribes are also dealt with. The reasons for why even after the completion of 55 years of Constitutional commencement, the socio-economic conditions of these people are not satisfactorily improved are also discussed. The empirical study on various problems of SC/ST will provide the factual reasons for non-implementation of Constitutional Mandates as well as Government Policies. It is hoped that this book would be more useful for policy implementers, administrators, Judicial officers and NGOs to understand the pathetic conditions of these people and to find out adequate remedies for their burning problems.

The restructuring and revising of my Ph. D. thesis has come out in the present form. In this connection, I sincerely thank all those who have extended their intellectual support and encouragement to complete this work. I always remember with gratitude my teachers whose discussions and deliberations, on the subject of Social Justice with reference to Scheduled Castes and Scheduled Tribes, have become more useful in shaping the thesis to the present form. I am also grateful to the Librarian and the authorities of the University for having assisted in all respects. I am also grateful to my Brother-in-Law, Prof. M. N. Javaraiah and my wife L. Hamsaveni for having extended moral supports all through my research work. I am grateful to Sri. S. K. Jha, Serials Publications, New Delhi, for publishing my thesis in the present impressive form.

C.B. Raju

1

INTRODUCTION

The struggle for "individual freedom" and "social justice" is as old as human existence. Although there is bound to be conflict between the claims of 'individual freedom' and those of 'social justice', these two values have assumed a significant place in the movement of Constitutionalism throughout the world during the 20th century. The reasons being that the Constitutionally guaranteed individual freedoms would lose much of their meaning, value and significance without adequate commitment to the Constitutional promise of social justice.

With the rapid growth of the concept of 'welfare state' in the 20th century, the conflict between the claims of these two competing values has become more pronounced and needed harmonisation. In view of this, realising that it would be impossible to give effect to these values in equal measures, different countries have adopted different Constitutional strategies to strike a harmonious balance between them. Thus, it may be seen that while the western capitalist countries have shaped their Constitutional strategies on the edifice of respect for individual freedoms, the socialist countries have pinned theirs to the bedrock of social justice. At the international level, ceaseless efforts are being made by the international community to harmonise the claims of the values of individual freedom and social justice by ushering in a new era of 'New International Economic Order'.

India, inspite of being a socialist democracy, opted for the liberal democratic model with due emphasis on the basic human rights. Consequently, the framers of the Indian Constitution attempted to strike a balance between the claims of the individual freedom and social justice by incorporating the 'individual freedom' in part III titled as 'Fundamental Rights' and the 'social justice' in part IV titled as 'Directive Principles of State Policy'. In this work, an attempt has been made to identify the Constitutional bottlenecks that have stood in the way of actualisation of the Constitutional goal of social justice enshrined in the 'Preamble' of the Constitution of India and to assess the actual position of their socio, economic and political situations. Besides, an attempt has also been made to trace the historical evolution of caste system, which is responsible for inequality, injustice, and discrimination between the haves and have-nots. In this author work the has confined his discussion on 'Social Justice as contemplated under the Constitution of India with special reference to the Scheduled Castes and Scheduled Tribes'.

MEANING OF THE TERM 'SOCIAL JUSTICE

The term 'social justice' may be defined as the right of the weak, aged, destitute, poor, women, children and other under-privileged persons to the protection of the State against the ruthless competition of life. It gives the necessary adventitious aids to the under-privileged so that they may have the equal opportunity with the more advanced sections of the society in the race of life. In other words, it is the balancing wheel between the 'haves and have-nots'. The concept of 'social justice' has emerged from the heritage of social injustice and it seeks to remove social disability by birth resulting in social and economic inequality. It ensures equality of status, equality of opportunity and developmental facilities to all. It has an important social content intended to promote public welfare. It not only provides for a just society, but also removes all patent sources of disunity and disharmony among the people. Thus social justice is of great value in providing a stable society and securing the unity of India.[1]

It may be said that 'social justice' is an art, which implies 'just, fair and reasonable' guidance to all the dispensers that "justice-according to law is necessary in society to establish some accepted standards of the common good". In *Prakash Cotton Mills V. Bombay*, Chief Justice Chagla said that 'social justice was hard to define, but submitted that court should import its own ideas of social justice in interpreting statutory provisions; social justice was an objective of the Constitution and it was an inarticulate major premise which was personal and individual to every court and every judge, depending on the judge's outlook on life and society; and laws cannot be interpreted without reference to social justice to the achievement of which our country was pledged'.

Justice Krishna Iyer is of the view that, 'social justice' in our socialist republic is 'socio-economic revolution in the current miasmic milieu'. He further explains the term 'social justice' as under:

> "The vice of social inequality assumes a particularly reprehensible form in relation to the backward classes and communities which are treated as Untouchables; and so, the problem of social justice is as urgent and important in India as is the problem of economic justice....... I am using the term 'social justice' in a comprehensive sense so as to include both economic justice and social justice. The concept of social justice thus takes within its sweep the objective of removing all inequalities and affording equal opportunities to all citizens in social affairs as well as economic activities."

According to former Chief Justice of India, K. Subba Rao, the word 'social justice has two-fold meaning. He said:

> "....... The expression 'social justice' has a limited as well as a wider meaning. In its limited sense it means the rectification of injustice in the personal relations of the people. In its larger sense it seeks to remove the imbalances in the political, social and economic life of the people. Social Justice is to be understood in the latter sense. As the three activities are inter connected, there cannot be social justice even in its limited sense, unless the society progresses in all directions. In short, social justice helps to bring about a just society...........".

This shows that, 'social justice' is a balancing wheel between the haves and have-nots. It is not aimed to pull down the advanced sections of society but only to uplift the backward sections thereof without unduly and unreasonably affecting the interests of the haves. It only prevents unjust enrichment at the expense of the under-privileged sections of the society. Besides, it ensures balanced development between rich and poor, equal opportunity for the under-privileged in public employment and education in various public institutions. The main object of this concept of 'social justice' is to transcend the welfare ideology of capitalist theory into the egalitarian goal of socialist system wherein there is a scope for upliftment and balanced development of every section of society. It disallows unjust enrichment and protects against undeserved wants. In short, it may be said that social justice means treating a human being as a human being. It includes equality of treatment, equal opportunities for betterment and equality of status.

NEED FOR THE PRESENT STUDY

The present study aims at analysing in a comprehensive manner, the problems, policies and issues pertaining to the development of the weaker sections of the society both in the urban as well as rural areas. There is a need to find out why even after 50 years of independence and the Constitution of India came into operation, the problems of the depressed classes including the Scheduled Castes and Scheduled Tribes have not been solved fully by the State. Besides, the study also focuses on Dr. Ambedkar's contribution for the upliftment of Untouchables and the depressed classes. Ambedkar's vision was to have an egalitarian society wherein there would be no injustice, inequality and social evils like Untouchability. He wanted to secure social justice to those people who were subjected to humiliation, torture, injustice and inequality by the caste Hindus. The study also focuses on the various Constitutional provisions which provide social, economic, and political justice to the Scheduled Castes and Scheduled Tribes.

DEGRADATION OF STATUS

To understand the status of Untouchables or the Scheduled Castes and Scheduled Tribes, who were considered as inferior to all other castes, we have to understand the nature and function of the caste system in the Hindu society. Caste has remained, since ages, as one of the exclusive characteristics of the Indian society particularly of the Hindu social system. It divides the people into inferior and superior castes and accords them lower and higher statuses respectively. It has also divided the Hindus into four major caste groups; Brahmins (priestly class), Kshatriya (warrior caste), Vaishyas (trading class), and Ati-Shudras or Untouchables (service caste). These have been arranged in a hierarchical social order with the Brahmins at the top followed by the Kshatriyas, Vaishyas, and Shudras. But later, Ati-Shudras or Untouchables were included to this social order placing them in the last category. Within each of these five major castes, there are innumerable sub-castes placed one over the other. Each caste in the past was supposedly associated with a particular occupation, which in turn determined the social and economic status of its members. While the Brahmins were considered to be the priests, teachers and advisors, the Kshatriyas were regarded as warriors or protectors or rulers. Similarly, the Vaishyas were considered as traders and the Shudras as cultivators and manual labourers. Untouchables were assigned menial and defiling occupations such as sweeping, scavenging, removing night soil etc. Besides, in the past, changing one's occupation from the given one was difficult and often discouraged. The other characteristics of the caste system such as endogamy, commensality, purity, and pollution were strictly observed and a few of these are observed even today. All these have cumulatively contributed to the degraded status of the Untouchables.

There are various historical reasons why the Untouchables or the Scheduled Castes and Scheduled Tribes have been socially degraded. For instance, the Racial Theory of Stanley Rice maintains that the present day Scheduled Castes and Scheduled Tribes are the descendants of the Indian aboriginals who were conquered and enslaved by Dravidians and Aryans and were reduced to assume the menial occupations. But Ambedkar rejected this view and states that there is no racial difference between the Untouchables and the Hindus, both of them belong to the same race. Ambedkar said, 'caste system is a result of super - imposition of endogamy over exogamy and there is nothing divine in its creation. The laws of Manu laid down in his Manusmriti were one sided as it extends undue support to the first three varnas and opposes social justice to the people of the fourth varna in the varna system. Manu does not allow the Shudras to perform sacraments and sanyasas, which sanctify the body and purify the sins committed. He prevents the Shudras from settling within the main village boundary but only at the outskirts.

Besides, Shudras were denied access to education in the past, which is a pre-requisite for the upliftment of every individual and community. They were not allowed to hear the Vedas, which was the only source of knowledge in the ancient time. Moreover, Brahmins alone had the right to teach the Vedas. The Shudras who attempted to study were dealt with inhuman indignities. It is stated that a "Shudra trying to hear the Vedic texts shall have his ears filled with molten tin or lac; if he recites the Veda, his tongue shall be cut off, and if he remembers it, he shall be dismembered. If he assumes a position of equality with the caste Hindus, he shall receive corporal punishment".[2] These were the laws that governed the social ranks of the four varnas which kept the Shudras always below the ranks of others.

The laws of Manu governing the social status of the Ati-shudras, or the panchamas (the fifth varna) or the chandalas or the Untouchables were inhuman. Some of these laws have direct bearing on the social degradation of the chandalas. For example, the Verse No.VIII, 281 of the Manusmriti declares, "A man of the lowest class (chandalas), who shall insolently place himself on the same seat with the upper caste, shall either be banished with a mark on his hidden parts, or the King shall cause a gash to be made on his buttock".[3] It also says that 'one who has touched a chandala must immediately bathe with his cloths on'.

The degraded social status of the Untouchables or Scheduled Castes and Scheduled Tribes is evident from the terms used to identify them. As early as nineteenth century, Jyotirao Phule used the term Dalit to describe them as the most oppressed and broken victims of the caste-ridden society. In the Vedas they had been described as 'Dasa' and 'Dasyu' depicting their unique dark colour complexion, which was considered to be inferior to a relatively fair complexion of the Aryans. They had also been described as 'Panchama', those forming the fifth Varna as Avarna i.e., people without Varna and thus inferior to those having Varna. The term Ati-Shudras depicts that they were below the status of the Shudras.

The social disabilities of the Untouchables or the Scheduled Castes and Scheduled Tribes were glaringly manifested at the community level where the services of community priests, barbers and washermen were denied to them. They were prohibited from walking through residential streets of the caste Hindus. Besides, they were prevented from bringing water from public wells and ponds, using public roads, streets, bathing ghats, burial and cremation grounds etc. They were also prohibited from using umbrellas, wearing sandals or foot wears. They were not allowed to enter the places of worship, hotels and restaurants to eat. They were not allowed to take out procession even during the auspicious occasions like wedding and religious festivals in the public roads. These practices continued till recently and continues in some places even today. In recent days, there were instances in which the Dalits or the Scheduled Castes and Scheduled Tribes were forced to eat human excreta and drink urine for participating in human rights activities. These inhuman treatments are meted out to them by the caste Hindus[4]. Such abominable practices continued against the Untouchables or the Scheduled Castes and Scheduled Tribes for centuries by the caste Hindus. Even today the social stigma attached to these people has not been removed fully by the State.

DEPRIVATION OF POWER

The problem that is faced by the Untouchables or the Scheduled Castes and Scheduled Tribes is their state of powerlessness. The power that could have ensured them economic independence and physical security, the power that could have protected their self-respect and dignity and the power that could have assured them equal opportunity in all spheres of their life is the power that they have been deprived of. Their powerlessness can be seen in terms of their deprivation of economic and political power.

DEPRIVATION OF ECONOMIC POWER

The deprivation of economic power of the Scheduled Castes and Scheduled Tribes or the Untouchables is not a recent development, but it has been in existence since Vedas. Manusmriti also depicts what should be the economic status of the untouchables, how should they earn their livelihood? Hinduism denies freedom of avocation, as the occupation of each caste being preordained, it has no relation to individual's capacity or to his inclination. By declaring that Shudra is born to serve the higher classes, Manu directs the king to see that all castes including Shudra do discharge their appointed tasks. Besides, Hinduism leaves no scope for the Shudras to accumulate wealth. Manu says " No collection of wealth must be made by a Shudra even though he be able to do it, for a

Shudra who has acquired wealth gives pain to Brahmana". Manu insists that "Shudra shall be servile, unfit for office, without education, without property and as a contemptible person, his personal property shall always be liable to be conscripted".[5]

This shows that the Shudras were not allowed to earn wealth vis-a-vis the caste Hindus. They were all assigned filthy, defiling and menial jobs with meagre income. They were meant for sweeping, cleaning streets, scavenging and removing dirty things. As a result, the Untouchables experienced acute poverty and were forced to depend on the mercy of the caste Hindus for their survival.

DEPRIVATION OF POLITICAL POWER

Throughout the history, the Untouchables were deprived of political power, which made them weak to protest against all indignities inflicted on them by the caste Hindus. Due to the lack of political power Untouchables or the Scheduled Castes and Scheduled Tribes seldom have had the courage to protest against the heinous crimes heaped on them by the caste Hindus. They could not get political power because they are scattered all over India, mostly in villages, towns and cities. Due to small in number in different villages, they could not fight for their political power. But the situation is different in urban areas where they are in a way socially and economically better off. Dr. Ambedkar is the champion to secure political power to the Scheduled Castes and Scheduled Tribes by demanding for 'right to vote' in the Constituent Assembly. He contended that unless political power is given to the Untouchables, their social and economic conditions cannot be improved. Therefore when the 'People's Representation Act' was enacted, right to vote and contest in the election was conferred to all citizens including Scheduled Castes and Scheduled Tribes.

CONSTITUTIONAL PROTECTIONS

The framers of the Constitution of India have provided a number of Constitutional safeguards to the Scheduled Castes and Scheduled Tribes. Being the architect and leader of the downtrodden, Ambedkar was able to get enshrined a number of provisions in the Constitution in favour of Scheduled Castes and

Scheduled Tribes. Some people call the act of providing certain exclusive special provisions in the Constitution for the Scheduled Castes and Scheduled Tribes as 'compensatory discrimination', others call it 'positive discrimination' or 'reverse discrimination' and some others term it as 'preferential treatment'.[6] The act of treating the Scheduled Castes and Scheduled Tribes as a special category is Constitutionally valid under Article 46 of the Directive Principles of the State Policy in part IV of the Indian Constitution.

Following are the specific Constitutional provisions guaranteed for safeguarding the socio, economic and political interests of the Scheduled Castes and Scheduled Tribes. For the purpose of protecting the interests of Scheduled Castes and Scheduled Tribes from all forms of social discrimination, the practice of Untouchability has been legally abolished under Article 17 of the Constitution. Accordingly, the Untouchability (Offences) Act, 1955 was passed, where under this Act, an offender could be fined upto Rs. 600/- or could be subjected to imprisonment. To enlarge the scope and to make the provisions still more stringent, the Act was subsequently amended in November 1976 and was renamed as the Protection of Civil Rights Act, 1976 (PCR Act). The cases filed under the PCR Act are cognisable and non-compoundable offences. As the Act failed to regulate the offences committed under this Act, as the punishment prescribed under this Act was less severe and not rigorous, as the offenders used to go scot free, the Parliament passed another Act called, 'The Scheduled Castes and Scheduled Tribes' (Prevention of Atrocities) Act, 1989. Under this Act certain offences were recognised as cognizable and non-compoundable. They are;

- Forcing any of the members of the Scheduled Castes and Scheduled Tribes to drink or eat obnoxious substances.
- Dumping excreta or waste matters in their premises or neighbourhood.
- Wrongful occupation of the land belonging to Scheduled Castes and Scheduled Tribes.
- Keeping Scheduled Castes and Scheduled Tribes as bonded labourers.
- Intimidating them during voting.

- Causing public humiliation to Scheduled Castes and Scheduled Tribes, intending to outrage the modesty of women belonging to this group, and exploiting them sexually.
- Denying the customary rights and forcing the members of the Scheduled Castes and Scheduled Tribes to live outside the town or village.

Any offence committed under this Act will be seriously taken note of and offenders shall be punished with an imprisonment of not less than six months extendable upto five years with fine. Offences of custodial rape, high way robbery and house breaking carry a maximum punishment of 10 years imprisonment under this Act.

The above provisions aim at protecting the self-respect and dignity of the Scheduled Caste and Scheduled Tribe. It helps them to stand on their own and protect themselves against all atrocities meted out to them by others. Besides, as nearly 83% of the bonded labourers belong to Scheduled Castes and Scheduled Tribes, the bonded labour system was formally abolished under the 'Bonded Labour System' (Abolition) Act, 1976. The Ministry of Information and Broadcasting through its various communication network, machineries like All India Radio, Doordarshan kendras, Press Information Bureau etc, have carried out a number of programmes highlighting the evils of Untouchability, caste discriminations, and atrocities on Scheduled Castes and Scheduled Tribes. Various Newspapers, Journals, and magazines have also involved in the task of creating awareness among the Scheduled Castes and Scheduled Tribes regarding their Constitutional protections and benefits.

In spite of legal abolition and a number of penal Acts, Untouchability is still practiced in many places. Although there is a marginal decline in the commission of atrocities on the Scheduled Castes and Scheduled Tribes, yet these atrocities are still continuing more in rural areas than in urban areas even today.

Another Constitutional safeguard provided to secure social justice to Scheduled Castes and Scheduled Tribes within the framework of the Constitution of India is the 'Reservation Policy'. This was Constitutionally guaranteed in 1950 with a view to ensuring opportunities for the Scheduled Castes and Scheduled

Tribes both in the field of public education and employment. The reservation policy has three important objectives;

1. Educational reservation ensuring admission to Scheduled Caste and Scheduled Tribe candidates in all educational institutions including engineering and medical colleges.
2. Job reservation ensuring their representation in all government departments and other public sector undertakings.
3. Political reservation ensuring their representation in Lok Sabha at the centre and Vidhana Sabhas at the State[7].

To ensure proper representation of Scheduled Caste and Scheduled Tribe candidates in all these three areas, under Article 338 of the Constitution, a commissioner for the Scheduled Castes and Scheduled Tribes is appointed to monitor all matters relating to these areas. Recently a Commission for Scheduled Castes and Scheduled Tribes was set up to investigate the problems of Scheduled Castes and Scheduled Tribes in various fields. According to the policy of reservation, Scheduled Castes and Scheduled Tribes are entitled for 15% and 7.5% (together 22.5%) reservation respectively in each of the above-mentioned areas. These are the important Constitutional protections provided to Scheduled Castes and Scheduled Tribes in the Constitution of India.

The objective of the study is to find out the actual application of various provisions of the Indian Constitution to secure social justice to the Untouchables i.e., Scheduled Castes and Scheduled Tribes. In the present welfare state, how are the problems of Scheduled Castes and Scheduled Tribes are being solved by the government in accordance with the Constitutional mandate? What are the measures that are being undertaken by the State to remove various disabilities of Scheduled Castes and Scheduled Tribes? The present study is also confined to the socio-economic and political problems of the Scheduled Castes and Scheduled Tribes. For this purpose, as a sample survey, three important taluks have been selected in the Mysore District, i.e., T.N. Pura, Hunsur, and Mysore. It is required to probe the various disabilities of the Scheduled Castes and Scheduled Tribes. It is also to be probed whether the Constitutional benefits given to Scheduled Castes and Scheduled

Tribes are reaching them properly. Besides, it is to be investigated whether the Scheduled Castes and Scheduled Tribes are still frequently subjected to atrocities, humiliation, degradation and Untouchability. It is important to know how far our Constitutional provisions secure safety and protections to these people.

The present study also focuses on how far our laws have been able to achieve the goals enshrined in the preamble to our Constitution i.e.,

- *Justice;* socio, economic, and political,
- *Liberty;* of thought, expression, belief, and faith,
- *Equality;* of status and opportunity

If the goals are not properly achieved even after 50 years of independence, what could be the reasons for this? It is also to be probed as to how far Scheduled Castes and Scheduled Tribes are participating in policy decisions that are undertaken in the Government. Besides, to achieve social justice and to remove all disabilities of these people, how far quota reservation helps them. It is also required to find out whether the Constitutionally conferred privileges are being utilised only by the elites among the Scheduled Castes and Scheduled Tribes or they are being shared equally among all. The idea is to find out why majority of the Scheduled Castes and Scheduled Tribes are still living below the poverty line, and are subjected to many disabilities, like Untouchability, degradation, inequality and injustice even though there are many legislations and enactments which protect their interest, and many welfare schemes and programmes that are being undertaken by the State to uplift these people. Besides, an attempt is also made to find out the extent of awareness of Scheduled Castes and Scheduled Tribes in relation to their Constitutional privileges and benefits conferred to them.

The present study is based upon both philosophical and empirical study. Intensive library research has been made to find out the reasons for the emergence of caste system in India. The researcher has relied on the secondary sources for highlighting the problems of untouchables or the Shudras from the time of Vedas till the constitution of India came into being. Various celebrated decisions of the Supreme Court of India and various High Courts have been used to discuss and to deliberate on the problems of Untouchables i.e. Scheduled Castes and Scheduled Tribes.

To find out the present socio and economic conditions of Scheduled Castes and Scheduled Tribes, Mysore district has been selected in which three taluks are chosen for my empirical study. They are T.N.Pura, Hunsur, and Mysore. In each of these taluks 10% of the villages have been selected for my empirical study. The total number of villages selected for my present study are 30 villages that consist of 600 respondents. This has been done as a sample survey to study the socio, economic and political conditions of the Scheduled Castes and Scheduled Tribes population living in these villages. As the social aspect is directly associated with the economic and political aspects, all the three factors are taken into consideration for my present study. The reasons for choosing the above three taluks are;

(a) All the three taluks are sensitive to the caste issues and prone to caste violence.

(b) The researcher is well familiar not only with the geographical location of these taluks but also the socio, economic and political conditions of Scheduled Castes and Scheduled Tribes and the language spoken by them i.e., Kannada.

(c) The researcher has intimate contact with these people as he often works with various Non- governmental organisations for the development of Scheduled Castes and Scheduled Tribes population in these taluks.

The introductory chapter focuses on the importance of the study, objectives of the study and the methodology employed to collect data relating to the socio-economic and political conditions of the Scheduled Castes and Scheduled Tribes. The second chapter deals with the historical evolution of caste system, which was responsible for the stratification of people into four varnas, i.e., Brahmanas, Kshatriyas, Vaishyas and Shudras on the functional basis. The third chapter contemplates on the origin of Untouchability. In this chapter, how the concept of Untouchability has emerged in the Hindu religion and what are the factors responsible for the emergence of Untouchability have been discusse. This chapter also focuses on the nature of 'Untouchability', the problems of Untouchables, and various attempts made to eradicate this social evil. The fourth chapter deals with the various Constitutional schemes and provisions provided under the Indian Constitution for securing justice to Scheduled Castes and Scheduled Tribes including socio, economic and political justice, equality of status and opportunity, liberty of thought, worship, belief, and various judicial responses. The fifth chapter focuses on the socio-economic conditions of Scheduled Castes and Scheduled Tribes-a case study of Mysore District. For this purpose, required statistics and data have been collected from three important taluks coming within the jurisdiction of Mysore District. An empirical study has been made to highlight the socio, economic and political conditions of Scheduled Castes and Scheduled Tribes relating to the above three taluks. The last and concluding chapter presents the findings, suggestions in respect of the actual working of the Constitutional mandates and provisions for the uplift of Scheduled Castes and Scheduled Tribes in India.

NOTES

1. P. Venugopal, *"Social Justice and Reservation"*, p. 2, 1990.
2. Gautama Dharmasutra, XII, 7.
3. Dr. B.R. Ambedkar, *"Writings and Speeches of Ambedkar"*, 1987.
4. The week, Oct. 1987, & Hindustan Times, May 24, 1988.
5. Opp. Cit. Note 3.
6. Articles 15 (4) and 16 (4).
7. Articles 330 and 332 respectively.

2

EVOLUTION OF CASTE SYSTEM –A HISTORICAL STUDY

"The caste system prevents common activity and by preventing it, it has prevented the Hindus from becoming a society with a unified life and consciousness of its own being. There is only individual share or part in the associated activity".

—B.R. Ambedkar

INTRODUCTION

One of the important burning social problems in India since several centuries is the problem of Injustice. The concept of 'Injustice' and 'Inequality' can be traced back to Vedic period. In this period, there were two varnas namely Arya Varna and Dasa Varna. But the society was divided into three orders: Brahma (Priests), Kshatra (Warriors) and Vis (Common people). There was no mentioning of the fourth order, that is, Shudra, though there was a reference to groups despised by the Aryans, like Ayogya, Chandala and Nishad, etc, in the Rig Veda [written in about 4000 B.C.]. But, during the closing period of the Vedic age, the Varna (the classes or castes) and 'Ashrama' (the four orders or stages of life) are the dominant features of the society. Grihya-sutra and Dharma-sutras were compiled during the first part of this period when the rules of castes and orders, domestic rites, ceremonies, general behaviour and customs were in prevalence.

Kautilya, in his "Arthashastra", has beautifully put in an analytical manner, the duties of the different castes as mentioned in the Dharma-sutras. He enumerates the duties of the Brahmins as;

(a) Adhyayana [study]
(b) Adhyapana [teaching]
(c) Yagna [worship]
(d) Yajana [officiating at worship]
(e) Dana [giving gifts] and
(f) Pratigraha [accepting gifts]

He enumerates the duties of Kshatriyas as;

(a) Adhyayana
(b) Yajana
(c) Dana
(d) Sastrajiva [profession of arms as source of livelihood] and
(e) Bhutarakshana [protection of living beings]

The duties of the Vaishyas are;

(a) Adhyayana
(b) Yajana
(c) Dana
(d) Krishi [agriculture]
(e) Pashupalya [cattle rearing] and
(f) Vanijya [trade];

The functions entrusted to the Shudras are;

(a) Dvijati susustra [menial service of the three twice-born castes]
(b) Varta [production of wealth]
(c) Karukarma [Arts] and
(d) Kusilava Karma [crafts]

From the above, it is evident that Kautilya points out the common duties of the three higher castes as 'study [Adhyayana], worship [Yajana], and giving gifts [Dana]'.

The above ideas are more or less reflected in the Dharma-shastras, which reflect the spirit of the Vedic literature in all respects. The stratification of society was made on functional basis. Out of four classifications, the first was accorded to Brahmanas. He occupied the highest offices of the State and the society by his character, knowledge and intelligence. Highest dignity and Status was also accorded to him because he was well versed in worshipping of Gods. So far as the Shudra was concerned, 'service' was his portion in life. He was not eligible for sacraments and was not allowed to hear sacred texts. But he was allowed to perform the rites of marriage, cooking of daily food in the grihya fires and funeral ceremonies [shraddha].

In Manu-smriti, Shudras had few privileges and many obligations or duties. The discriminating laws against him and his social disabilities were an inheritance of the past. The jataka stories also describe how the Chandalas were treated as despised outcastes doomed to live outside the city or village and their very sight was considered as impure. Due to these disparities, the caste system was emerged with its many rigidities, which is attributed to the writings of Manu. The time of Manu Dharma Shastra is again somewhat hazy, but nevertheless, these writings testify the crystallization of caste from the open class to a closed system[1]. The four-fold Varna division Brahmana, Kshatriya, Vaishya and Shudra still remained the broad categories of classification. Birth became the basis of one's status in society. Consequently, occupation, food, ritual status, choice of mate, social and physical distance between different castes became well defined. Anybody who transgresses these rules became an outcaste. These 'outcastes' were later on reduced to the status of Untouchables or the 'panchamas' who constituted the fifth Varna.

A Brahmana was well versed in the vedas and other sacred literature. He was a scholar, priest and a teacher who enjoyed the highest status and was ritually 'pure'. The Kshatriyas symbolised physical prowess, constituted a military and ruling class. The Vaishyas were involved in trade and business. The Shudras constituted a class of manual workers involved in cultivation and obeying the orders of the other three upper caste groups. These people were not given any opportunity to read the vedas or any other holy literature. But the fifth Varna consisting of several outcasts was considered as low and was placed at the bottom of the system. This stratification and how it evolved needs to be analyzed.

EVOLUTION OF CASTE SYSTEM

Vedic Period

The feature of Indian society that strikes a foreign observer as distinctive of it, is what is termed as 'caste' and what Hindus call 'varnashrama-dharma'. All the literary accounts of the important aspects of caste, centre around the four orders in society namely, Brahmana, Kshatriya, Vaishya and Shudra. In the Rig-Veda, three classes of society were frequently mentioned and named as Brahma, Kshatra and Visha. The first two represented the two professions of the poet-priest and the warrior-chief. The third group consisted of all common people in the society. It is the only in the hymns of the celebrated Purusha Sukta that the reference of the fourth order of the society was mentioned. The names of those four orders are mentioned as Brahmana, Rajanya, Vaishya and Shudra who are said to have come from mouth, the arms, the thighs and the feet of the creator respectively appeared in the Purusha Sukta.

> *"The Brahmana was his mouth,*
> *The Rajanya was made of his two arms;*
> *His thighs became the Vaishyas;*
> *From his feet was produced the* Shudra".[2]

The Brahmana has been called the mouth of the Purusha and is placed highest in society. His special function pertains to speech. Being a priest, invoking gods is his privilege. The second rank, Rajanya, is born of arms of Purusha and has the privilege of wielding arms. The thighs of the Purusha become Vaishya. The occupation of Vaishya is agriculture and trade. From his feet was produced the Shudra. Just as the feet are the lowest in the body, Shudras are the lowest in the society. The particular limbs associated with these divisions and the order in which they are mentioned indicate their status in the society of the time, though no such interpretation is directly given in the hymn.[3]

This origin of four classes is repeated in the later works with slight modification. The *"Taittiriya Samhita"* accepts the origins of those four classes to the four limbs of the creator and explains that the 'Brahmanas' are declared to be the 'chief' as they were created from mouth, the 'Rajanya' are vigorous because they were created from vigor, the 'Vaishyas' are meant to eat because they were created from the stomach and the 'Shudras' were created from the feet as he is to be the transporter of others and to subsist by feet.[4] In this particular account of the creation, not only is the origin of the classes interpreted theologically, but also a divine justification is sought to be given to their functions and status. These classes or orders are reformed frequently in many later literatures as "varnas" to such an extent that Hindu religion has come to be defined as 'Varnashrama Dharma'. It is to be remembered that the 'Varna' is never used to any one of these classes in 'Rig Veda'. But in the 'Shatapatha Brahmana', four classes are described as the four varnas. The word 'varna' means 'colour' and it was in this sense that the word 'varna' seems to have been used in contrasting the 'Arya' and the 'Dasa' i.e., fair and dark colours respectively. Rig Veda literature emphasizes strongly the difference between the Arya and the Dasa not only in their colour, but also in their speech, religious practices and physical features. The Brahmin is said to be superior to the Kshatriya, who is able to embroil with his incantations or with his ritualistic knowledge. He is said to ensure a king's safety in battle by his prayers. The main functions of a Brahmana may be said to be teaching and officiating at sacrifices, as he was proficient in sacred knowledge.

The 'Kshatriya' was known as the 'Rajanya' in the Rig-Veda who was placed in the second order in the society. This class is usually represented as inferior to the Brahmin, but in 'Kathaka Samhita', the Kshatriya is raised over the Brahmin. The occupations of the class consisted of administrative and military duties. 'Upanishadic' literature points out that some of the kings of the age were not only the patrons of philosophers but were themselves well versed in the profound philosophical speculations of their times.[5] The third order in the society namely, the 'Vaishyas' figures little in Vedic literature. The 'Aitareya Brahmana' describes him as a tributary to another, "to be lived upon by another, to be suppressed at will".[6] In comparison to the Brahminic class, the Vaishyas position was rather insignificant yet the class was definitely better than the Shudra class.

The last class in the society was Shudra who represented domestic servants, whose status was very close to the position of slaves. The 'Shudras' are described as "the servant of another, to be expelled at will, and to be slain at will".[7] The milk, which was used to be used for fire-oblation was not allowed to be milked by a Shudra. Besides, he was not to be addressed by a person consecrated for sacrifice. The 'Shatapatha Brahmana' goes to the length of declaring the Shudra as untruth itself. The Shudra, though he was received within the precincts of the Aryan fold, yet he was kept away from following the religious practices of the Aryans. The ideas of Untouchability were first given literary expression in connection with the Shudras and the sacrifice. Besides, there were many inequalities in the matter of religious practices between three other classes. Each order seems to have been habitually endogamous in marriage though occasionally Brahmins married Kshatriya females.

Post-Vedic Period

In the post-Vedic period, the Brahminic literature also contemplates only four varnas. Among the four varnas, the old distinction of 'Arya' and 'Shudra' appears so predominantly as 'Dvija' and 'Shudra'. The first three varnas are called 'Dvijas [twice born]' because they have to go through the initiation ceremony, which is symbolic of rebirth. As this privilege is denied to the Shudra, he is called 'ekajati' [once born]. In this period, a great consolidation of the position of the Brahmin class can be found contrasting with the degrading position of Shudras due to the growing superiority of the Brahmins. Vashistha quotes that a 'Brahmin is born with three debts, viz., to the gods, to the manes and to the sages'. The discharge of these was to be achieved through sacrifices, progeny and Vedic studies. The privilege of officiating at sacrificial sessions and other religious ceremonies was exclusively confined to the Brahmins as a hereditary function. Apasthamba declares that a king, who without prejudice to his servants gives land and money to deserving Brahmins, gains endless heavenly worlds.[8] The pre-eminence of the Brahmins was so great that the Mahabharatha declared that there was only one Varna viz., the Brahmin and the other varnas were merely it's modifications. The superiority of a child-Brahmin over an aged Kshatriya is supported by Apasthamba. Gouthama also quotes the Vedic text and observes that the Kshatriyas were assisted by the Brahmins to prosper and the union of the two alone upholds the moral order. Besides, he never forgets to point out that when a king and a Brahmin pass along the same road, the road belongs to the Brahmin and not to the king. This clearly indicates that there was a domination of the Brahmins over the kings also. Gouthama observes that all varnas must serve their superiors, i.e., the Brahmins, as the most superior Varna among the other varnas. They were exempted from all taxes; if they followed their lawful occupation and found a treasure, they were not required to hand it over to the king. Both their property and person were not subject to violation. If the gold belonging to a Brahmin is stolen or if he was killed, both acts were regarded as heinous sins [mahapataka]. Willful murder of a Brahmin was considered as inexpiable. Besides, he was also exempted from any corporal punishments. He must not be forced to be a witness at the instance of a non-Brahmin unless whose name is already mentioned in the plaint. Above all, the lawgivers insist from time to time that the Brahmin shall keep to the moral discipline of his class and honestly perform the duties assigned to him. If he deviates from his path, he is equated to a Shudra. It is well known that in the story of the Ramayana, Rama is represented to have killed a Shudra who was practicing austerities. From this it is evident that, the Shudra could not perform a sacrifice, could not listen to or recite the Vedic texts, nor could he practice austerities. In addition to this, he was denied the right of initiation and the first stage of individual life [ashrama] i.e. the studentship. Apasthamba opines that the Shudra is not entitled to the rite of initiation, the study of the Veda and kindling of the sacred fire. He says that, food brought by an impure Shudra must not be eaten.[9] Besides, Apasthamba provides the same penance for killing a Shudra as he provides for killing a crow, chameleon, a peacock, a duck, a frog, a mongoose, a muskrat or a dog.[10] But according to Gouthama, some people allow a Shudra to offer 'pakayajnas' [minor sacrifices to be offered in the fire kept at home, as distinguished from major sacrifices offered in the Vedic fire]. A 'pakayajna' may be offered on his behalf without he being initiated for it. The views are also recognized by Mahabharatha regarding the Shudra's religious duties. Therefore, the above facts clearly indicate that the Shudra had no right to perform any important ceremonies, sacrifices and sacraments. One of the eminent sociologists like Ghurye does not agree the observations made by Professor Max Muller when he says that the Grihya sutras never expressly exclude the Shudra from the rites of initiation. Ghurye observes that the ages at which this rite was to be performed are laid down only for the three classes and not for the Shudras. The Shudra was debarred incessantly from the study of Veda and to hear Vedic recitations.

According to Mahabharatha, the Shudra can have no absolute property, as his wealth can be appropriated by his master at his will. If the master of a Shudra has fallen into distress, the latter shall be placed at the disposal of the poor-master. The king is pleased to appoint only persons belonging to the first three classes over villages and towns for their protection. If a Shudra intentionally listens to the recitation of the Vedas, his ears shall be filled with molten lead or lac; if he recites Vedic texts, his tongue shall be cut off; if he remembers any verses of Veda, he shall be dismembered.[11] If he assumes a position of equality with caste-Hindus, either in sitting or conversing or going along the road, he shall receive corporal punishment. If a Shudra commits adultery with women of first three castes of the social order, he shall receive capital punishment, or shall be burnt alive or tied up in straw.[12] All members of the Brahmana varnas were expected to maintain a close vigil over the Shudras to prevent them even from listening to Vedic recitations. Any kind of self-assertion on the part of a Shudra amounted to a crime according to the Dharmasutras. Thus, the Shudras had no civil or religious rights to perform them independently. But the fact remains that the Shudra is not totally neglected, rather, the sentiments of compassion about him are expressed in many places. For example, a master is exhorted to support his Shudra servant when he is unable to work and to offer funeral oblation for him in case he dies without any child.

British Period

It is evident from the previous discussion that the Brahmin was at the apex of the hierarchical organization of caste and the Hindu kings upheld the institution with the help of their civil power. With the advent of British rule in India and they being the political head of society, things were bound to change. The establishment of British Courts administered a uniform criminal law in many matters. For example, questions of assault, adultery, rape were taken before the British Courts for decision. Consequently caste councils lost their importance and the British Courts acquired prominence to deal with many matters. In the matters of civil law like marriage, divorce, the British Courts set aside the authority of caste. The hereditary and prescriptive right of the Brahmins to act as priests to all castes of Hindu fold has been the one uniform and general principle inherent in a caste society through all its vicissitudes. But later, due to the decision of the High Courts in the three presidency towns the Brahmins were dislodged from their monopoly of priesthood. In Bengal and in some parts in North India, generally it is now settled that there is no office of priest recognised as such in law and a householder may employ anyone he likes for the performance of any priestly service and pay the fees to him.[13] Several non-Brahmins reformists started to perform their religious rites without the assistance of the Brahmin priests. Many Brahmin priests lodged complaints against such acts in the High Court of Bombay asking for an injunction against those persons who were violating their rights. But the High Court rejected the petition and held that people could engage any priest they liked and were not at all bound to call for the services of the hereditary priest. On the other hand, the hereditary priest must be paid some fees by way of compensation. This decision revoked the employment of hereditary priest for the performance of ritualistic ceremonies. Besides, the British Courts have given different opinions regarding the prohibition against a marriage, which takes place outside the caste. In early cases, it was observed that marriages between persons belonging to different divisions of the Brahmins or Shudras were invalid unless specially sanctioned by their respective custom in their caste. But later, in a Madras case, when a Hindu, belonging to the Shudra class married a Christian woman turned into a Hindu, the marriage was accepted as one between members of different divisions of the Shudra class and declared as valid one. Many social reformers were not happy with the existing state of affairs and consequently, the legislators tried to introduce a bill, which legalises such inter-caste marriages. Therefore the 'Special Marriage Act' of 1872 was enacted in which an Indian of whatever caste or creed could enter into a valid marriage with a person belonging to any caste or creed, provided, the parties registered the contract of marriage declaring 'interalia' that they did not belong to any religion. Soon after this, " Special Marriage Amendment Act" of 1923 was enacted where persons marrying under the provisions of this Act, whatever caste they may belong, need not make any declaration as prescribed in the Act of 1872. For example, if two Hindus belonging to different caste marry under this Act, they need not renounce their religion through declaration but have to forfeit certain of their personal rights as Hindus.

Besides, some sections of Hindu society, under the old regime of caste, were denied some civil rights e.g. Untouchables. The British administrators several times thought that the disabilities of the Untouchables should be removed and they should be placed on par with the caste Hindus. In 1856, the Government of Bombay had to consider the case of a 'Mahar' boy, who was not given admission to the government school at Dharwar. Ultimately, in the year 1858, the Government announced in a press-note that;

> "Although the Governor-in-Council does not contemplate the introduction of low-caste pupils into schools, the expenses of which are shared with the Government by local contributors and patrons who object to such a measure, he reserves to himself the full right of refusing the support of Government to any partially aided school in which the benefits of education are withheld from any class of persons on account of caste or race, and further resolves that all schools maintained at the sole cost of Government shall be opened to all classes of its subjects without distinction".

In the press-note of 1915, again the problem of an Untouchable was referred to the "familiar sight of Mahar and other depressed class boys in village schools where the boys are often not allowed to enter the school room but were accommodated on the verandah". In the year 1923, the Government issued a notification that 'no grants would be paid to any aided educational institutions, which refused admission to the children of the depressed classes. Consequent to this, the practice of segregating the depressed class boys disappeared in the Central Division of the Presidency and thereafter the boys from depressed classes were allowed to sit in their classes along with the boys and girls of caste-Hindus'.

Likewise, in 1925, a bill was introduced in the Madras Legislative Council to put under the Statute to throw open all public roads, streets or pathways, giving access to any public office, well, tank or place of public resort, to all classes of people including the depressed classes. In old regime, one caste used to file the petition to the sovereign to obstruct another caste from carrying any procession through a particular street or from using a particular mark. This practice was deliberately discouraged through the declared policy of the British Government in India and thus removed some of the occasions for a demonstration of the bitter caste-spirit.[14] The object of the British Government's administrative measures and promulgation of the uniform law virtually was to remove all legal inequality, injustice in the treatment of different caste – particularly the so called low-castes. One of the disabilities the depressed class had was that they were denied access to Hindu temples. Besides, they were required to stand outside the temple and satisfy themselves so that they had a glimpse of the idol of god. For example, the famous Parvati temple at Poona was one such, where even if the depressed classes wanted to enter the temple as other caste-Hindus would, the trustees of the temple refused to allow them the entry into the temple. When this was the situation, the Government of Bombay, which was producing substantial grants towards the maintenance of the temple, removed all restrictions on the entry of depressed classes to the Parvati temple. The Government directed all the public temples, which were obtaining Government grants, to throw open the temples, to all the people including the depressed classes. From the above facts, it is evident that, the British Government showed sympathy and consideration to bring equality among all castes in India. Through the uniform laws enforced by the British, many prejudices, inequality and ill will among many castes were removed and whoever discriminated and treated with contempt were punished under the law. Although the British brought this uniform law through the territory of India for their survival and safety in their administration, yet it also helped for the removal of many social disabilities, which existed in the Hindu society to some extent.

THEORIES RELATING TO THE ORIGIN OF CASTE SYSTEM

Many theories have advanced to explain the origin of castes in India. Among these theories, Traditional theory, Brahminical theory, Racial theory, Occupational theory, Ketkar's theory,

Senart's theory and Hutton's theory are very important for our study.

Traditional Theory

A number of western scholars have described Hindu society as super-natural centered society in which people are lured by abstract rules and search for it through mysticism and not through science. According to some scholars, Hindus seek intimacy with the ultimate reality and explain everything in terms of god and religion.[15] The Traditional theory believes that the caste system has been established by divine ordinance or atleast with divine approval. This theory has two versions namely mythical and metaphysical.

The mythical version regards four 'varnas' as four castes and believes that these four 'castes' have emerged from different parts from Brahma's body. It considers caste as a naturally determined organisation of social functions and explains the membership of an individual in a particular caste in terms of 'karma' and 'Dharma' doctrines. Even lord Krishna in Bhagavath Gita has said: "The four fold system [chathur varnya] was created by me according to the division of qualities [gunas] and functions [karma]". According to the 'Dharma doctrine', a man who accepts the caste system and the norms of his particular caste is living according to 'Dharma', while a man who questions them is violating 'Dharma'. Living according to 'Dharma' is rewarded while violation of 'Dharma' is punished both here and hereafter. If he observes the rule of 'Dharma', he will be born in his next birth in a high and rich caste, otherwise he will be born in a low and poor caste. But according to the 'karma doctrine', a man is born in a particular caste because of his actions performed in his previous birth [incarnation]. If he had performed better actions, he would have been in a higher caste, i.e., birth in a particular caste is not an accident. He was born in that caste because he deserved to be born there.

Whereas metaphysical version explains the fixed functions, hierarchy and other characteristics of a caste. Each caste has a separate function and this function is determined by the nature [swabhav] and the qualities [gunas] of the caste members. According to the Hindu view, 'swabhav' of an individual comprises of two sets of qualities–'gotrika' and 'namika'. The former is hereditary qualities which the individual inherits from his gotra [lineage] and which he shares with all the members of his family; and the latter is the individual qualities which are specifically one's owned and which does not share with any other member of his family. So, when the 'namika [individual]' qualities differentiate an individual from other individuals, the 'gotrika' qualities identify him to a particular group. It is these 'gotrika' qualities, which determined his ascriptive nature and entitled him the status in a 'jati [caste]'. This explains the characteristics of hereditary members of the caste system. Swabhav [nature] and action [occupation] cannot be separated from each other. This again explains the characteristics of caste, namely, the fixed occupation. To understand this, we have to look into the different kinds of functions.

1. Ordinary
2. Extraordinary

Ordinary function requires no special skills for their performance and the extraordinary function requires specialised knowledge. Extraordinary functions are again of three types: techno-economic functions, politico-legal functions and cultural-religious functions. The first are means-oriented, the second are end-oriented and the last are agent-oriented. As the agent-oriented, cultural-religious functions aim at the ultimate end of life, those who perform them get the highest status in the society. On the other hand, those who perform ordinary functions get the lowest status. In between these two functions, there are some people who are engaged in administrative-military [politico-legal] and economic-commercial [techno-economic] functions. The Brahmins are engaged in cultural-religious functions, Kshatriyas in politico-legal functions, Vaishyas in techno-economic functions and Shudras in ordinary functions. This clearly explains the hierarchical arrangements of four varnas considered as four castes in the Traditional theory.

Brahminical Theory

According to Ghurye, one of the renowned Sociologists of the world, he believes in the role of Brahmins in the origin of caste and supports the Brahminical theory. He says that, the various factors that characterises caste systems were the result of the attempts on the part of the upholders of the Brahminic civilization to exclude the aborigines and the Shudras from religious and social communion with themselves. When the Aryans entered India, they had three well-defined classes. But when the fourth class of the Shudras was formulated, the Brahminic literature contemplated it as in contradiction to the other three classes. Thus the Vedic opposition between the Arya and the Dasa was replaced by Brahminic classification of the 'dvijati' and the 'ekajati' [Shudra]. As an important constituent of Brahminic culture, in connection with the sacrificial rituals, the Aryan notion of ceremonial purity took on an exaggerated aspect. Brahmins, partly out of their honest desire to preserve the purity of Vedic ritual, partly being the victims of their own ideas of ceremonial purity and partly also owning to their consciousness of superiority over their aborigines, first enacted rules for the guidance of their own members.[16] Therefore, Ghurye observes that caste in India is a Brahminic child of the Indo-Aryan culture, cradled in the land of the Ganga and the Yamuni and then transferred to other parts of the country.

Racial Theory

Herbert Risley was the ardent exponent of this theory. According to this theory, the clash of cultures and the contact of races crystallized castes in India. In the world history, whenever one person has subdued another, the conquerors have not only taken women as concubines or wives from the conquered group but have also refused to give their own daughters in marriage to them. When these two are of the same race, or at any rate of the same colour, complete amalgamation between them took place. But if they belong to two different races and colours they run on different lines.

In India also, the migrant Aryans, had their own ideas of ceremonial purity. They considered the original inhabitants as inferior to them. They married with the daughters of the aboriginal but refused to give their daughters to them. The children who were born out of such marriages had to be assigned the lowest position in the society and were called 'chandals'. Thus, the origin of the group of 'half-breeds' as well as the feeling of racial superiority ultimately became responsible for the origin of the caste system.

Herbert Risley refers to four processes in the formation of castes;

(a) Change in traditional occupation: By adopting a new occupation, either a caste or a sub-division of a caste ultimately develops into a distinct caste.

(b) Migration: In early periods, when the means of transportation and communications were not fully developed, when a section of a caste wanted to migrate to other region, it became difficult for it to maintain contacts with the parental caste. Gradually it was cut off from the parental caste and developed as a new caste.

(c) Change in customs: Whenever people discarded old customs and usages and adopted new practices, there emerged a new form of caste system in the earliest times.

(d) Preservation of old traditions: In this process, 'certain castes cherish the traditions of bygone sovereignty and preserve old traces of an organization. To separate themselves from those who have assumed new traditions and customs, they take up new names and thus a new caste comes into existence'.

From the above theory, i.e., racial theory, it is evident that, being civilized and fair in colour, in comparison to the natives, the Vedic Aryans tried to show off their exclusiveness. They had developed exclusive spirit in social behaviour and had preserved the ideas of ceremonial purity. They used strong expression against the natives and imposed several restrictions in social interaction with the natives. As the Aryan religion represented the early Vedic religion, we can call them as 'Vedic Indians'. These Vedic Indians spoke of themselves as 'Arya' and described the native population as 'dark coloured' people and applied to them the word 'Dasa'. So far as the matters of religious faith and practice, though they began by stigmatizing the faith and practice of the natives, they did not develop the extreme intolerance. The Aryans not only tolerated the beliefs and practices of the natives, even though they are not in harmony with their central doctrines, but also assimilated a number of them in their own faith and practices. Thus the caste system was the modus operandi accommodating diversity of faiths and practices. Besides, Ghurye, Majumdar and Westermarck have also supported the racial theory of the origin of the caste system.

Hutton also considers racial factor as one of the factors in the origin of the caste system.

Occupational Theory

Nesfield, the profounder of this theory believed that, the origin of the caste has nothing to do with racial affinity or religion, but it is mainly due to functions and occupations. He believes that the technical skill of the occupation was passed on hereditarily from one generation to another generation and because of practicing the same occupation over a long period of time, 'occupational guilds' came into existence, later, which came to be called 'castes'. According to Nesfield, the hierarchy in the caste system was the result of the feeling of superiority and inferiority of occupations. He also believes that, the rank of any caste as high and low depends upon whether the industry represented by the caste belongs to an advanced or backward stage of culture. He provides an example of artisans working in metals ranking themselves higher than the basket makers and other primitive callings, which do not involve the use of metals. He takes an example of Brahmins to show how they got the highest status in the collective caste hierarchy. He says Brahmins were specialized in the 'occupation' of sacrifices and hymns and rituals. As sacrifices were very important in the social life of the people, Brahmins became the most important and respected people in the society. Brahmin was thus the first born of castes, the model upon which all other castes were subsequently formed. However, in the beginning, priesthood was not an exclusive monopoly of the Brahmins. It was only when they organized themselves as an exclusive privileged class that priesthood became hereditary.

D.N. Majumdar criticizes Nesfield's idea of the hierarchy of castes in terms of the superiority or the inferiority of the occupations. He says that the status of castes depends not on the superiority or the inferiority of occupation but upon the degree of purity of blood and the extent of isolation maintained by the groups. Inspite of this criticism, one cannot totally discard the occupational theory. This theory has some sociological significance. Sociologically speaking, the study of caste groups is the study of particular aspect of social stratification and every human society comes to be stratified into various groups when work becomes specialized and the number of occupational roles becomes so great.

Ketkar's Theory

Ketkar traces the origin of castes from the early tribes and the psychologically prejudicial tendencies of human beings. He believes that castes have developed from tribes or converted classes. Various tribes, which were living in different parts of India, existed as different units and after the custom of endogamy was introduced, they did not fuse. Many of these tribes were in struggle with each other because their heads had quarreled either over boundaries or because a person from one tribe had kidnapped a girl from other tribe. Because of these conflicts, many people avoided other tribes in marriage and social relations and started to confine social interaction to the members of their tribes. Ketkar proceeds to give what he calls the 'psychological' explanation to each characteristics of the caste system. He takes the most important element of endogamy in the caste system and says that this endogamy came to be practiced because of three factors.

1. Due to the feelings of sympathy and affection for the members of one's own group;
2. To maintain blood purity;
3. Because it makes the social adjustment with the partner easier.

According to Ketkar, feeling of superiority and inferiority is either the cause or the result of endogamy. A race of people who regard themselves as superior to another will not intermarry with one that is thought of as inferior. He illustrates this with examples. When Indians first migrated to Africa, they did not marry natives because they considered themselves superior to them. Similarly, Chinese, after migration to America, had also confined their marital relations to their own community as they were filled with prejudice against the white people. Ketkar's theory cannot be accepted fully. There are various other factors apart from the psychological factors, which construed as the important factors in the origin of castes. For example, Brahmin's concept of ceremonial purity and the Vedic Aryan's idea of preserving their racial superiority.

Senart's Theory

Senart seeks the origin of the caste system to the Aryan sources. He holds that the characteristics of the caste system form part of usage and tradition common to all branches of the Aryan race.

Senart compares the practices, which prevailed in ancient Indian society, ancient Roman and Greek societies. And these common characteristics are the jurisdiction, which somewhat tyrannically regulates private life, marriage, food, ceremonial usages, and the habitual practice of certain special cults. Indians, Greeks and Romans are all Aryans and their civilizations are the oldest ones. Senart finds certain similarities in the three systems, each of them have three groups namely, *family, gotra* and *caste* in India; *gens, curia* and *tribe* in Rome; and *family, phratria* and *phyle* in Greece. Just as *'gotra'* is an exogamous group in India, *'gens'* in Rome and *'phratria'* in Greece also confined their marriages to their own groups. Both Indian Brahmins and Roman Patricians enjoy the hypergamous right of marriage. Just as in India, there is a custom that after marriage, woman transfers from her *'gotra'* to that of her husband's *gotra,* the same type of custom existed in Rome also in Roman confarratio. Lastly, just as caste panchayats exist in India and its head [sarpanch] is a powerful man, in Rome and Greece too, there are similar councils with similar powers. So, on the basis of this comparison, Senart observes that, caste is the normal development of ancient Aryan institutions.

Hutton's Theory of Mana

Hutton emphasizes on the primitive conception of *'Mana'* in the formation of castes. According to him, *'Mana'* is a mysterious impersonal power attached to individuals, objects and places. It is believed to have powers to harm people. Wherever the belief in *'Mana'* prevails, a corresponding belief in the value of taboo as a protective measure is also to be found. Taboos were imposed in commensality, inter-marriage and interaction etc., to save or protect the members of one's tribe from the *'Mana'* of the other tribes. According to Hutton, tribals consider the food of strangers as dangerous. The restriction on sharing food with others and having contacts with them is based on the belief that these may be infected with the dangerous soul-matter of strangers. It is such beliefs that led to the origin of the commensal taboo. In Hutton's study of Nagas in 1923-24, it was found that in some villages, people were not accepting presents or money from the strangers or parting with any possession to them for fear of the influence to which they might thus become subject by proxy as it were, but they used to destroy mats and other property, lent to visitors (strangers) when they had used them and gone.

From the above theories, it is evident that, the superiority feeling of the Vedic Aryans over the natives due to the racial differentiation, occupational distinctiveness, the monopolistic priesthood of Brahmins, the religious ideas of ceremonial purity and pollution applied first to Shudras (native aboriginals) in connection with the sacrificial ritual and then extended to other groups because of the theoretical impurity of certain occupations. These were the important factors in the origin of the caste system in India.

SOCIAL JUSTICE THROUGH CONSTITUTIONAL RIGHTS AND SAFEGUARDS

Over a long period of time, in the Hindu society, there was no mobility for the depressed classes, because, the upper caste Hindus were not allowing the depressed classes to enjoy some privileges. Besides, the upper castes had occupied important positions in the Hindu society, where the depressed classes were socially, educationally and economically poor enough as not to claim some benefits. At this point of time, where the caste prejudice was so high, some social reformers and Constitutional-makers thought that, unless this caste prejudice, inequality, discrimination were removed from the society, it was not possible to have a welfare and egalitarian society. The members of the Constituent Assembly took interest in removing inequality, discrimination and caste prejudices from the Hindu society. Therefore, the first step, which they undertook, was to insist for various rights and privileges for the depressed classes in British India as well as in the Constituent Assembly. Being the most articulate spokesman of the exploited and the downtrodden in Indian society during British time, Ambedkar insisted that, the depressed classes, including the Scheduled Castes and the Scheduled Tribes, should be provided with various rights and freedoms. On 29th May 1928, Ambedkar submitted a statement before the Indian Statutory Commission[16(a)] [i.e. Simon Commission] on its arrival in India. The statement concerns the safeguards for the protection of the interests of the depressed classes as a minority in the Bombay Presidency. Before the Simon Commission, it was also contended that, proper protection through adequate representation should be given to the depressed classes. A demand was also made that the education of the depressed classes shall be recognized as the first charge on the revenue of the province as well as the right of the depressed classes to unrestricted recruitment in the Army, Navy and the Police shall be recognized without any limitation as to caste. Besides, for a period of thirty years, the Provincial Government shall recognize the right of the depressed classes for priority in the matter of recruitment to all posts in all civil services. Ambedkar said, "Surely, the first essential of any scheme of reform is that, adequate safeguards should be provided for the good Government of the inarticulate masses of the population"[17].

In November 1928, Government of Bombay constituted a committee to enquire into the educational, economical and social conditions of the depressed classes and the aboriginal tribes in the Presidency and to recommend measures for their upliftment. This committee was popularly known as the Starte committee. The committee in its report recommended scholarships and hostels for students. To uplift the backward classes, it stressed for the need to recruit depressed Classes in the police and urged that the present ban on the recruitment of the depressed classes in the Army should be removed and housing schemes for the backward classes should be promoted. The committee recommended for a legislation to prevent dedication of '*devadasis*' and that social boycott is checked by propaganda and legislation. At the Round Table Conference held in London during 1930-32, some members of the Constituent Assembly including Ambedkar, played a vital role in focusing the British and World attention to the problems of the depressed classes and other weaker sections in India.

At the first Round Table Conference, Ambedkar disclosed his 'scheme of political safeguards' for the protection of the depressed classes in the future Constitution of India. He also demanded that in the future Constitution of India, the depressed classes should be given "a fundamental right enacted in the Constitution which will declare 'Untouchability' to be illegal for all public purposes... Secondly, this fundamental right must also invalidate and nullify all such disabilities and all such discrimination as may have been made hitherto"[18]. In 19th January 1931, the British Government was reminded of its responsibilities towards the depressed classes and said "the British Parliament and those who speak for it, have always stated that they are trustees for the depressed classes........ It is the bounden duty of any Government to see that trust is not betrayed... the depressed classes would regard it as the greatest betrayal.... If it were to leave us to the mercy of those who have taken no interest in our welfare and whose prosperity and greatness is founded on our ruination and degradation"[19]. The incessant role played by Ambedkar in ensuring social justice for the depressed classes had its desired effect upon the British authorities. Consequently, the Prime Minister Macdonald announced the communal Award, creating separate electorates for the depressed classes on 17th August 1932. The announcement appeared to mark the culmination of a long and bitter struggle for the adequate representation for the Untouchables on their own terms. A separate status was sanctioned to the depressed classes by the British authorities. But Gandhiji did not tolerate this separate status, as it would divide the Hindus and lead to the disintegration. Immediately, Gandhiji announced his decision to fast unto death to resist the Communal Award. Ambedkar endeavored to defend the communal Award and tried to convince Gandhiji but failed. Finally, Ambedkar had to agree to amend the communal Award in a manner acceptable to Gandhiji. Thus Ambedkar, Gandhiji and others signed an agreement, which was popularly known as 'Poona Pact'[20] on 24th September 1932. But unfortunately, the understanding made between Ambedkar and Gandhiji regarding the 'Poona Pact' failed in sending true representation of the depressed classes to the legislature. Ambedkar felt disappointed about his understanding with Gandhiji as well as the way the Britishers also betrayed the depressed classes. Then Ambedkar came forward with the following proposals as a programme to ameliorate the conditions of the depressed classes. He wanted these to be incorporated in the Constitution that was going to govern India when it becomes free.

(a) All educational facilities should be provided to the depressed classes.

(b) Depressed classes should be given representation in States and Central Legislative Councils on the basis of their population, needs and importance.

(c) Jobs in the State and Central Government services should be reserved.

(d) Depressed classes should be given representation in all the democratic bodies of the country.

(e) Provision of separate electorates should be made for the depressed classes.

(f) Separate settlements should be established for the depressed classes.[21]

QUEST FOR SOCIAL JUSTICE IN THE CONSTITUENT ASSEMBLY

The primary objective of the Constituent Assembly was to provide social, economical and political Justice to all. Ambedkar's name came to be closely associated with the drafting of a Constitution for free India as the Chairman of the drafting committee and as a member of the Advisory Committee on Minorities and Fundamental Rights. There was a general consensus in the Constituent Assembly that the term 'backward classes' would cover three principal components, the Scheduled Castes, the Scheduled Tribes and the other backward classes. The Constituent Assembly fought for the task of securing social justice for all the backward classes in the country under the mandate of a new Constitution. Therefore, it was unanimously agreed to incorporate two important chapters like, 'Fundamental rights' and 'Directive Principles of State Policy' to the new Constitution for the protection of the interests of backward classes including Scheduled Castes and Scheduled Tribes.

THE FUNDAMENTAL RIGHTS

Ambedkar, being the leader of the downtrodden, thought that there was a need for a 'Bill of Rights' in the Indian Constitution. He insisted for an elaborate system of fundamental rights for the downtrodden in particular and for all citizens in general. He was also of the opinion that social justice could not be secured to all unless it was enshrined or guaranteed in the Indian Constitution.[22] The first step, which was taken up by the Constituent Assembly, was the formulation of a 'Bill of Rights' to secure social justice and equality. Consequently, the Bill of Rights was incorporated in the Constitution of India in the form of fundamental rights.

The provisions of the Constitution, which aimed at preventing discrimination and promoting social justice, are;

1. The fundamental rights guaranteeing equality before the law and equal protection of law (Article 14);
2. Prohibition of discrimination on grounds of religion, race, caste, sex, or place of birth (Article 15);
3. Equality of opportunity in matters of public employment (Article 16);
4. Abolition of 'Untouchability' (Article 17); and
5. Prohibition of traffic in human beings and forced labour (Article 23).

The above provisions clearly indicate that Ambedkar and the founding fathers made sincere effort to provide Constitutionally guaranteed equality to the oppressed and disadvantaged sections of the population. Besides, the above provisions clearly show the concerted effort "to abolish social inequality, social stigma and social disabilities in our society".[23]

The Constitution-makers emphasized that the objective of the Constitution was to establish an egalitarian society where rights were guaranteed not to a few but to all. They believed that the right to equality of opportunity has no meaning unless the vast disparities between the rich and the poor are reduced. Besides, right to private property has no sense for those who have no roofs over their heads. Therefore, importance was accorded to the rights of the masses, of the minorities and of the under-privileged classes of the society in the Indian Constitution as against the political and civil rights of a few individuals, entrenched interests or propertied classes.[24]

THE DIRECTIVE PRINCIPLES OF STATE POLICY

It was also the intention of the Constitution-makers to incorporate into the Constitution certain principles and concepts that should determine Governmental activity which enables to secure economic and social justice to the people of India. While the fundamental rights guarantee the rights and liberties of the individuals against arbitrary state action, the Directive Principles seek to emphasize economic and social goals to be achieved. Both

Ambedkar and Nehru believed that India's survival depended on the success of the social and economic revolution in the country. In the Constituent Assembly Debates, Ambedkar stressed the importance of Directive Principles of State Policy in the following words:

> "Whoever captures power will not be free to do what he likes with it. In the exercise of it, he will have to respect these instruments of instructions, which are called the Directive Principles. He cannot ignore them. He may not have to answer for their breach in a Court of Law, but he will certainly have to answer for them before the electorate at election time. What great value these Directive Principles possess, will be realized better when the forces of right contrive to capture power".

Besides, it was also pointed out that Directive Principles were not intended to be mere pious declarations. "It is the intention of the Constituent Assembly that in future, both the Legislature and the Executive should not merely pay lip service to these principles enacted in this part, but that they should be made the basis of all executive and legislative actions that may be taken hereafter in the matter of the governance of the country". This shows that, the purpose of incorporating Directive Principles of State Policy in the Constitution of India was to secure social and economic justice as well as to create a Welfare State and just social order. This significance is incorporated in Article 38, which contemplates that "the State shall strive to promote the welfare of the people by securing and protecting as effectively as it may a social order in which justice–social, economic and political, shall inform all the institutions of National life".

Ambedkar and the founding fathers also fought for the inclusion of some special provisions to the Constitution relating to certain classes–the Scheduled Castes and Scheduled Tribes, the Anglo-Indians and the socially and educationally backward classes. Articles of the Indian Constitution like 330 and 332 provide that seats shall be reserved for the Scheduled Castes and Scheduled Tribes in the House of the People and the State Legislative Assemblies. Article 331 and 333 provide representation for Anglo-Indian community by nomination by the President and the Governor respectively, provided the community is not adequately represented in the Union and the States lower Houses. To protect the interests of the Scheduled Castes and Scheduled Tribes under the Article 338, a special officer is appointed by the President whose duty is to investigate all matters relating to the safeguards provided for the Scheduled Castes and Scheduled Tribes and to report to the President. Besides, under Article 340, the President may appoint a commission to investigate the conditions of socially and educationally backward classes within the territory of India and the difficulties under which they labour and to make recommendations as to the steps that should be taken by the Union or any State to remove such difficulties and to improve their conditions.

There were many objections raised by the members of the Constituent Assembly to the special provisions providing for reservation. Some members viewed that providing reservation is 'the very negation of efficiency and good Government'. But there was a general consensus among the members in favour of reservation of jobs for Scheduled Castes and Scheduled Tribes. Ambedkar strongly emphasized for the reservation to meet the 'demand of communities which have not so far been represented in the State'.

From the above, it is clear that, the members of the Constituent Assembly wanted to ensure social justice and social change through Constitutional means. They wanted to create a society where there is no inequality, injustice, discrimination and exploitation through the process of Constitutional making. Besides, being the leader of the Untouchables, Ambedkar wanted to have India free from 'Untouchability', degradation and caste prejudices.

CONCLUSION

The foregoing discussion shows that how the caste system which evolved among the Hindus gradually became rigid and hierarchical with its own discriminatory practices.

There were many attempts by social reformers who wanted to bring about changes in this social system and how at the time of India's Independence and the Constitutional organization of free India, these reforms were given effect to create an egalitarian society. These depressed classes were provided not only with equal rights and privileges but also political representation. The

Constitution-makers deliberately included chapters on 'Fundamental Rights'[25] and 'Directive Principles of State Policy'[26] which guaranteed various fundamental rights including 'Right to equality, abolition of Untouchability, freedom of speech and expression, freedom of association, freedom of movement, freedom of religion, and Right to life and liberty'. To ensure social welfare programmes to the depressed classes including Scheduled Castes and Scheduled Tribes, Directive Principles of State Policy was also included. The main objective of the framers of the Indian Constitution was to establish a society free from all discriminations, inequality, injustice and social disabilities. These objectives became reality to some extent when the Constitution of India came into operation.

NOTES

1. C. Parvathamma, *"Scheduled Castes at the cross roads"*, p. 15.
2. Rigveda, X.XC, 12.
3. G.S. Ghurye – *"Caste and Race in India"*.
4. Ibid., p. 45.
5. Ibid., p. 48.
6. Ibid., p. 49.
7. Ibid., p. 49.
8. Ibid., p. 56.
9. Apasthamba Dharmasutra, 15.16.22.
10. Apasthamba Dharmasutra, 1.9.25.13.
11. Gautama Dharmasutra, XII. 7.
12. Apasthamba Dharmasutra, I, 5.16.22; Baudhayana Dharmasutra, II 2.1.
13. G.S. Ghurye – *"Caste, Class and Occupation"*, [Popular Book Depot, Bombay], 1961, p. 181.
14. Ibid., p. 187.
15. Ram Ahuja–*"Indian Social System"*, Rawat Publications, New Delhi.
16. G.S. Ghurye – *"Caste and Race in India"*, Opp. Cit., p. 174.

16(a) Text of the Simon Commission is included in the Appendix.

17. Vasant Moon (Ed)–*"Dr. Babasaheb Ambedkar: Writings and Speeches"*, Vol. 2, Education Department of Maharashtra, 1982, p. 445.
18. Vasant Moon, Opp. Cit., p. 532.

19. Ibid., p. 598.
20. Text of the Poona Act is inserted in the Appendix.
21. Ashok S. Chousalkar, *"Indian Idea of political resistance"*, Aurobindo, Tilak, Gandhi and Ambedkar [Delhi Publications, 1990], p.102-3.
22. A.M. Rajashekaraiah – *"B.R. Ambedkar: The quest for Social Justice"*, [New Delhi, Uppal Publishing House, 1989], p.199.
23. Constituent Assembly Debate, Vol. 7, p. 666.
24. V.T. Patil – *"Studies in Ambedkar"*, [Devika Publications, New Delhi, 1995], p. 113.
25. Part–III of the Constitution of India.
26. Part–IV of the Constitution of India.

3

CONSTITUTIONAL PROVISIONS FOR SECURING SOCIAL JUSTICE AND JUDICIAL RESPONSE

INTRODUCTION

The struggle for 'individual freedom' and 'social justice'[1] is as old as human history. There is always a conflict between the claims of 'individual freedom' and those of 'social justice'. With the emergence of the concept of 'welfare State' in the 20th Century, the conflict between the claims of these two competing values have become more pronounced and needed harmonization. Various Countries have adopted different Constitutional strategies on the edifice of respect for 'individual freedoms'; the socialist countries have adopted their strategies on the bedrock of 'social justice'. India being a socialist democracy opted for the liberal democratic model with due emphasis on the basic human rights.[2] The Indian Constitution makers have tried to strike a balance between the claims of the individual freedom and social justice by including 'Fundamental Rights' and 'Directive Principles of State Policy'.

In this chapter, an attempt has been made to explain some of the provisions of the Constitution of India, which secure social justice to the people of India in general, and Scheduled Castes and Scheduled Tribes in particular. The challenge of social justice is in essence the challenge for equal opportunity and for equal protection of the laws. The challenge before the legislators and judicial statesmen today is to develop appropriate policies and to forge relevant tools to promote equality with freedom and protect fundamental rights with social justice.[3]

Besides, the Constitution-makers were aware of the social, economic and political inequalities, which existed in the country due to historical reasons and were anxious to remove these inequalities by positive State measures, even if these measures imposed unequal burden on those individuals who had hitherto enjoyed undue advantages. The framers of the Constitution were also aware of the prevailing miserable and appalling conditions of backward classes that had remained far behind and separated from national and social life. They continued to be socially oppressed and economically exploited for centuries because of various disabilities. They believed that in a caste-ridden society like ours where due to the 'historical reasons' certain castes and classes were for decades socially oppressed, economically continued to live the life of poverty and educationally coerced to learn the family trade or occupation and to take to education set out for each caste and class by the society'. So a doctrinaire insistence on formal equality would in fact aggravate and perpetuate inequality.[4] In the above background the following Constitutional provisions, which secure not only social and economic justice to the Scheduled Castes and Scheduled Tribes but also political justice along with the judicial responses wherever required, have been discussed elaborately.

PREAMBLE OF THE CONSTITUTION OF INDIA

The promise of 'social justice' finds expression in the very preamble to the Constitution of India. The preamble says;

> "We, the people of India, having solemnly resolved to constitute India into a SOVEREIGN, SOCIALIST, SECULAR, DEMOCRATIC, REPUBLIC and to secure to all its citizens;
>
> ***JUSTICE*** – social, economic and political;
>
> ***LIBERTY***- of thought, expression, belief, faith and worship;
>
> ***EQUALITY***- of status and of opportunity and to promote among them all;
>
> ***FRATERNITY*** – assuring the dignity of the individual and the unity and integrity of the Nation;

In Our Constituent Assembly, This Twenty Sixth Day of November 1949, Do Hereby Adopt, Enact and Give to Ourselves This Constitution".

The above principle incorporated in the preamble envisages that, Justice–social, economic and political, assuring equality of status and of opportunity is the declared goal of the Supreme Law, which the people gave to themselves through the Constituent Assembly.

The preambular conception of equality of status and opportunities, justice–social, economic and political, fraternity and individual dignity, principle of equality and amelioration of weaker sections through a time bound protective discrimination policy, the scope for reasonable restrictions upon liberties and freedoms under part III of the Constitution, and to implement various socio-economic goal values under part IV of the Constitution can be considered as providing a Constitutional drive and thrust for social advancement.[5] Social justice does not act alone. It acts with political justice and economic justice. Social justice role is to correct and rectify past injustices perpetrated upon socially handicapped classes.[6]

The preamble to the Indian Constitution sets out the aims and aspirations of the people of India and these have been translated into the various provisions of the Constitution. The aim of the Constitution-makers was to have a welfare State and an egalitarian society to overcome from all types of discrimination, inequalities, humiliation, exploitation suffered by various sections of society. Besides, the philosophy of the Indian Constitution is found in the Preamble, which secures to its citizen justice, liberty, equality and fraternity. The fact that the preamble provides that it is the people of India who have enacted and given to themselves the Constitution, the successful working of the Constitution and its continued acceptance by the people over the years leads to the conclusion that, the binding force of the Constitution is the sovereign will of the people of India.[7] At one point of time an opinion prevailed that the preamble to the Constitution was not a part of the Constitution.[8] But in Keshavananda Bharati Case, the Supreme Court opined that the preamble is a part of the Constitution.[9] This shows that, the ideals enshrined in the preamble are the part of the Constitution. As such, the State while making any legislation should keep in mind the ideals like Justice–Socio, economic and political, Equality, Liberty and Fraternity. These are the essential characteristics of a democracy, which are declared in the Preamble to the Constitution as its very objectives.

FUNDAMENTAL RIGHTS

In order to achieve social justice and to provide certain basic rights to the people in general and Scheduled Castes and Scheduled Tribes in particular, the Constitution-makers have included various fundamental rights to the citizens and non-citizens of India. The Constitution has regulated the State power from legislating in a manner not permissible under the Constitution.

Following are the fundamental rights conferred in part III of the Constitution:

1. Article 14 contemplates that, 'the State shall not deny to any person equality before the law or equal protection of the laws within the territory of India'.
2. Under Article 15 (1), 'the State shall not discriminate against any citizen on grounds only of religion, race, caste, sex, place of birth or any of them'.

   Clause (2) of this Article says, 'No citizen shall on grounds only of religion, race, caste, sex, place of birth or any of them, be subject to any disability, liability, restriction or condition with regard to–

   (a) Access to shops, public restaurants, hotels and places of public entertainment; or

   (b) The use of wells, tanks, bathing ghats, roads and places of public resort maintained wholly or partly out of State funds or dedicated to the use of general public.

   Clause (3) says, 'Nothing in this Article shall prevent the State from making any special provision for women and children'.

   Clause (4) says, 'Nothing in this Article shall prevent the State from making any special provision for the advancement of any socially and educationally backward classes of citizens or for the Scheduled Castes and the Scheduled Tribes.

3. Article 16 (1) provides that there shall be equality of opportunity for all citizens in matters relating to employment or appointment to any office under the State.

   Clause (2) contemplates that 'No citizen shall on grounds only of religion, race, caste, sex, descent, place of birth, residence or any of them be ineligible for, or discriminated against in respect of, any employment or office under the State'.

   Clause (4) of this Article provides that 'Nothing in this Article shall prevent the State from making any provision for the reservation to appointments or posts in favour of any backward class of citizens which in the opinion of the State is not adequately represented in the services under the State'.
4. Article 17 contemplates that 'Untouchability is abolished and its practice in any form is forbidden. The enforcement of any disability arising out of 'Untouchability' shall be an offence punishable in accordance with law'.
5. Article 19 states that 'All citizens shall have the rights to:
   (a) Freedom of speech and expression;
   (b) Assemble peaceably and without arms;
   (c) Form associations or unions;
   (d) Move freely throughout the territory of India;
   (e) Reside and settle in any part of the territory of India.
   (f) To practice any profession, or to carry on any occupation, trade or business'.
6. Article 21 provides that 'No person shall be deprived of his life or personal liberty except according to procedure established by law'.
7. Article 23 (1) says 'Traffic in human beings and begging and other similar forms of forced labour is prohibited...'.
8. Article 24 contemplates that 'No child below the age of fourteen years shall be employed to work in any factory or mine or engaged in any other hazardous employment'.
9. Article 25 (1) provides that 'Subject to public order, morality and health and to other provisions of this part, all persons are equally entitled to freedom of conscience and the right to freely profess, practice and propagate religion....'.

10. Article 29 (2) states that 'No citizen shall be denied admission into any educational institution maintained by the State or receiving aid out of State funds on grounds only of religion, race, caste, language or any of them'.
11. Article 30 (1) says 'All minorities, whether based on religion or language, shall have the right to establish and administer educational institutions of their choice....'.

    The Constitution has also provided Constitutional remedies to enforce the above fundamental rights if they are violated by the State under Article 32 and 226 of the Constitution.
12. Article 32 (1) says 'The Supreme Court shall have the power to issue directions or orders or writs, including writs in the nature of 'Habeas Corpus, Mandamus, prohibition, Quo-warranto, and Certiorari', whichever may be appropriate for the enforcement of any of the rights conferred by this part.

The above fundamental rights are an integral part of the Constitution, which secure social justice, equality and welfare to the people of India in general, and Scheduled Castes and Scheduled Tribes in particular. The framers of the Indian Constitution have deliberately included 'equality Provisions' in part III of the Constitution to treat all people equally irrespective of their race, caste, religion, sex, language and place of birth. For instance, Article 14 of the Constitution secures to all citizens the freedom from discrimination on grounds of religion, race and caste.[10] Besides, State is forbidden to discriminate against any citizen on the grounds of place of birth[11], caste, race, residence, descent, sex, and language. This shows that the Constitution has expressly prohibited any discrimination made against any person on the above grounds, for promoting equality to all the citizens and non-citizens. When Article 14 was being drafted, the main thrust was given to secure equality to the depressed classes including the Scheduled Castes and Scheduled Tribes who were subjected to inequality, discrimination and degradation in the caste system prevalent in the Hindu social order. If any person is discriminated on the grounds mentioned in Articles 15, 16, 29, 325 and 350, he can challenge such discrimination in a court of law and enforce his fundamental rights or any other Constitutional rights.

The Constitution of India has provided formal equality under Article 15 and 16. The contents of these Articles clearly show that 'formal equality' requires the absence of any discrimination in the words of Law. The implication is that similar cases must be treated similarly, according to one and the same rule.

The opening words of Article 14 say, 'the State shall not deny to any person equality before the law or the equal protection of the laws within the territory of India'. The expression 'equality before law' indicates the absence of any special privileges in favour of any individual. That is whatever be his rank or position; he is subject to the jurisdiction of the ordinary courts. It is worthwhile to quote what Professor Dicey says about the legal equality;

> "With us every official, from the Prime Minister down to a constable or a collector of taxes, is under the same responsibility for every act done without any legal justification as any other citizen'.[12]

The expression 'the equal protection of the laws indicate that equal protection shall be provided to all persons within the territorial jurisdiction of the union in the enjoyment of their rights and privileges without favouritism or discrimination.[13] Besides, the essence of Article 14, i.e., Equality, is that all persons and things similarly circumstanced shall be treated alike both in privileges conferred and liabilities imposed.[14] 'Equality before law' means that amongst equals the law should be equal and should be treated alike.[15] This indicates that Article 14 forbids discrimination between persons who are substantially in similar circumstances and conditions. But this Article allows different treatment of unequals. The Supreme Court of India has observed that, 'equal treatment of unequals is as bad as unequal treatment of equals'.[16] This is because all persons are not alike or equal in all respects. Therefore the application of same laws uniformly to all sections of the society is inconsistent with the principle of 'equality' contemplated under Article 14 of the Constitution. The general principle of 'Equality' indicates that 'no person shall be discriminated on the grounds of race, caste, colour, sex and place of birth. This is to provide opportunity and justice to all the citizens without taking into consideration various factors. This broader and general principle of 'equality' is also found in the preamble, where Constitution secures to all its citizens 'equality of status and opportunity'. The

Constitution-makers after several discussions deliberately included this equality clause in the Constitution to provide social, economic and political justice to all people of India and to have a welfare and egalitarian State.

EQUALITY AND PROTECTIVE DISCRIMINATION

'Equality' and 'protective discrimination' are two different principles adopted in the Constitution of India to secure social, economic and political justice to all citizens. The 'equality' concept contemplates that all persons are equal before the law and equal protection shall be given to all people living in India. But as the Indian society has been highly stratified on the basis of caste hierarchy, many sections of the population born into the lower castes have been incessantly oppressed and exploited for many centuries, which led to entrenched group inequalities denying equal opportunity to large masses of people. On the other hand, some sections of the society, by virtue of their birth enjoyed privileges and many opportunities for advancement in life. The colonial regime consciously pursued a policy of preserving the caste-based inequalities and religion-based discrimination, as they were more concerned with order than justice.[17] The Indian leaders, who participated in the Freedom Movement, including Gandhiji, protested against this unjust legal regime and they later mobilized the public opinion for bringing social reformation and legal change. When India got independence, these leaders wanted to have a just society where there would be no discrimination and exploitation. Therefore, the idea of 'equality' became the central theme for achieving social justice. Ultimately, the 'equality' provision or principle found expression in Article 14, 15, 16, 17, 38 and 46 of the Indian Constitution.

The framers of the Constitution also thought that with the formal equality [absence of discrimination], it is not possible to secure social, economic and political justice to the oppressed and exploited classes, especially Scheduled Castes and Scheduled Tribes. They were aware that, social realities could not be wished away by policy declaration and therefore, they evolved a discriminatory scheme and included in the Constitution to remove centuries old inequalities entrenched in the Indian social fabric. This arrangement is called 'protective or compensatory discrimination' in favour of some groups. This is a deliberate departure from the formal equality contemplated under the Constitution. The phrase 'Protective Discrimination' indicates the preference given in admission to public educational institutions and in public employment to the Scheduled Castes and Scheduled Tribes and other backward classes. This also includes reservation of seats in legislatures for the above groups. The preferential treatment given to the Scheduled Castes and Scheduled Tribes is in the form of assistance and reservation in various fields.

The Constitution-makers had also determined that social justice should be achieved without any violence and it should be secured within the framework of the Constitution. The conflict between the claims of the individual to enforce his Constitutional rights to formal or legal equality on the one hand and the concern of the State on the other to accord preferential treatment to the weaker sections of the society and in particular to the Scheduled Castes and Scheduled Tribes who constitute more than one-fifth of India's total population, in order to make the fundamental right to equality really meaningful to them, has presented many challenges not only to the Government but also to the judiciary. Many special provisions were incorporated to protect the interests of Scheduled Castes and Scheduled Tribes. For example, a provision has been made in the Constitution of India to reserve some seats for Scheduled Castes and Scheduled Tribes in the House of the People[18] and Legislative Assemblies of the States.[19] Besides, provisions were also made for the reservation of seats in educational institutions[20] and employment in State services.[21] These special provisions were incorporated in the Constitution by the Constitution-makers with a hope that with the increased educational opportunities and providing more representation in the public services and the Legislatures, the Scheduled Castes and Scheduled Tribes and other backward classes would be given more 'equal' opportunity guaranteed by the Constitution. A question would arise, who are these Scheduled Castes and Scheduled Tribes, who avail these special privileges conferred under the Constitution? The Untouchables are called Scheduled Castes because of their special relationship with the Government and they are selected by the President in the Presidential order, on the basis of their low ritual standing.[22] Besides, a Scheduled Caste is one whose name appears in a list issued by President under Article 341 (1) of the Constitution. The Constitution (Scheduled Castes) Order, 1950 specifies several 'castes', 'races' and 'tribes' and paragraph 3 of the order imposes a religious qualification for being a member of the Scheduled Caste. It reveals that 'No person who professes a religion different from Hinduism shall be deemed to be a member of Scheduled Caste'. As the Scheduled Castes population constitutes about 15% of India's population, Protective Discrimination is identified in the form of reservation of seats in the legislative assemblies, educational institutions, scholarships, housing allotments, land allotments, providing free hostel facilities and free training programmes in various fields. In case of Scheduled Tribe, the position is similar to that of Scheduled Castes as mentioned above. But these people live in exclusive territorial communities. Their disabilities can be identified in their physical isolation from the society and their exploitation by non-tribals. The population of this group can be found in States like Meghalaya, Dadra and Nagarhaveli to the extent of 80%. Therefore, to provide special privileges to these classes, the Constitution itself has guaranteed certain rights. Besides, the preambular premise of 'equality' of status and of opportunity has been concretized and clothed with flesh and blood by the provisions of Articles 14, 15 and 16 read with Articles 38, 46 and 335 of the Constitution. Thus Article 38 obligates the State among other things to minimise the inequalities in status, facilities and opportunities not only amongst individuals but also amongst classes of individuals living in the country. In this context, a special Constitutional obligation is imposed on the State by Article 46 to promote with special care the educational and economic interests of the weaker sections of the people and in particular, the Scheduled Castes and Scheduled Tribes. In order to enable the State to discharge the Constitutional obligation imposed by these directives, the right to equality embodied in Articles 14 and 16 (1) should be given a very liberal interpretation so that the right is made really meaningful to the Scheduled Castes and Scheduled Tribes and other backward classes of the Indian citizens.

It may be said that the Constitutional goal of 'equality' enshrined in the preamble of the Constitution is wide enough in its import to embrace both the concepts of formal and substantive equality.[23] Its import is also wide enough to obligate the State to bring about substantive equality by according, if necessary, favored or preferential treatment to those who deserve and need it. Strict adherence to the concept of formal equality would not only mean aggravation and perpetuation of the existing inequalities, but also a total negation of the preambular promise of equality of status and of opportunity. Therefore, the idea of substantive equality would and should necessarily admit the rational classification for preferential treatment in favour of Scheduled Castes and Scheduled Tribes with the consequent discrimination against the privileged classes of the society. The preferential treatment implicit in the idea of substantive equality may relate to the reservation of appointments in the State services or of seats in educational institutions. Besides, the idea of protective discrimination enjoins the State not only to make reservation in favour of the socially and educationally backward classes, Scheduled Castes and Scheduled Tribes, but also not to close to the members of these communities the doors of merit or open competition. Therefore, the main question in this context is; what are the Constitutional limitations on the power of the State to enforce substantive equality? To answer this question, we have to look to the Constitutional provisions and their judicial treatment.

THE ROLE OF JUDICIARY IN PROTECTIVE DISCRIMINATION

The concept of 'Protective discrimination' contemplates all kinds of preferential treatment provided to backward classes of people including Scheduled Castes and Scheduled Tribes in matters of availing opportunities in educational institutions, public employment and public life. The State provides various assistances to the backward classes including Scheduled Castes and Scheduled Tribes through its policies time and again. But the questions encountered by the Supreme Court in a number of cases were on the policies relating to 'reservation'.

Firstly, in **State of Madras** *V.* **Champakam Dorairajan,**[24] Madras Government, with a view to help backward classes, issued a Government Order providing for community wise reservation of seats in educational institutions such as Medical and Engineering colleges in the State, i.e., for Brahmins, Hindus, Muslims and Christians. The Supreme Court struck down the communal

Government Order as being violative of Article 15 (1) and Article 29 (2). The State tried to convince the Supreme Court saying that the State was under an obligation under Article 37 of the Constitution of India to give effect to the provisions of Article 46. The court observed that although the Directive Principles of State policy lay down that the State should promote with special care the education and economic interests of weaker section of the people and to protect them from social injustice, but the framers of the Constitution did not intend to give special preference to backward classes in educational institutions as they intended to give them in State services under Article 16 (4). The Supreme Court also pointed out that, apart from Article 16 (4), there is no provision authorising reservation or any kind of preferential treatment to these classes of people. Because the Constitution, as originally stood, contained only one clause i.e., Article 16 (4) in part III expressly authorising reservation in appointments and posts in public services for Scheduled Castes, Scheduled Tribes and other backward classes.

To overcome from the effect of this judgement of Supreme Court, Parliament inserted clause (4) to Article 15 to secure preferential treatment to backward classes and Scheduled Castes and Scheduled Tribes.[25] Article 15 (4) authorises the State to make special provisions for the advancement of socially and educationally backward classes of people. This provision covers reservation policy and various types of assistance to help them to overcome from their disabilities. In **Balaji V. State of Mysore,**[26] the Supreme Court was confronted with the problem of the term 'backwardness' in Article 15 (4); could 'Caste' be treated as a criterion for determining backwardness of a class? The Supreme Court declared that the use of 'Caste' as a sole criterion of classification of socially and educationally backward classes of citizens was violative of Article 15 (4) of the Constitution. Justice Gajendragadkar observed:

> "We are satisfied that the classification of the socially backward classes of citizens made by the State proceeds on the consideration only on their castes without regard to the other factors which are undoubtedly relevant. If that be the social backwardness of the communities to whom the impugned order applies has been determined in a manner which is not permissible under Article 15 (4) and that would introduce an infirmity which is fatal to the validity of the said classification".

The court also observed that 'Caste' could be a relevant factor for determining backwardness. Besides, it also pointed out that poverty, occupation and place of habitation could also contribute to backwardness and such factors could not be ignored.

In **R. Chitralekha V. State of Mysore,**[27] a question arose before the Supreme Court, whether an order specifying tests other than caste tests was a valid order? In this case, the Government of Mysore, by an order defined 'backward classes' and directed that 30% of the seats in professional and technical colleges and institutions shall be reserved for them and 18% shall be reserved for Scheduled Castes and Scheduled Tribes. The Supreme Court, by relying on Balaji's case, pointed out that if in a given selection 'Caste' is excluded in ascertaining a class within the meaning of Article 15 (4), it does not vitiate the classification if it satisfies the other tests. This shows that the court tried to base the determination of backwardness solely on secular, scientific and rational criterion ignoring the other factors. Justice Subba Rao also supported this view saying that Article 15, which used the expression 'classes' and not 'castes'. Both are not synonymous. But the Supreme Court in **P. Rajendran V. State of Madras**[28] upheld a classification made solely on terms of caste, but the court did not fully depart from the Balaji's decision. The court observed that;

> "If the reservation in question had been based only on caste and had not taken into account the social and educational backwardness of the caste in question, it would be violative of Article 15 (1). But it must not be forgotten that a caste is also a class of citizens and if the caste as a whole is socially and educationally backward, reservation can be made in favour of such a caste on the ground that it is socially and educationally backward class of citizens within the meaning of Article 15 (4). It is true that in the present case, the list of socially and educationally backward classes has been specified by caste. But that does not necessarily mean that the caste was the sole consideration and that persons belonging to these castes are not also a class of socially and educationally backward citizens".

Again in **State of Andhra Pradesh V. P. Sagar,**[29] Justice Shah interpreted non-absentee clause and clarified that;

> 'The criterion for determining the 'backward' must not solely be on religion, race, caste, sex or place of birth and the backwardness being

social and educational must be similar to the backwardness from which the Scheduled Castes and Scheduled Tribes suffer'.

The formula evolved in Rajendran's case had suffered a setback in P. Sagar's case and again it was revived by the Supreme Court in **State of Andhra Pradesh V. Balram**,[30] case. In this case, the Andhra Pradesh backward classes commission, in 1970, had drawn up a list of 92 communities. The Supreme Court upheld the list, which was based on 'castes' and 'communities'. The Court observed that, in determining 'backwardness', the Government could take into account the percentage of educated boys in a caste or community and after assessing their poverty and social status if it was found that a 'caste' was educationally and socially backward, its inclusion in the list of backward classes would be valid. In **K.S. Jayashree V. State of Kerala**,[31] the Supreme Court upheld the denial of protective discrimination in admission to medical colleges to the families among the backward classes whose income exceeded Rs. 10,000 per annum. The Court also pointed out that 'poverty' and 'caste' are both relevant for determining the backwardness. Besides, the Court said, neither the 'caste' alone nor 'poverty' alone will be the determining factor. It was emphasized that, there is a need for adopting means-cum-caste/ community test in classifying backward classes. Further, it stressed that the rich people among the backward castes/communities ceased to be socially and educationally backward classes even though they had not acquired any high level of education. The above facts clearly show that, in order to avail protective discrimination, the class must be identified both as socially and educationally backward. For this 'backwardness', the factors like both poverty and caste shall be taken into consideration to identify the backwardness of the caste or community.

THE EXTENT OF RESERVATION TO MEET SOCIAL JUSTICE

The main feature of the reservation policy under the Indian Constitution is that it bears a close resemblance to the population of Scheduled Castes and Scheduled Tribes. The Constitution of India has not fixed any maximum or minimum limit of reservation. Dr. Ambedkar observed in the Constituent Assembly: 'Supposing, for instance, reservations were made for a community or a collection of communities, the total of which came to something like 70% of the total posts under the State and only 30% are retained as the unreserved, could anybody say that the reservation of 30% as open to general competition would be satisfactory from the point of view of giving effect to the first principle namely, that there shall be equality of opportunity? It cannot be in my judgement'.[32]

In the absence of Constitutional prescription, the task of identifying how much reservation is to be fixed fell on the Courts and to determine the limits of reservation. The Supreme Court first considered the nature and extent of reservation of seats in educational institutions in **M.R. Balaji V. State of Mysore**.[33] In this case, the State of Mysore made its reservation through its Government Order, to the extent of 68% of the seats in the State's engineering and medical colleges in favour of socially and educationally backward classes of citizens including Scheduled Castes and Scheduled Tribes. The Supreme Court struck down the reservation of 68% as excessive and held that, the maximum percentage of seats that can be reserved in a year was 50%. The Court also observed that such excessive reservation amounted to a fraud on the Constitution. Besides, it also pointed out that, Article 15 (4), being in the nature of exception to the main rule embodied in the Article 15 (1), cannot be allowed to eat away the main rule and therefore, reservation in favour of socially and educationally backward classes of citizens must be less than 50% of the total available seats. But the Court has not said how much less than 50% reservation shall be fixed. It is left to the State to fix depending on the relevant prevailing circumstances in each case.[34]

The reservation of 68% here is plainly inconsistent with Article 15 (4). This is a clear inconsistency with the concept of the special provision, combined with sole reliance on caste as a criterion for selecting these classes, was such a covert or latent transgression of the Constitutional power as to amount to a "fraud on the Constitution".[35] The question regarding the quantum of reservation again came up for consideration in **T. Devadasan** *V.* **Union of India**[36] **and Rangachari cases**.[37] In Devadasan's case, the Supreme Court struck down the 'carry forward rule' which enabled excessive reservation to the backward classes including Scheduled Castes and Scheduled Tribes in the public services. The Court observed that where the reservation was so excessive in its character as to deny in practice a reasonable opportunity to other classes, it was a fraud upon the Constitution. This was because, in the instant case, the number of vacancies which came to be reserved by virtue of 'carry forward rule' could be upto 54% of the total vacancies, which was not below 50% limit fixed by the Supreme Court in Balaji's case. The Court also observed that, the carry forward rule is valid so long as the actual reservation in a particular year does not exceed 50% of the vacancies. The 50% limit has to be worked out on the basis of the total vacancies in a particular year and not in the services on total that is contemplated.

In the above case, the Central Government provides reservations of 12½% for Scheduled Castes and 5% for Scheduled Tribes for promotions from Grade IV to Grade III posts in the Central Secretariat service to be filled by competitive examination. The Government applied 'carry forward rule' under which unfilled reservations from the previous two years were added to the reservation for the current year. A total of 45 appointments were made, of which 29 (64.4%) were from Scheduled Castes and Scheduled Tribes.[38] Finding that the carry forward rule permitted reservations of over 50% (in the third year), the Supreme Court considered the scheme as ultravires or unconstitutional. Article 16 (4) says, the majority of judges in Devadasan case, is "a proviso or an exception" to Article 16 (1) and cannot be interpreted to nullify or destroy the main provision. "To hold that unlimited reservation could be made under clause (4) would in effect efface the guarantee contained in Clause (1) or at best make it illusory".[39] Therefore, the overriding effect of Clause (4) on Clauses (1) and (2) of Article 16 could only extend to the making of a reasonable number of reservations of appointments and posts in certain circumstances.[40]

Thus, reservations are legitimate to the extent that they provide backward classes with an "opportunity equal to that of members of the more advanced classes"; apparently they are excessive if they do more than provide equal opportunity. But Justice Subba Rao's dissenting opinion in the Devadasan's case is pertinent. He suggests that, the reasonableness of a reservation is to be measured by its relation to total cadre strength; a reservation is Constitutional so long as the "privileged" groups do not make up a disproportionate part of the total complement of employees. According to Subba Rao, the words "any provisions" in Article 16

(4) are broad enough to cover schemes of reservation, which operate over several years and in relation to the entire strength of the cadre; reasonableness is not to be determined on the basis of the percentage of seats reserved on one particular occasion. The State may use any method, including reservation of 100% of posts until the prescribed level is reached.[41]

Again, in **General Manager, S. Rly. V. Rangachari,**[42] a question arose before the Supreme Court whether benefit of reservation is applicable only for initial appointments or it can be extended to selection posts or promotional posts?

The Supreme Court observed that the power of reservation, which is conferred on the State, could be exercised by it not only to provide reservation of appointments but also to provide reservation in selection posts as well as promotional posts. But the Supreme Court in Mandal Commission case[43] has overruled this decision, wherein the Court pointed out that reservations can be made only in respect of direct recruitment at any level but not in respect of promotions. Consequent to this judgement, the Parliament brought an amendment to Article 16 (4) and added clause-(A)[43(a)] which says "nothing in this Article shall prevent the State from making any provision for reservation in matters of promotion of any class or classes of posts in the services under the State in favour of Scheduled Castes and Scheduled Tribes which in the opinion of the State are not adequately represented in the services under the State".

The question of quantum of reservation came in for consideration before the Supreme Court in **Thomas Case**.[44] This case involved the validity of a scheme showing favour to the Scheduled Castes and Scheduled Tribes employees by exempting them from the necessity of passing the departmental test for promotion in services. In the State of Kerala, a large number of Government servants belonging to Scheduled Castes and Scheduled Tribes were unable to get their promotions from lower division clerks to upper division clerks in the registration department. To provide relief to the backward classes of citizens, the Government incorporated rule 13AA under the Kerala State and Subordinate Service Rules 1958 enabling the Government to give exemption for two years to the Scheduled Castes and

Scheduled Tribes from passing the necessary tests. As a result of this, thirty-four out of fifty one posts were filled up by the members of the Scheduled Castes and Scheduled Tribes without passing the tests. The petitioner, N.M. Thomas, a lower division clerk was not promoted despite his passing the test. The petitioner questioned the validity of Rule 13AA as violative of Article 16 (1) and not protected by Article 16 (4) before the High Court of Kerala. The Kerala High Court observed that the impugned rule was invalid under Article 16 (1). It was also observed that the impugned scheme resulting in promotion of over 60% employees of the preferred group was too excessive and not conducive to the administrative efficiency. But when an appeal was made to the Supreme Court against the judgement of the Kerala High Court, the Supreme Court by 5 : 2 upheld the rule 13AA as a valid protective discrimination under Article 16 (1) because the implementation of Article 46 required the State to promote with special care the educational and economic interests of the weaker sections of the people and in particular the Scheduled Castes and Scheduled Tribes.[45] Chief Justice Ray, Justice Mathew, Justice Krishna Iyer, Justice Fazal Ali took the view that Article 16 (1) permits reasonable classification just as Article 14 does and as such the State could adopt any method or technique under Article 16 (4) to ensure adequate representation of the Scheduled Castes and Scheduled Tribes in public services. Justice Ray observed that the extent of reservation should be considered in the context of total position of promotions in services. The Court also pointed out, through these Judges, that the impugned rule in no way affected the efficiency of the administration as the beneficiaries of the rule were given only a temporary and not total exemption from passing the promotional tests. The judgement clearly shows that, in order to provide adequate representation to the Scheduled Castes and Scheduled Tribes, the State can adopt any technique or method to secure justice to these classes of people. Besides, the Government should adopt new strategy to repair the depressed lot of the backward classes in order to level them up to the rest of the society.[46] This advice of the Supreme Court is in due recognition of the ineffectiveness of the method of 'reservation', the benefits of which are snatched away by the creamy elites among the backward classes leaving the weakest and the most needy in the same condition of utter deprivation and backwardness.[47] The importance of this decision is to extend the State authority to confer preferential treatment and to provide all opportunities and incentives to the backward classes including Scheduled Castes and Scheduled Tribes to improve their living standards vis-à-vis the rest of the society.

Again the Supreme Court was confronted with the problem of 'quantum of reservations' to be given to the backward classes including Scheduled Castes and Scheduled Tribes, in **Akhil Bharathiya Shoshit Karamchari Sangh [Rly] V. Union of India.**[48] In this case, the validity of the Railway Board circulars, which provided reservation in selection for the Scheduled Caste and Scheduled Tribe candidates, were challenged. The Supreme Court upheld those Railway Board circulars and carry-forward rule, which provided for reservation. In the instant case, the carry forward rule was extended from 2 to 3 years. As a result of this rule, the reservation quota came to about 64.4%. But the Supreme Court held that this was not excessive.[49]

Besides, the Court also insisted that, the quantum of reservation has to be seen in the context of overall representation of the Scheduled Castes and Scheduled Tribes and not in a particular year. Justice Krishna Iyer observed:

> "In no year Scheduled Caste and Scheduled Tribe candidates are actually appointed to substantially more than 50% of the promotional posts. Some excess will not affect as mathematical precision is difficult in human affairs, but substantial excess will void the selection"

In order to protect the interests of SC/ST's, the parliament brought an amendment to Article 16(4) and inserted clause (4B) in the year 2000 which came in to effect from 9-6-2000. According to this 16 (4B), the State is permitted to consider any unfilled vacancies of a year which are reserved for being filled up that year in accordance with any provision for reservation made under clause (4) or clause (4A) as a separate class of vacancies to be filled up in any suceeding year or years and such class of vacancies shall not be considered together with the vacancies of the year in which they are being filled up for determining the ceiling of fifty per cent reservation on total number of vacancies of that year.

Justice Chinnappa Reddy also observed that, the rule of 50% laid down in earlier cases was only for the guidance of judges and were not bound by it. But in *K.C. Vasanth Kumar V. State of Karnataka,*[50] the Government sought some guidelines from the Supreme Court to fix reservation to the backward classes. After a thorough discussion of the earlier cases, the Court gave the guidelines of caste-cum-means test. The Court observed that, it is on the basis of multiple factors that a community as a whole will be considered as a backward class; it is by application of means test that the 'forward' within the 'backward class' will have to be excluded from such benefit. This enables the State to provide benefits of reservation to the most needy.

The above decisions of the Supreme Court indicate that, the doctrine of protective discrimination is Constitutionally permitted in Articles 14, 15 (4), 16 (1) and 16 (4). The State can adopt any measures to provide justice to the backward classes including Scheduled Castes and Scheduled Tribes. But it is also clear that no fundamental right to protective discrimination in the sense of imposing an affirmative duty on the State to ensure substantive equality is expressly embodied in the Constitution. Wide discretionary powers are given to the State to make various special provisions to the backward classes including the Scheduled Castes and Scheduled Tribes in such a way that it shall not eat away the benefits conferred to the others in the main provisions of the Constitution. In *Indra Sawhney V. Union of India,*[51] popularly known as Mandal Commission case, Constitution Bench of the Supreme Court by 6 : 3 majority *[Justice B.P. Jeevan Reddy, C.J. M.H. Kania, M.N. Venkatachalaiah, A.M. Ahmadi with S.R. Pandian and S.B. Sawant]* held that the decision of the Union Government to reserve 27% Government jobs for backward classes provided to socially advanced persons i.e., creamy layer among them, are to be eliminated. With a view to provide reservation benefits to the backward classes under Article 16 (4), the Court observed that 'creamy layer' among the backward classes should be eliminated from the purview of reservation benefits. This is due to the fact that, the benefits of social privileges like job reservations in Central and State services, admission to public educational institutions are mostly chewed up by the richer or more affluent sections of the backward class. The poorer and really backward sections among them keep on getting poorer and more backward. The Court also directed the Union Government to set up a Commission within four months from this decision to apply socio-economic criteria to exclude socially advanced persons from the backward classes group. The real objective of this decision is to secure reservation benefits to those needy and socially and economically disadvantaged members of the backward class.

When this criterion of 'creamy layer' extended even to the Scheduled Castes and Scheduled Tribes in providing reservation benefits, the real needy and disadvantaged persons will be benefited and their economic and social conditions may be improved. Gradually, it enables them to join the main stream of the society.

SINGLE POST RESERVATION

One of the important methods through which 'social justice' can be secured to the depressed classes including the Scheduled Castes and Scheduled Tribes is 'reservation'. A question arose before the Supreme Court of India, whether reservation can be made to 'single post' available in a particular year? This question was answered by the Supreme Court in **Dr. Chakradhar Paswan** *V.* **State of Bihar**.[52] The facts of the instant case are; in the State Directorate of Indigenous Medicines, Bihar, initially, there were three class–I posts i.e., Director of Indigenous Medicines, Deputy Director (Homeopathic) and Deputy Director (Unani). Later the post of Deputy Director (Ayurvedic) had also been added. The post of Director was the highest in the Directorate of Indigenous Medicines as a whole and not of any particular speciality of Indigenous Medicines.

The State Government of Bihar, in its circular dated November 8th, 1975, prescribed a 50-point roster to implement the policy of reservation to posts and appointments for members of the backward classes under Article 16 (4). It was laid down that, "if in any grade, there is only one vacancy for the first time, then it will be deemed to be unreserved and for the second time also, if there be only one vacancy, then it will be deemed to be reserved". For the purpose of determining the quantum of reservation according to the roster, the Government grouped together all the class-I posts viz., the posts of Director as well as Deputy Directors and as the post of Director had already been filled up treating it to be unreserved, the second post viz., the Deputy Director (Homeopathic) was treated as reserved. Accordingly, the State Public Service Commission issued advertisement-inviting applications from Scheduled Caste candidates for selection to the same posts and ultimately the State Government appointed a member of Scheduled Caste to the post of Deputy Director (Homeopathic). Immediately a writ petition was filed before the High Court of Patna by the general candidates challenging the advertisement issued by the State Public Service Commission and the consequent order of appointment. The High Court quashed the impugned advertisement and the appointment order. An appeal was made to the Supreme Court against the judgement and order of the Patna High Court. The appeal was dismissed by the Supreme Court and it held that, in service jurisprudence, the term 'cadre' has a definite legal connotation. It is not synonymous with 'service'. It is open to the Government to constitute as many cadres in any particular service as it may choose according to the administrative convenience and expediency and it cannot be said that, the establishment of the Directorate constituted the formation of a joint cadre of the Director and Deputy Directors because the posts are not interchangeable and the incumbents do not perform the same duties or carry the same responsibilities or draw the same pay.[53] The posts of the Director and those of the Deputy Directors constitute different cadres of the service. The first vacancy in the cadre of the Deputy Directors was that of the Deputy Director (Homeopathic) and it had to be treated as unreserved, the second reserved and the third unreserved. The Court also observed that, the whole concept of reservation for application of the 50-point roster is that, there are more than one post and the reservation can be made upto 50%. If there is only one post in the cadre, there can be no reservation with reference to the post either for recruitment at the initial stage or for filling up a future vacancy in respect of that post. Besides, the Court also held that, for implementing the 50-point roster, isolated and separate posts in different specialities couldn't be clubbed together. Reservation of posts, by applying the roster, can be made only where there is more than one post. That means, any reservation that comes under Article 16 (4) presupposes the availability of atleast more than one post in that cadre. No reservation could be made under Article 16 (4) so as to create a monopoly; otherwise it would render the guarantee of equal opportunity contained in the Article 16 (1) and (2) wholly meaningless and illusory.[54] Therefore, the reservation of the post of Deputy Director (Homeopathic) amounted to 100% reservation, which was impermissible under Article 16 (4). As the three posts of Deputy Directors of Homeopathic, Unani and Ayurvedic are distinct and separate as they pertain to different discipline and each one is an isolated post by itself carried in the same cadre, there can be no reservation for a single post in a cadre under Article 16 (4) of the Constitution of India.

But in **Madhav V. Union of India**[55], the Supreme Court took a different view on the single post reservation. The facts of the instant case are as follows;

In the National Savings Scheme service, there were various posts but there was only one post of Secretary. The Government applied the rule of reservation to that post by rotating the vacancies in accordance with the 40-point roster. When point no. 4 vacancy in that post, reserved for Scheduled Tribe, was filled by promoting an Scheduled Tribe candidate from the post below, such promotion was set aside by the Central Administrative Tribunal on the ground that the post of Secretary being a single point post, granting of reservation was unconstitutional. An appeal was made to the Supreme Court by the Government wherein the Court observed that 'reservation could be provided even to the isolated posts on the basis of rotation'. Extension of reservation in such cases is not unconstitutional.[56]

The Court also observed that, appointment to an office or post under the State is one of the means to render socio-economic justice. Article 16 (4-A) introduced in the Constitution of India in 1995 has resuscitated the objectives of the preamble to and Articles 46 and 335 of the Constitution of India to enable the Dalit and Scheduled Tribe employees to improve excellence in higher echelons of service and a source of equality of opportunity in the matter of social and economic status. As a consequence, Parliament has removed the lacuna pointed out by the Supreme Court in Indra Sawhney case. Thus, the legal position settled by the Supreme Court in *Rangachari's* case has been restored and held that; reservation of appointment by promotion would be available to the members of the Scheduled Castes and Scheduled Tribes as per

50% quota maintained in *Indra Sawhney's* case. The Court observed that, if the Government has applied the rule of rotation and the roster point to the vacancies that had arisen in the single point post and filled up by the candidates belonging to the reserved categories at the point on which they are eligible to be considered, such a rule is not violative of Article 16 (1) of the Constitution. Therefore, it was observed that, the roster point No. 4 in the vacancy of the Secretary reserved for the Scheduled Tribes was valid and Constitutional.

But in **Post-Graduate Institute of Medical Education & Research, Chandigarh V. Faculty Association**,[57] the Supreme Court held that, where there is a single post cadre, it cannot be reserved neither directly nor by device of rotation of roster point. The Court observed that, if reservation is made to a single post cadre through a device of rotation of roster point to the exclusion of the general members of the public would amount to 100% reservation which is not permissible within the Constitutional framework. Therefore, until there is plurality of posts in a cadre, the question of reservation will not arise. The Court was of the view that, Article 16 (4-A) relates to reservation in promotional posts in the cadre, but it does not deal with the question of reservation in a single cadre post.

From the above cases, it is evident that, wherever there is single cadre post, reservation cannot be made through any methods including the device of rotation of roster point. But this view is not correct and reasonable to secure social justice, which is a well-settled principle that Preamble is part of the Constitution. In **S.R. Bommai V. Union of India**,[58] the Court held that, 'Preamble to the Constitution is a part of its basic structure. Socio-economic justice, equality of opportunity and of status, dignity of persons is the arch of the Constitution. The Supreme Court also pointed out that, 'Social Justice' is a fundamental right as held in *Life Insurance Corporation V. Consumer Education and Research Centre*.[59] Article 335 mandates the State to take into consideration the claims of the Scheduled Castes and the Scheduled Tribes for appointment to a post or office under the State, consistent with efficiency of administration. Besides, providing reservation by the Government in posts or offices under the State is one of the modes to secure socio-economic justice to Scheduled Castes and Scheduled Tribes.

It may be submitted that the nation has yet to go a long way in the direction of ensuring substantive equality to the backward classes including the Scheduled Castes and Scheduled Tribes in the country.

ABOLITION OF UNTOUCHABILITY

The problem of Untouchables is an age-old concept, where some sections of the society were denied some privileges. They were prevented from entering into temples, public places, restaurants, educational institutions and socially they were boycotted in their villages by the caste Hindus. Therefore, the framers deliberately included a provision to eradicate Untouchability and to provide equal status to them along with the caste Hindus.

Mahatma Gandhi said, "What I want, what I am living for and what I should delight in dying for is the eradication of Untouchability root and branch".

Jawaharlal Nehru said, "We shall look to the common and forgotten man in India and seek to bring him relief and raise his standard of living. We shall continue to fight against curse of 'Untouchability' and other forms of enforced inequality and shall especially try to help those who are economically or otherwise backward".

Dr. B.R. Ambedkar said, "Annihilation of Untouchability is my birth right. The Untouchability has ruined the Untouchables, the Hindus and ultimately the nation as a whole".

Historically speaking, the term 'Untouchability' is associated with the origin of caste system [Varnashrama]. This caste system assumed a great complexity and rigidity and ultimately resulted into widespread Untouchability. The ideas of 'Untouchability' and 'Unapproachability' arose out of the ideas of ceremonial and occupational purity. The idea of purity not only centered around food and drink but also covered every human activity. A section of the Hindu society was debarred from keeping certain domestic animals, using certain metals for ornaments or household utensils, drawing water from public wells entering into temples, enjoying services of watermen and barbers and celebrating various festivals with others. The social disabilities of Untouchables were numerous and severe. Attempts were made from 18th century to eradicate this social evil. Many social reformers made sincere efforts to eradicate this evil to mitigate the rigour of the caste system. Even the Britishers were also not interested in eradicating this social evil of Untouchability. The Indian National Congress took up the cause of Untouchables very seriously and started a movement to give them an honored place in the Hindu society. It was Mahatma Gandhi who favored a change in the Hindu heart instead of resort to coercive measures. Gandhiji said:

> "To remove 'Untouchability' is a penance that caste Hindus owe to Hinduism and to themselves. The purification required is not of 'Untouchables' but of the so-called superior castes. There is no vice that is special to the 'Untouchables', nor even dirt and insanitation. It is our arrogance which binds us, superior Hindus, to our blemishes and which magnifies those of our downtrodden brethren whom we have suppressed and whom we keep under suppression".[60]

Gandhiji, further, believed that the caste Hindus should change their attitude towards Untouchables and to remove the rigidity of the Caste System.

In the year 1920, the Congress included the issue of eradicating Untouchability as an important item of the political programme. It was considered that to attain 'swaraj', it was necessary to eradicate this social evil of Untouchability from the Hindu society. Besides, the 'All Parties Committee' headed by Motilal Nehru in 1923, which recommended for an Indian Constitution also stressed for the removal of Untouchability and other caste disabilities. In 1929, a committee was appointed by the Congress to arouse a better public opinion in favour of the removal of caste disabilities. Due to the committee's efforts, many schools, wells and temples were thrown open to suppressed classes.

In the Constituent Assembly, the framers adopted the historic objectives resolution on 22nd January 1947, moved by Jawaharlal Nehru and declared their firm and solemn resolve to frame a Constitution wherein the people of India would be guaranteed and secured, interalia, socio, economic and political justice; and equality of status, of opportunity before the law and wherein, interalia, the depressed and backward classes would be provided with adequate safeguards. Later the Constituent Assembly elected the Advisory Committee on minorities, which submitted its reports, on fundamental rights, to the Constituent Assembly in April and August 1947. The report contained various rights including right to equality. This right provides for the removal of certain disabilities and abolition of Untouchability. Later, the drafting committee drafted equality provisions, headed by Dr. B.R. Ambedkar. In the first reading, one of the draft Articles provided, interalia, that on grounds of religion, race, castes and sex, citizens would not be subjected to any disability, liability, restrictions or condition with regard to;

1. Access to shops[61], hotels and places of public entertainments, public restaurants.
2. The use of wells, tanks, roads and places of public resort[62] maintained wholly or partly out of the State revenue or dedicated to the use of public.

Another draft Article declared the abolition of Untouchability and forbade its practice in any form. Further, it declared that the enforcement of any disability arising out of Untouchability would be an offence punishable under the law. One of the members of the Constituent Assembly said:

> "[The Draft Article] about Untouchability is one of the most important of the fundamental rights. This ...... does not propose to give any special privileges and safeguards to some minority community, but it proposed to save one-sixth of the Indian population from perpetual subjection and despair, from perpetual humiliation and disgrace. The custom of Untouchability has not only thrown millions of the ...... population into the dark abyss of gloom and despair, shame and disgrace but it has also eaten into the very vitality of our nation. I have not a jot of doubt ...... that this provision will be accepted by this House unanimously; not only the Indian National Congress is pledged to it, but for the sake of fairness and justice to the millions of Untouchables of this land, for the sake of sustaining our good will and reputation beyond the boundaries of India. This ...... must find a place in the Constitution of free and independent India ...... so ...... today the 29th November 1948 is a great and memorable day for us, the Untouchables. This day will go down in history as the day of deliverance, as the day of resurrection of the 5 crores of Indian people. Standing on the threshold of this new era, at least for ...... the Untouchables, I hear distinctly the words of Mahatma Gandhi ......[who said]; I do not want to be reborn, but if I am reborn, I wish

> that I should be born as a Harijan, as an Untouchable, so that I may lead a continuous struggle, life long struggle against the oppressions and indignities that have been heaped upon these classes of people".[63]

The final draft was adopted on 26th November signed on 24th January 1950 and enforced on 26th January. The relevant provisions are;

PREAMBLE: .... equality of status and of opportunity.

ARTICLE 15 (2): No citizen shall, on grounds only of religion, race, caste, sex, place of birth or any of them, be subject to any disability, liability, restriction or condition with regard to:

(a) Access to shops, public restaurants, hotels and places of entertainments; or

(b) The use of wells, tanks, bathing ghats and places of public resort maintained wholly or partly out of State funds or dedicated to the use of general public.

ARTICLE 17: " 'Untouchability' is abolished and its practice in any form is forbidden. The enforcement of any disability arising out of 'Untouchability' shall be an offence punishable in accordance with law".

This is one of the important provisions included in the Constitution of India for the complete removal of age-old social practice of 'Untouchability' from the Hindu social order. The Constitution-makers deliberately included this provision to provide equal status to the Scheduled Castes and Scheduled Tribes vis-à-vis the caste Hindus and to establish an egalitarian society. Therefore, the Constitution of India under Article 35 has empowered the Parliament to make suitable enactments to punish those individuals and institutions who infringe the fundamental rights guaranteed under Article 15 and 17 of the Constitution. The concept of 'Untouchability' and its eradication as contemplated under the Constitution of India and various enactments relating to it have been elaborately discussed in the subsequent chapter.[64]

PROTECTION OF 'LIFE AND PERSONAL LIBERTY' UNDER ARTICLE 21:

One of the important and inevitable rights guaranteed in the Constitution of India by the framers is 'Right to Life and Personal

Liberty' of an individual under Article 21. This Article contemplates that "No person shall be deprived of his life or personal liberty except according to procedure established by law". This Article guarantees twin rights like 'right to life' and 'personal liberty' to all persons against the executive and legislative actions. But under this Article a person's 'life and personal liberty' can be taken away through a procedure prescribed by law, provided that procedure is just, fair and reasonable.[65]

The Supreme Court of India, in several cases, has interpreted the word 'right to life and personal liberty' and given a literal meaning to them. For the first time, the Supreme Court in **A.K. Gopalan** *V.* **State of Madras**[66] interpreted the word ' personal liberty' and observed that, the word 'personal liberty' was confined only to freedom from arrest, detention or physical restraint. It also observed that, the term 'personal liberty' is confined or limited to freedom from punitive and preventive detention. Again the question of interpreting the word 'personal liberty' came up before the Supreme Court in **Kharak Singh** *V.* **State of Uttar Pradesh**.[67] In this case, Kharak Singh had been charged in a dacoity case but later he was released, as there was no evidence available against him. But he was kept under police surveillance and his name was recorded in the 'history-sheet' maintained by the police in accordance with the Uttar Pradesh police regulations. The term 'surveillance' defined in the police regulation included secret picketing of the house, domiciliary visits at night, periodical inquiries about the person and an eye on his movements. This regulation was challenged by the petitioner as violative of his fundamental right to movement guaranteed in Article 19 (1) (d) and 'personal liberty' in Article 21. Speaking for the majority, Justice Ayyangar struck down the earlier interpretation of the word 'personal liberty' confined to 'freedom from physical restraint or freedom from confinement within the bounds of a prison' and observed that "personal liberty is used in the Article as a compendious term to include within itself all the varieties of rights which go to make up the 'personal liberties' of man other than those dealt with in Article 19 (1). In other words, while Article 19 (1) deals with particular species or attributes of that freedom, 'personal liberty' in Article 21 takes in and comprises the residue". The court pointed out that, an unauthorised intrusion into a person's home and the disturbance caused to him is the violation of the personal liberty of the individual. Therefore, the police regulations authorizing domiciliary visits were violative of fundamental right guaranteed in Article 21 of the Constitution.

Again, the Supreme Court had an occasion to interpret the expression 'right to life' in **Francis Coralie** *V.* **Union Territory of Delhi.**[68] In this case, the court observed that 'right to live is not confined to the protection of any faculty or limb through which life is enjoyed or the soul communicates with the outside world, but it also includes the right to live with human dignity'. That means, right to live is not restricted to mere animal existence, but it is more than just physical survival. It includes, 'the right to live with human dignity', and all that goes along with it, namely the bare necessities of life such as adequate nutrition, clothing and shelter and facilities for reading, writing and expressing our views in diverse forms, freely moving about and mixing with fellow human beings.

RIGHT TO LIFE AND ITS BASIC NECESSITIES

Right to Livelihood

Article 21 of the Constitution guarantees the most fundamental of all rights, namely, the 'Right to Life'. This is the foundation on which the superstructure of other rights are built. In **Bandhu Mukti Morcha** *V.* **Union of India,**[69] Justice P.N. Bhagawati observed that "it is the fundamental right of every one in this country to live with human dignity, free from exploitation'. The right to live with human dignity derives its life breath from the Directive Principles of State Policy, particularly clauses (e) and (f) of Article 39 and Articles 41, 42 of the Constitution. Thus human dignity must include protection of health and strength of workers, tender age of children against abuse, opportunities and facilities for children to develop in a healthy manner and conditions of freedom and dignity, educational facilities, just and humane conditions of work". In **Peoples Union for Democratic Rights** *V.* **Union of India,**[70] the Supreme Court of India observed that non-payment of minimum wages to the workers employed in various Asiad projects in Delhi was a denial to them of their 'right to live with basic human dignity' and violative of Article 21 of the Constitution of India. Justice Bhagawati pointed out that "the rights and benefits conferred on the workmen employed by a contractor under various labour laws are clearly intended to ensure basic human dignity to workmen and if the workmen are deprived of any of these rights and benefits, that would clearly be a violation of Article 21". Besides, he also said, the non-implementation by the private contractors and non-enforcement by the State authorities of the various provisions of labour laws violated the fundamental right of workers 'to live with human dignity'.

For the first time, the Supreme Court gave a wider meaning to the expression 'right to life' in **Olga Tellis** *V.* **Bombay Municipal Corporation**.[71] In this case the court held that the expression 'Right to Life' in Article 21 includes 'Right to Livelihood' also. It observed that the sweep of Article 21 is wide enough to cover livelihood also. Because no person can live without the means of living, i.e., livelihood. If the 'right to livelihood' is not treated as an integral part of the Constitutional right to life, then it is easy to deprive a persons livelihood by depriving his right to life. This would make life impossible to live. The court said;

> "It does not mean merely that life cannot be extinguished or taken away as, for example, by the imposition and execution of death sentence, except according to the procedure established by law. That is but one aspect of the 'right to life'. An equally important facet of that right is the 'right to livelihood' because no person can live without the means of livelihood. If the right to livelihood is not treated as part of Constitutional right to life, the easiest way of depriving a person of his right to life would be to deprive him of his means of livelihood. In view of Article 39 (A) and 41 require the State to secure to the citizen an adequate means of livelihood and the right to work, it would be sheer pedantry to exclude the right to livelihood from the content of the right to life".

Therefore, when a person is deprived of his 'right to livelihood' except according to just and fair procedure established by law, he can challenge such deprivation as it offends his 'right to life'.

In **Neeraja Chaudhury** *V.* **State of Madhya Pradesh**,[72] the Supreme Court, through Justice Bhagawati, has observed that failure of the State to identify the bonded labourers, to release them from their bondage and to rehabilitate them as envisaged by the Bonded Labour System Act, 1976, violates Article 21 and 23 of the

Constitution. If these labourers are not rehabilitated by the State, they would be driven to poverty, helplessness and despair. This enables them to live with utter poverty, and without dignified life. Therefore, 'right to livelihood' is an integral part of 'right to life' in Article 21.

In **State of Himachal Pradesh** *V.* **Umed Ram**,[73] a question arose before the Supreme Court whether 'Right to access to road' is also included in 'Right to life' under Article 21. The court observed that, the right to life in Article 21 "embraces not only physical existence of life but also the quality of life for residents of hilly areas, access to road is access to life itself".[74] By interpreting the expression 'right to life', the court said the 'right to life' includes 'right to livelihood also'. In this case, the Scheduled Castes who were living in the hilly region of Himachal Pradesh had no access to road to earn their daily bread, which affected their livelihood.

Right to Shelter

In a civilized society, every individual requires 'Shelter' to have a decent and dignified life. Therefore, the Supreme Court in several cases has observed that 'right to shelter' is an integral part of 'right to life' under Article 21 of the Constitution. For instance, in **Chameli Singh** *V.* **State of Uttar Pradesh**,[75] the Supreme Court observed that, the 'right to shelter' is a fundamental right as 'right to live' guaranteed in any civilized society implies the right to food, water, decent environment, education, medical care and shelter. These are the basic human rights known to any civilized society. All civil, political, social and cultural rights enshrined in the Universal Declaration of Human Rights and Convention or under the Constitution of India cannot be exercised without these basic human rights. Therefore, 'Shelter' for human being is not a mere protection of his life and limb, but it includes home where an individual will have an opportunity to grow physically, mentally, intellectually and spiritually. Therefore, 'Right to Shelter' includes adequate living space, safe and decent structure, clean and decent surroundings, sufficient light, pure air, water, electricity, sanitation and other civic amenities like roads etc, so as to have easy access to his daily avocation. Therefore, 'right to shelter' does not mean a mere 'right to a roof' over one's head but right to all the infrastructure necessary to enable them to live and develop as a human being. The court also pointed out that, it is the duty of the State to provide housing facilities to Scheduled Castes and Scheduled Tribes, to enable them to join the main stream of the national life.

In **Ahmedabad Municipal Corporation** *V.* **Nawab Khan Gulab Khan**,[76] the question was whether, removing of pavement dwellers from footpaths or public streets would be violative of 'right to life' under Article 21? The Supreme Court once again gave a wider meaning to the expression 'right to life' by saying that, 'Shelter' is an aspect of right to life and it is the duty of the State to provide adequate facilities and opportunities to the pavement dwellers for the erection of shelter over their heads to make the 'right to life' meaningful, effective and fruitful. The court also observed that, though no person has a right to encroach and erect structures or otherwise on footpaths, public streets or any other place reserved for public purpose, it is the Constitutional duty of the State to provide necessary facilities to them to carry on their business for their livelihood. The deprivation of 'right to life' in that context would not only denude life of effective content and meaningfulness, but it would make life miserable and impossible to live.

Right to Medical Aid & Health of Workers

One of the important factors, which go to make life meaningful and dignified, is the 'right to medical aid and health'. In the light of the importance of 'right to medical aid and health', the Supreme Court has interpreted the word 'right to life' elaborately in **Consumer Education and Research Centre** *V.* **Union of India**[77] and observed that 'right to health and medical aid' is an integral part of 'right to life' in Article 21 of the Constitution. In this case, the workers who were working in asbestos industry were affected by asbestosis and became prone to lung cancer and related ailments. In the light of these facts, the court held that, 'right to life' under Article 21 includes right to health and medical care. It also observed that, the State, be it Union or State government or an industry, whether public or private is obligated to take all actions which will promote health, strength and vigour of the workmen during and after service. The 'right to life' with human dignity encompasses within its fold, some of the finer facets of human civilization, which makes life worth living.

In order to make the lives of the workmen meaningful, the Supreme Court laid down the following guidelines to be followed by the asbestos industries in India;

(a) All asbestos industries must take health insurance of workers employed in industry;

(b) Every worker suffering from occupational health hazards would be entitled for compensation of Rs.1 lakh;

(c) All asbestos industries must maintain the health record of every worker up to a minimum period of 40 years from the beginning of the employment or 15 years after retirement or cessation of the employment whichever is later.

(d) "Membrane filter test" to detect asbestos fiber should be adopted by all the factories on par with Metalliferous Mines Regulations, 1961 and Vienna Convention.

(e) All the factories whether covered by the Employees State Insurance Act, or Workmen's Compensation Act or otherwise, should insure health coverage to every worker.

In **Paramananda Katara** *V.* **Union of India**[78] a question arose whether providing immediate medical aid to an injured person is also included to 'Right to life' under Article 21 of the Constitution? The Supreme Court has observed that, it is the professional obligation of all doctors, whether government or private, to extend medical aid to the injured immediately to preserve life without waiting for any legal formalities to be complied with by the police under Criminal Procedure Code. Failure to provide immediate medical aid to an injured person would be violative of 'Right to life' guaranteed in Article 21. The court, through Justice Oza, also pointed out that 'when a man is in a miserable state hanging between life and death reaches the medical practitioner either in a hospital run or managed by the State public authority or a private person or a medical professional doing only private practice he is always called upon to rush to help such an injured person and to do all that is within his power to save his life. It is a duty coupled with human instinct, which needs neither decision nor any code of ethics or any rule or law'.[79] The court also observed that Article 21 of the Constitution casts the obligation on the State to preserve life. No law or State action can intervene to delay the discharge of the obligation to provide immediate medical aid by the members of the medical profession. This obligation being total, absolute and paramount, laws of procedure whether in statutes or otherwise which would interfere with the discharge of this obligation cannot be sustained and must therefore, give way. Therefore, the court pointed out that 'Right to life' in Article 21 includes right to provide immediate medical aid to injured person to make the life meaningful and dignified.

The question of right to health in the context of emergency medical treatment again came up before the Supreme Court in **Paschim Banga Khet Mazdoor Samiti** *V.* **State of West Bengal**.[79(a)] In this case, a person fell down from a running train and sustained severe head injuries. Immediately, he was taken to nearby hospital where he was denied admission on the grounds that there were no vacant beds. Eventually he was admitted to a private hospital incurring heavy expenditure for the emergency treatment. Later, a suit was filed in the Supreme Court against the State for failure to provide immediate emergency treatment. Supreme Court observed that, failure to provide timely emergency treatment to a person who was in need of such treatment violated his 'right to life' guaranteed under Article 21 of the Constitution. It also pointed out that, Article 21 imposes an obligation on the State to safeguard the right to life of every person. Preservation of human life is thus of paramount importance. Therefore, failure to provide immediate medical treatment by the medical practitioners to an injured person would take away the life of such individual and thereby violative of 'Right to life' under Article 21 of the Constitution.

The importance of 'Right to life' has also been recognised by the Supreme Court in **Kirloskar Brothers Ltd.** *V.* **Employees State Insurance Corporation**.[79(b)] In this case, the Court observed that, 'right to health' is a fundamental right of the workmen within the meaning of Article 21 of the Constitution. For the purpose of ensuring safety and protection to the workmen, the Court held that, this right is not only available against the State and its instrumentalities but also to private industries to ensure to the workmen basic facilities and opportunities for the maintenance of health and vigour as guaranteed in part-IV of the Constitution i.e., Directive Principles of State Policies', which are integral part of right to life under Article 21. As health is a state of complete physical, mental and social well being of a workman, it should be protected by the employer to make the right to life meaningful.

Right to Education

For the first time Supreme Court of India has observed, in **Mohini Jain** *V.* **State of Karnataka**,[80] that the 'right to education' is a fundamental right under Article 21 of the Constitution which cannot be denied to a citizen by charging higher capitation fee. The right to life under Article 21 and the dignity of an individual cannot be assured unless it is accompanied by the right to education, as this right flows directly from 'right to life'. In this case, a writ petition was filed by Miss. Mohini Jain of Meerut, Uttar Pradesh challenging the validity of the notification issued by the Government of Karnataka under Karnataka Educational Institutions (Prohibition of Capitation Fee) Act, 1984, which was passed to regulate the capitation fee collected by the private Medical College in the State.

The petitioner, Miss. Mohini Jain was denied admission to Medical College as she refused to pay the tuition fee of Rs. 60000 per annum as per the notification. Justice Kuldip Singh and R.N. Sahai observed that 'right to education at all level (including professional education like Medicine and Engineering) is a fundamental right of citizen under Article 21 of the Constitution and charging exorbitant capitation fee for admission to educational institutions is violative of Right to life in Article 21'. Because, imposing of exorbitant capitation fee makes the availability of education beyond the reach of poor people. The right to education is concomitant to the fundamental rights enshrined under part-III of the Constitution. Therefore, in order to have meaningful and dignified life, education is a must and inevitable. The same view was reiterated by the Supreme Court in **Unnikrishnan** *V.* **State of Andhra Pradesh**[81] and held that 'right to education' is a fundamental right under Article 21 of the Constitution. But the Court partly overruled the Mohini Jain's case and observed that 'every child/ citizen of this country has a right to free education until he/she completes the age of fourteen years. Thereafter, his right to education is subject to the limits of economic capacity and development of the State'.[82]

Right to Environment

In the area of environmental law, judiciary has been playing an activist role to protect the humanity against the adverse effects of environmental pollution and ecological imbalances. The reason is that, the pollution problem threatens the very survival of human race. Article 48 A of the Indian Constitution directs the State to endeavour to protect and improve the environment and to safeguard the forests. There are number of enactments to control pollution, namely, the Water (prevention and control of pollution) Act, 1974 and Air (prevention and control of pollution) Act, 1981. Despite all these enactments, every day chemical industries and other sources are polluting the atmosphere due to gas leaks and discharge of wastes.

In '**Rural Litigation and Entitlement Kendra, Dehradoon** *V.* **State of Uttar Pradesh**'[83], a rural activist group filed a writ petition in the Supreme Court based on Article 21 and 48 A to enjoin limestone quarrying that was causing irreparable damage to hill sides, villages and surrounding farm land in the Doon valley. It was alleged that mining operations in lime quarries of Missouri hills had adverse impact on ecological balance. Besides it was also alleged that the manner of working of these quarries was disturbing the ecological balance and threatening human health by polluting the environment. Immediately the court appointed an expert committee under the chairmanship of Sri. D.N. Bhargava, Controller General of Indian Bureau of Mines, Nagpur, for the purpose of inspecting limestone quarries and to report about their working and impact on ecology. The committee submitted its report to the Supreme Court. Based on the report, the court ordered the closing of almost all the quarries, and conditional renewal of leases for the rest of them. The court also ordered land reclamation and employment programs, and leasing practices that would solve the problems of those whose jobs or businesses were disrupted by the closures. Through this decision, the court protected the health and environment of the people who are not even parties to the writ petition. To make 'life' meaningful, State should take measures to regulate those industries, which pollute the environment and discharge waste products. The judgment is a landmark in judicial history illustrating the anxiety of the court to ensure pollution free atmosphere, which goes a long way in making the 'right to life' as meaningful and dignified as contemplated under Article 21 of the Constitution.

In **M.C. Mehta** *V.* **Union of India**,[83(a)] through Public Interest Litigation, the problem of Ganga water was brought before the Supreme Court. The Contention of the petitioner was that the water from the river Ganga is being contaminated to a dangerous level by industrial effluents and domestic sewage which violates the citizens' fundamental right to a clean and hygienic environment which is an aspect of 'Right to life' under Article 21 of the Constitution. The Supreme Court in its historic judgement on September 27th, 1987, ordered the closure of a number of tanneries near Kanpur city, which were found guilty of discharging directly or indirectly toxic effluents into the river. The Court also took note of the fact that many provisions of the pollution prevention laws had just remained on paper without any action being taken by the authorities and on account of the failure to obey the statutory duties for several years, the water of river Ganga had become so polluted that it could no longer be used either for drinking or for bathing. The Court also observed that tanneries, which claimed that they had no money to establish primary treatment plants, couldn't be allowed to exist, just as an industry must close down if it cannot pay maximum wages to its workers.

In **Delhi water supply and sewage disposal undertaking** *V.* **State of Haryana**,[83(b)] the Supreme Court again observed that, "water is a gift of nature. Human hand cannot be permitted to convert this bounty into a curse, oppression The primary use to which water is put being drinking, it would be mocking nature to force the people who live on the bank of a river to remain thirsty". It further held that, 'drinking is the most beneficial use of water and this need is so paramount that it cannot be made subservient to any other use of water, like irrigation. So the right to use of water for domestic purpose would prevail over other needs'.

From the above cases it is evident that Article 21 of the Constitution of India has guaranteed 'right to life' to the people of India, which includes Scheduled Castes and Scheduled Tribes. The Article has also imposed an obligation on the State to provide basic facilities to the people of India in general and Scheduled Castes and Scheduled tribes in particular. This is to make the 'right to life' more meaningful and dignified as required under the

Constitution. Whatever the basic facilities provided to the people in general, will also be applicable to the Scheduled Castes and Scheduled Tribes. Therefore the 'right to life' in Article 21 protects the life of Scheduled Castes and Scheduled Tribes to make their life meaningful and dignified.

Constitutional Remedies

The framers of Constitution have also made provisions in the Constitution to protect various fundamental rights conferred to the individuals. That means, any violation of these rights by any authority, the Supreme Courts and High Courts, are empowered to enforce those rights under Article 32 and 226 of the Constitution respectively.

Article 32 guarantees the right to move the Supreme Court by "appropriate proceedings" for the enforcement of the fundamental rights conferred under part III of the Constitution. Clause (2) of Article 32 confers power on the Supreme Court to issue appropriate directions, orders or writs, including writs in the nature of Habeas Corpus, Mandamus, Prohibition, Quo Warranto and Certiorari for the enforcement of any of the rights conferred by part III of the Constitution. Under Article 226, the High Courts are given the same power, but it can issue any of the above writs not only for enforcement of fundamental rights but also for any other purpose.

The significance of Article 32 has been emphasised by Justice Bhagawati in **Bandhu Mukti Morcha case**[84] as follows;

> "Article 32 does not merely confer power on the Court to issue direction, order or writ for the enforcement of fundamental rights but it also lays a Constitutional obligation on this Court to protect the fundamental rights of the people and for that purpose this Court has all incidental and ancillary powers including to forge new remedies and fashion new strategies designed to enforce fundamental rights. It is in realisation of this Constitutional obligation that this Court has innovated new methods and strategies particularly for enforcing the fundamental rights of the poor and disadvantaged who are denied their human rights and to whom freedom and liberty have no meaning".

This shows that, even the poor and disadvantaged sections of the society, particularly the members of Scheduled Castes and Scheduled Tribes, can also seek quick remedy either in the Supreme

Court or in the High Courts, if their fundamental or any other Constitutional rights are violated by the State or by any private individuals. Therefore, the Supreme Court has adopted a new strategy like 'Public Interest Litigation' wherein the public-spirited citizens can move the Supreme Court or the High Courts for the enforcement of fundamental rights and Constitutional rights respectively. In **Bandhu Mukti Morcha** *V.* **Union of India**, an organisation dedicated to the cause of the release of bonded labourers, informed the Supreme Court through a letter that, they conducted a survey of the stone-quarries situated in Faridabad district of the State of Haryana and found that there were a large number of labourers working in the stone-quarries under 'inhuman and intolerable conditions' and many of them were bonded labourers. The organisation prayed for a writ to be issued against the State for proper implementation of the various provisions of the Constitution and statutes to liberate the bonded labourers, who were suffering from torture and exploitation, immediately. The Supreme Court treated the letter as a writ petition and appointed a commission to visit these stone-quarries and to submit its report on the actual suffering and misery of the bonded labourers. Speaking for the majority Justice Bhagawati explained the nature and purpose of the Public Interest Litigation as follows;

> "Public Interest Litigation is not in the nature of adversary litigation but it is a challenge and an opportunity to the Government and its officers to make basic human rights meaningful to the deprived and vulnerable sections of the community and to assure them social and economic justice which is the significant tune of our Constitution. The Government and its officers must welcome Public Interest Litigation because it would provide them an access to examine whether the poor and the downtrodden are getting their social and economic entitlements or whether they are continuing to remain victims of the deception and exploitation at the hands of strong and powerful sections of the community ...... when the Court entertains Public Interest Litigation, it does not do so in a caviling spirit or in a controversial mood or with a view to tilting at executive authority or seeking to usurp it, but its attempt is only to endure observance of social and economic programmes framed for the benefit of the have-nots and the handicapped and to protect them against violation of their basic human rights, which is also the Constitutional obligation of the executive. The Court is thus assisting in the realisation of the Constitutional objective".[85]

Through the Public Interest Litigation cases, the Supreme Court has emerged as the defender and champion of the have-nots. Today, under trials,[86] convicted prisoners,[87] bonded labourers,[88] unorganized labourers,[89] Scheduled Castes and Scheduled Tribes,[90] exploited women,[91] slum dwellers,[92] victims of police tortures[93] and other vulnerable sections of the society, until now voiceless and invisible, have access to the Supreme Court and the High Courts for securing their human rights. Besides, the new strategies of the Public Interest Litigation has awakened the consciousness of the public regarding the dignity of the human life, the importance of liberty and the right to equal justice. By introducing this new mode of litigation in the judicial system, the Supreme Court has demonstrated a non-violent means to prevent the exploitation of the poor and to promote social justice.

In **State of Himachal Pradesh** *V.* **Umed Ram Sharma**,[94] some poor Harijans addressed a letter to the Chief Justice of the High Court complaining that, in 1972, the State Government had sanctioned road but it was not constructed till 1980 and was causing immense hardship. The High Court treated the letter as a writ petition, allowed the petition and issued the necessary instructions and directed the State Government to place before the Court the progress report. The State Government approached the Supreme Court against the High Court order. The Supreme Court recognised the 'locus standi' of the residents of the hilly area to approach the Court, and treating a right of access to road as right to life. The Supreme Court observed;

> "The entire State of Himachal Pradesh is in hills and without workable roads, no communication is possible. Every person is entitled to life as envisaged in Article 21 of the Constitution and in the facts of this case read in conjunction with Article 19 (1) (d) of the Constitution and in the background of Article 38 (2) of the Constitution, every person has right under Article 19 (1) (d) to move freely throughout the territory of India and he has also the right under Article 21 to his life and that right, under Article 21 embraces not only physical existence of life but also the quality of life and for residents of hilly area, access to road is access to life itself".

From all the above instances, it is evident that, the Constitutional remedies incorporated in the Constitution of India under Article 32 and 226 protects the interests and rights of the weaker sections of the society in getting social and economic justice. Through Articles 32 & 226 of the Constitution, the downtrodden sections of the society may invoke the jurisdiction of the Supreme Court as well as the High Courts for the enforcement of their human rights to secure social justice if they are deprived of these rights by the State.

DIRECTIVE PRINCIPLES OF STATE POLICY

Under part IV of the Constitution of India a number of State policies are envisaged for achieving welfare and social justice, ensuring social order and dignity to the individuals, not only to the few privileged persons but also to the entire masses of the country including the have-nots and the depressed classes. Although the Directive Principles of State Policies are not enforceable in a Court of law unlike fundamental rights, they are nevertheless fundamental in the governance of the country. Besides, it is the duty of the State to apply these principles while making various laws. These Directive Principles are as important as fundamental rights. Because, while fundamental rights are aimed at assuring political freedom to the citizens, the Directive Principles are intended to foster social and economic democracy. Explaining the object in laying down these principles Dr. Ambedkar said;[95]

> "It is no use giving a fixed, rigid form to something which is not rigid, which is fundamentally changing and having regard to the circumstances and keep on changing. It is therefore, no use saying that the Directive Principles have no value. In my judgement, the Directive Principles have a great value, for they lay down that our ideal is economic democracy. Because we did not want merely a Parliamentary form of Government to be instituted through various mechanisms provided in the Constitution, without any directions as to what our economic ideal or as to what our social order ought to be, we deliberately included the Directive Principles in our Constitution. I think, if the friends who are agitated over this question bear in mind what I have just said that our objective in framing this Constitution is really two folds.
>
> (i) To lay down the form of political democracy and
>
> (ii) To lay down that our ideal is economic democracy and also to prescribe that every Government whoever it is in power, shall strive to bring about economic democracy much of the

misunderstanding under which most members are labouring will disappear".

Besides, Ambedkar added that the Directive Principles are in the nature of instructions issued to future legislators and executives for their guidance. He said;[96]

"But whoever captures power will not be free to do what he likes with it. In the exercise of it, he will have to respect these instruments of instructions, which are called Directives Principles. He cannot ignore them. He may not have to answer for their breach in a Court of law. But he will certainly have to answer for their breach before the electorate at election time".

This shows that, both Fundamental Rights and Directive Principles of State Policies aim at establishing a just social order based on the philosophy of social justice. So the concept of social justice is a living concept or revolutionary import. It provides sustenance to the rule of law and meaning and significance to the ideals of a welfare State. This is basically founded on the basic ideal of socio-economic equality and its objective is to help in the removal of socio-economic inequalities and disparities. The various freedoms and rights guaranteed under the Constitution are not an end in itself, but they are the means to achieve social justice. Besides, our Constitution is the unique document for the upliftment of downtrodden and weaker sections of the society. The greatest need of hour in our society is social integration of the weaker and oppressed sections of the people with the rest of the society. Therefore, the Constitution-framers have included some Directive Principles of State Policies to the Constitution of India in part IV to achieve social justice. These are;

State to Secure a Social Order for the Promotion of Welfare of the People

Article 38 of the Constitution says 'the State shall strive to promote the welfare of the people by securing and protecting as effectively as it may be a social order in which justice, social, economic and political, shall inform all the institutions of the National life'.

Clause (2) of this Article says 'the State shall in particular, strive to minimise the inequalities in income and endeavour to eliminate inequalities in status, facilities and opportunities, not only amongst individuals but also amongst groups of people residing in different areas or engaged in different vocations'.

The above Article obligates the State to promote the welfare of the people and to secure to all, political justice, economic justice as well as social justice. At the same time, the State shall eradicate inequalities in status, facilities and opportunities. Through these measures, it is possible to secure social order and to ensure dignity to the individuals.

Certain Principles of Policy to be Followed by the State

Article 39 of the Constitution contemplates that 'the State shall direct its policy towards securing;

(i) That the citizens, men and women equally, have the right to an adequate means of livelihood.

(ii) That the ownership and control of the material resources of the community are so distributed as best to sub serve the common good.

(iii) That the operation of the economic system does not result in the concentration of wealth and means of production to the common detriment.

(iv) That there is equal pay for equal work for both men and women.[97]

(v) That the health and strength of workers, men and women, and the tender age of children are not abused and that citizens are not forced by economic necessity to enter avocations unsuited to their age and strength.

(vi) That the children are given opportunities and facilities to develop in a healthy manner and in conditions of freedom and dignity and that childhood and youth are protected against exploitation and against moral and material abandonment.

The above Article imposes an obligation on the State to ensure and to provide its people sufficient means of livelihood, equal pay for equal work, fair distribution of wealth and protection to children and labour. The objective is to secure egalitarian society where there shall be no discrimination, inequality, injustice and exploitation in the State. Moreover, our Constitution assigns a prominent role to and imposes heavy responsibilities upon the State to assure a dignified life to all individuals irrespective of his race, caste, colour, language, religion and status. In a way it incorporates the need-based principle of justice. The need-based principle is richer in content and has close proximity with social justice than the merit-based principle.[131] In order to ameliorate the weaker sections of the society and to reduce their number to a minimum level, need-based principle of justice should be strictly followed by the State. This principle secures to every human being, including the downtrodden sections of the society, the basic necessities to life like food, clothing, housing, medicine, education etc. This is infact Dr. Ambedkar's voice of social justice and Constitutional vision.

Equal Justice and Free Legal Aid

The State shall secure that the operation of the legal system promotes justice, on the basis of equal opportunity and shall in particular provide free legal aid, by suitable legislation or schemes or in any other way, to ensure that opportunities for securing justice are not denied to any citizen by reason of economic or other disabilities.[99]

This Article emphasizes that free legal service is an inalienable element of 'reasonable, fair and just' procedure for without it a person suffering from economic or other disabilities would be deprived of the opportunity for securing Justice. Therefore, the right to free legal services is clearly an essential ingredient of 'reasonable, fair and just' procedure for a person accused of an offence and it must be held implicit in the guarantee of the Article 21 of the Constitution of India. This is a Constitutional right of every accused person who is unable to engage a lawyer and secure legal services on account of reasons such as poverty, indigence or incommunicado situation. The State is under an obligation to provide a lawyer to an accused person if the circumstances of the case and the needs of justice so required. If our legal system fails to take cognisance of this free legal services to the economically and socially weaker sections of the society, it loses its credibility. Therefore, we should inject equal justice into legality and that can be done only by dynamic and activist scheme of legal services. In this connection, the famous words of Justice Mr. Brennan are noteworthy;

'Nothing rankles more in the human heart than a brooding sense of injustice, illness, we can put up with. But injustice makes us want to pull things down. When only the rich can enjoy the law, as a doubtful luxury and the poor, who need it most, cannot have it because its expenses puts it beyond their reach. The threat to the continued existence of free democracy is not imaginary but very real because democracy's very life depends upon making the machinery of justice so effective that every citizen shall believe in and benefit by its impartiality and fairness".

The Supreme Court of India in **Hussainara Khatoon** *V.* **State of Bihar,**[100] through Justice Bhagawati, strongly recommended to the Government of India and the State Governments that it is high time that a comprehensive legal service programme is to be introduced in the country. That is, not only a mandate of equal justice implicit in Article 14 and 'right to life and liberty' conferred by Article 21, but also the compulsion of the Constitutional directive embodied in Article 39-A. The Court has also observed that, it is the Constitutional right of every accused person who is unable to engage a lawyer and secure legal services on account of reasons such as poverty, indigence or incommunicado situations to have free legal services provided to him by the State.[101] Besides, the State is under a Constitutional mandate to provide a lawyer to such accused person if the ends of justice so require. If any State Government fails to set up any machinery for the purpose of providing free legal services to the persons who are accused of offences and who are not able to engage a lawyer on account of poverty or indigence, it amounts to the deprivation of liberty guaranteed by the Constitution of India under Article 21. If the free legal services are not provided to the accused by the State, the trial itself may run the risk of being vitiated as contravening Article 21 of the Constitution.

Now it is a settled law that 'free legal assistance at State cost is a fundamental right of a person accused of an offence which may involve jeopardy to his life or personal liberty and this fundamental right is implicit in the requirement of reasonable, fair and just procedure prescribed by Article 21.[102] But it must be recognised that there may be cases involving offences such as economic offences or offences against law, prohibiting prostitution or child abuse where social justice may require that free legal service may not be provided by the State.

A question arose, is the exercise of this fundamental right conditional upon the accused applying for free legal assistance? The Supreme Court answered this question in **Khatri** *V.* **State of Bihar**[103] wherein it observed that the Magistrate or the Sessions Judge before whom an accused appears, must be held to be under an obligation to inform the accused that if he is unable to engage the services of a lawyer on account of poverty or indigence, he is entitled to obtain free legal services at the cost of the State. In the above case, the accused persons were blinded prisoners who were not provided with legal assistance to defend themselves. The Judicial Magistrate contended that no legal representation had been asked for by the blinded prisoners and hence none was provided with legal assistance by the State. This was rejected by the Supreme Court and held that it is the duty of the Magistrates and the Sessions Judges to inform every accused who appears before them and who is not represented by a lawyer on account of his poverty or ignorance that he is entitled to free legal services at the cost of the State.

In **Centre of Legal Research** *V.* **State of Kerala**,[104] the Supreme Court of India was confronted with a question as to whether voluntary organisations or social action groups engaged in the legal aid programme should be supported by the State Government and if so, to what extent and under what conditions?

Chief Justice Bhagawati observed that, 'it is absolutely essential that people should be involved in the legal aid programme because the legal aid programme is not a charity or bounty but it is a social entitlement of the people and those in need of legal assistance cannot be looked upon as mere beneficiaries of the legal aid programme but they should be regarded as participants in it.[105] The best way of securing people's participation and involvement in the legal aid programme is to operate through voluntary organisations and social action groups. As these groups are working amongst the deprived and vulnerable sections of the community at the grass-root level, they know the problems and difficulties encountered by these neglected sections of the Indian society. Besides, these organisations have their finger on the pulse of the people and they know what are the sources of exploitation and injustice to the underprivileged segments of the society and what measures are required to be taken for the purpose of eradicating exploitation and injustice and to achieve social and distributive justice to them. Therefore, voluntary organisations and social action groups must be encouraged and supported by the State in taking up the legal aid programmes. The Court has also observed that, the legal aid programmes, which are inevitable for the purpose of securing social justice to the people, cannot afford to remain or confine to the traditional or litigation oriented legal aid programme, but it must take into account the socio-economic conditions prevailing in the country and adopt a more dynamic posture and take within its sweep aid schemes or the State Legal Aid and Advice Board. But such voluntary organisations and social actions groups shall not be under the control or direction or supervision of the State Government or the State Legal Aid and Advice Board, rather they should be free to take up many legal aid programmes for securing social justice to all vulnerable sections of the Indian society.

Provisions for Just and Humane Conditions of Work and Maternity Relief

Article 42 of the Constitution of India provides that, 'the State shall make provision for securing just and humane conditions of work and for maternity relief'.

The framers of the Constitution have not only provided the right to work in the Directive Principles of State Policies, but also provided the right to secure just and humane conditions of work. They have been influenced by various International Covenants, which provide these rights.[106]

From this it is clear that, every individual shall get favourable and just conditions of work in their respective establishments. It is the duty of the State to secure and to ensure humane conditions as well as favourable atmosphere to all the workers to work in the work places.

The factories Act 1948, enacted by the Central Government has provided many provisions to ensure humane conditions of work to the workers. Section 11 of the Act provides that, every factory shall be kept clean and free from effusive arising from any drain, or other nuisances. This includes;

(a) Accumulation of dirt and refuse shall be removed daily from the floors and benches of work rooms;

(b) The floor of every workroom shall be cleaned at least once in every week by washing;

(c) Effective means of drainage shall be provided and maintained.

Besides, Section 12 of the Act provides that, proper arrangements shall be made for the disposal of waste and effluents from the work place. The Act also contemplates that proper and suitable measures shall be taken to ensure adequate ventilation and temperature to the workers. Besides, the State is required, under the Act, to provide sufficient supply of water to the workers both for cleaning and drinking purposes and to provide proper safeguards to the workers while working with the dangerous machines.

The above measures which are required to be taken up by the State shows that, every individual has a Constitutional right to have just and humane conditions of work in their respective workplaces. If any State fails to ensure these rights to the workers would be violative of 'Right to life' guaranteed under Article 21 of the Constitution of India. Therefore, to make the 'Right to Life' meaningful, it is the primary duty of the State to ensure proper atmosphere, adequate humane conditions of work to the individuals who work in different establishments.

The second part to Article 42 of the Constitution specifically provides that, 'the State shall make provision for securing maternity relief". This is infact an important provision of the Constitution, which provides social justice to the women before their pregnancy and after their pregnancy. The same right has also been provided in the International Covenant[107].

In pursuance of Article 42 of the Constitution, the Parliament has enacted 'the Maternity Benefit Act 1961'. The main objective of this Act is to regulate the employment of women in certain establishments for certain periods before and after childbirth and to provide maternity benefits and certain other benefits. The

Maternity Benefit is intended to achieve the object of doing social justice to women workers. Section 4 of this Act prohibits any employer from knowingly employing any woman in any establishment during the six weeks immediately following the day of her delivery or her miscarriage. It also contemplates that, 'No woman shall work in any establishments during 6 weeks immediately following the day of her delivery or her miscarriage. Further, it also provides that, 'No pregnant woman shall, on a request made by her, be given any work of the following nature during the period of one month immediately preceding the period of six weeks before the date of her expected delivery and during the said period of six weeks for which the pregnant woman does not avail of the leave of absence;

(a) Any work, which is of arduous nature.

(b) Any work, which involves long hours of standing.

(c) Any work which in any way is likely to interfere with her pregnancy or the normal development of the feotus or is likely to cause her miscarriage or otherwise adversely affect her health.

Under Section 5 (3) of the Act, it is provided that, 'a woman shall be entitled for 'Maternity Benefit' for a maximum period of twelve weeks that is, six weeks upto and including the day of her delivery and six weeks immediately following that day'.

In a case,[108] the Supreme Court of India has observed that, in interpreting the provisions of the Maternity Benefit Act, 1961, beneficent rule of construction should be adopted by the courts which would enable the women workers not only to subsist but also to make up her dissipated energy, nurse her child, preserve her efficiency as a worker and to maintain the level of her previous efficiency and output.

Power of the Central Government to give Directions

Section 25 of this Act empowers the Central Government to issue such directions as it may deem necessary to a State Government regarding the carrying into executions of the provisions of this Act and the State Government shall comply with such directions. This shows that, the Central Government has got wide discretionary powers, under this Act, to compel the State Governments to implement various provisions for securing social justice to women.

Penalty for Non-compliance to the Act

Section 21 of this Act provides that, 'if any employer contravenes the provisions of this Act or the rules made there under, he shall be punishable with imprisonment, which may extend to three months or with fine which may extent to five hundred rupees, or with both.

From the above facts, it is evident that, the Maternity Benefit Act 1961 plays an important and crucial role in protecting the interests of the pregnant workingwomen in various establishments. The Act also ensures certain benefits to the pregnant women to meet social justice. Now almost all State Governments have brought this Act into force and thereby India has fulfilled the International obligations with respect to the Maternity Relief.

Living Wages etc., for Workers

The Constitution of India under Article 43 provides that, 'the State shall endeavour to secure, by suitable legislation or economic organisations or in any other way, to all workers, agricultural, industrial or otherwise, work, a living wage, conditions of work ensuring a decent standard of life and full enjoyment of leisure and social and cultural opportunities and in particular, the State shall endeavour to promote cottage industries on an individual or co-operative basis in rural areas'.

The above provision envisages for 'living wages', which includes provisions for education of children and insurance in addition to the bare necessities of life such as food, shelter and clothing. The concept of 'living wage' has been elaborately discussed by the Supreme Court in **Standard Vacuum Refining Co. of India** *V.* **Workmen**[109] and **Express Newspapers (Pvt.) Ltd., V. Union of India**.[110] The essence of this concept is that every workman shall have a wage, which enables him to maintain the highest state of industrial efficiency which in turn provides to his family all materials which are required to maintain health and physical well-being, for enabling him to discharge his duties as a citizen.

Justice Gajendragadkar observed that, "the concept of living wage is not a static concept; it is expanding and the number of its constituents and their respective contents are bound to expand and widen with the development and growth of the national economy. That is why, it would be impossible to attempt the task of determining the extent of the requirements of the said concept in the context of today in terms of rupees, annas and pies on the scanty material placed before us in the present proceedings. We apprehend that it would be inexpedient and unwise to make an effort to concretise the said concept in monetary terms with any degree of definiteness or precision even if a fuller enquiry is held. Indeed, it may be true to say that, in an underdeveloped country, it would be idle to describe any wage structure as containing the ideal of living wage, though in some cases, wages paid by certain employers may appear to be higher than those paid by others".[111]

According to the fair wages committee report submitted in 1949, 'the living wage' should enable the male earner to provide for himself and his family not merely the bare essentials of food, clothing and shelter, but a measure of frugal comfort including education for the children, protection against ill-health, requirements of essential social needs and a measure of insurance against the more important misfortunes including old age'. The committee also emphasised that, 'the minimum wage must provide not merely the bare sustenance of life but for the preservation of the efficiency of the worker'. For this purpose, the minimum wages also provide some measure of education, medical requirements and basic amenities. The same benefit has also been conferred in various international instruments.[112]

All the above provisions show that a worker shall be given living wage for enabling him to have decent living in the society, which includes bare necessities, education to his children and insurances for old age. This is the ideal, which is contemplated under Article 43 of the Constitution of India. If this is not done by the State, social justice to the workers cannot be ensured, as it is one of the objectives enshrined in the Directive Principles of the State Policies. A worker's decent standard of life depends upon the living wage that he gets.

Provisions for free and Compulsory Education for Children

The Constitution of India does not expressly guarantee the fundamental right to education but Article 41 which falls under Directive Principles of the State policy, directs the State to make effective provisions for securing the right of education. Article 45 of the Constitution states that, 'the State shall endeavour to provide, within a period of ten years from the commencement of this Constitution, free and compulsory education for all children until they complete the age of fourteen years'. The same right is also recognised in the Universal Declaration of Human Rights[113] and International Covenant on Economic, Social and Cultural Rights.[114]

All the above provisions envisage that, there shall be free and compulsory education to all persons, including the children, irrespective of their race, colour, caste, religion and language. Under Article 45 of the Constitution of India, a time limit has been fixed, i.e. 25th January 1960, within which the goal set forth in the Article was to be achieved. But unfortunately, the goal continues to remain very far from the ground realities. The Supreme Court of India in **Miss Mohini Jain** *V*. **State of Karnataka**[115] has observed that the directive principles, which are fundamental in the governance of the country, cannot be isolated from the fundamental rights guaranteed under part III of the Constitution. These principles have to be read into the fundamental rights, as they are supplementary to each other. The State is under a Constitutional mandate to create conditions in which the fundamental rights guaranteed to the individuals under part III could be enjoyed by all. Without making "right to education", under Article 41 of the Constitution, a reality, the fundamental rights under part III shall remain beyond the reach of large majority who are illiterate. Besides, the fundamental rights guaranteed under part III of the Constitution including the rights under Article 19 cannot be appreciated and fully enjoyed unless a citizen is educated and conscious of his individualistic dignity.

Therefore, the right to education is concomitant to the fundamental rights enshrined under part III of the Constitution. The State is under a Constitutional mandate to provide the educational institutions at all levels for the benefit of the citizens.

The educational institutions must function to the best advantage of the citizens and the opportunity to acquire education should not be confined to the elite sections of the society.

In a landmark judgement in **Unnikrishnan** *V.* **State of Andhra Pradesh**,[116] the Supreme Court of India opined that, 'Right to Education' upto the age of 14 years is a fundamental right within the meaning of Article 21 of the Constitution. The Court also observed that, 'the right to education flows directly from the right to life'.

Impact of Article 21 on 'Right to Education'

The guarantee of personal liberty in Article 21 of the Constitution is not only a restraint on the Government but also a part of the cultural and social consciousness of the community. It determines to a great extent the quality of life in the context of Individual and State relationship. In recent times, judicial activism has taken a lead to nurture the right to life and personal liberty in Article 21 of the Constitution. This Article says, "No person shall be deprived of his life or personal liberty except according to the procedure established by law".

The expression 'personal liberty' in Article 21 is of the widest amplitude and it covers a variety of rights which go to constitute the personal liberty of man and some of them have been raised to the status of distinct fundamental rights and given additional protection under Article 19.[117] Justice Bhagawati observed that, Article 21 covers variety of human rights including 'right to education', which is the basic need to lead a dignified life.

In one case[118], the High Court of Andhra Pradesh observed that, 'right to education to Dalits is a fundamental right and it is the mandatory duty of the State to provide adequate opportunities to advance their economic and educational interests by establishing schools'. In *Unnikrishnan V. State of Andhra Pradesh,* the Supreme Court by 3 : 2 observed that 'every Indian child till the age of 14 years has the fundamental right to primary education which can be enforced through the Courts, as this right flows from the content of Article 21 of the Constitution'.

From the above observations, it is evident that it is only through education that Scheduled Caste and Scheduled Tribe people could be made to reap the Constitutional benefits provided to them under various Articles of the Constitution. Besides, education is a potent agent not only for their social and psychological changes, but it may influence productivity and economic change and improvement in their profession. With this object in view, education has been made as a Constitutionally guaranteed right by the Supreme Court of India. Various legislations have been enacted in different States for the introduction of compulsory primary education. To strengthen the educational base for Scheduled Castes and Scheduled Tribes at the elementary and higher secondary level, various kinds of scholarships, stipends, hostel facilities, books, mid-day meals, uniforms etc., are being provided for them. Besides, the scheme for the grant of National Overseas Scholarships for Scheduled Castes and Scheduled Tribes have been started by the Government of India to take up Post Graduate Studies and Research abroad in the subjects for which suitable facilities are not available in India.

By providing these facilities to the Scheduled Caste and Scheduled Tribe people, their educational standards may be upgraded, in turn that enables them to acquire better positions in the society along with the others. Once the educational standards of these people are improved, they can compete with the others to get better facilities and good positions in the Government.

Promotion of Educational and Economic Interests of Scheduled Castes and Scheduled Tribes and other Weaker Sections:

Article 46 of the Constitution says that, "the State shall promote with special care the educational and economic interests of the weaker sections of the people, and in particular, of the Scheduled Castes and the Scheduled Tribes and shall protect them from social injustice and all forms of exploitation".

This Article imposes an obligation on the State to take up all possible means to promote the standard of educational and economic interests of the Scheduled Castes and Scheduled Tribes including the weaker sections of the society. With a view to promote the Scheduled Castes and Scheduled Tribes and weaker sections of the society educationally, for the first time the State of Madras, through its communal Government Order (G.O.), reserved seats in the State Medical and Engineering colleges for different communities in certain proportions on the basis of race, caste and religion. This communal Government Order was challenged by the petitioner in **State of Madras** *V.* **Champakam Dorairajan**[119]. The State of Madras defended its Government Order on the ground that State is permitted, under Article 46 of the Constitution, to promote with special care the educational and economic interests of the weaker sections of the people including Scheduled Castes and Scheduled Tribes and to promote the social justice to some section of the society as required under Article 46 of the Directive Principles of State Policy. The Supreme Court struck down the Communal Government Order of the Madras Government as unconstitutional and held that, 'the Directive Principles of State Policy cannot override the fundamental rights guaranteed under Article 15 of the Constitution'.

In another case,[120] the state Government of Bombay ordered for the requisitioning land for the construction of Harijan colony. This was challenged by the petitioner as violating his fundamental right under Article 15 (1) of the Constitution. But the Government defended its action on the ground of protecting the interests of the Scheduled Castes and Scheduled Tribes provided under Article 46 of the Constitution. But the Bombay High Court struck down the act of Bombay Government and held to be void under Article 15 (1) of the Constitution. Consequent to these two decisions, the Parliament amended Article 15 by the Constitution [1st Amendment] Act, 1951 and incorporated clause (4) to Article 15. Now Article 15 (4) enables the State to make special provisions for the educational, economic or social advancement of socially and educationally backward classes of citizens or for the Scheduled Castes and Scheduled Tribes. After this amendment, now, the State is empowered to put up a Harijan colony in order to advance the interests of the weaker sections of the society including Scheduled Castes and Scheduled Tribes. Again in *Balaji V. State of Madras,*[121] the Government of Mysore State issued an order reserving seats in the Medical and Engineering colleges in the State as mentioned under;

Backward classes:	28%
More backward classes:	20%
Scheduled Castes & Tribes:	18%

Thus 68% of the seats available in both Medical and Engineering colleges were reserved and only 32% were made available to the merit pool. The validity of such reservation made under the order was challenged by the candidates who did not get admission only by reason of Government Order. The contention of the Government was that, with a view to ensure social justice and to protect the interests of the backward classes, including Scheduled Castes and Scheduled Tribes, as provided under clause (4) of Article 15, such a reservation policy was made. But the Supreme Court struck down the sub-classification made by the order between 'backward classes' and 'more backward classes' as unconstitutional and unjustifiable under Article 15 (4). The Court observed that, clause (4) of Article 15 only enables the State to make special provision but not exclusive provision for the backward classes. Besides, the court also held that 'the State cannot ignore or exclude altogether the advancement of the rest of the society in its zeal to promote the welfare of the backward classes'. For the first time the Supreme Court said, 'the special provision which is made by the State should be less than 50%'. This observation clearly indicates that, under the guise of special provision under Article 15 (4), the State cannot defeat the interests of the other advanced sections of the society. But the above observation was overruled by the same Court in *State of Andhra Pradesh V. Balram,*[155] and *K.C. Vasanth Kumar V. State of Karnataka.*[123] In the former case, the Supreme Court held that;

> "A caste is also a class of citizens and that a caste as such may be socially and educationally backward. If after collecting the necessary data, it is found that the caste as a whole is socially and educationally backward ... the reservation made of such persons will have to be upheld not withstanding the fact that a few individuals in that group may be both socially and educationally above the general average".

Again in **Akhil Bharatiya Shoshit Karamchari Sangh (Rly.) V. Union of India,**[124] the Railway Board issued a circular under which reservations were made in selection of posts of the Scheduled Caste and Scheduled Tribe candidates to promote their interests as contemplated under Article 16 (4) and 46 of the Constitution. The circular provides promotions by selection from class III to class II, eligible Scheduled Caste and Scheduled Tribe candidates were given one grade higher than that which were due to them on the basis of their record of service. The circular also provided for 'carry forward rule' under which 17% posts are reserved. These benefits conferred to Scheduled Castes and Scheduled Tribes were challenged as discriminatory against the vast number of employees of the railways. The Supreme Court dismissed the challenge and upheld the validity of the Railway Board circular. The Court also observed that, the classification of Scheduled Castes and Scheduled Tribes separately from the rest of the communities for the purpose of reservation is just and reasonable, as they constitute a class by themselves because of their social backwardness. The Court also upheld the 'carry forward rule'. As a result of this rule, the quota of reservation came to about 64.4%, but the Court said it was not excessive. Justice Krishna Iyer words are noteworthy, where he observed that, 'some excess reservation will not affect the general categories, but substantial excess will vitiate the selection'.

Recently, the Supreme Court of India was confronted with a question whether State can acquire a land, belonging to private persons, for the purpose of an Harijan Welfare Scheme? This question was affirmatively answered by the Court in **State of Tamil Nadu** *V.* **Ananthi Ammal.**[125] In this case, the impugned legislation passed by the Tamil Nadu Assembly i.e., 'The Tamil Nadu Acquisition of Land for Harijan Welfare Scheme Act, 1978' was challenged by the petitioner in the High Court of Tamil Nadu. Under this Act, Section 3 defines, 'A Harijan Welfare Scheme is to mean any scheme for provision of house, sites for Harijans, for constructing, extending or improving any dwelling house for Harijans, for providing any pathways leading to such dwelling house, burial or burning ground or providing any other amenities for the benefit of Harijans'. Section 4 (1) confers powers to District Collector to acquire land if he is satisfied that for the purpose of any Harijan Welfare Scheme, it is necessary to acquire any land, he may acquire the land by publishing in the District Gazette a notice to the effect that he has decided to acquire the land in pursuance of this Section.

Section 4 (2) says, 'before publishing a notice under sub-sec (1), the District Collector or any officer authorised by the District collector in this behalf, shall call upon the owner or any person, who, in the opinion of the District Collector or the Officer so authorised, may be interested in such land, to show cause why it should not be acquired. Besides, Section 20 of the above Act states that, 'the provisions of the Land Acquisition Act, 1894, save as provided in the said Act, shall cease to apply to any land which is required for the purpose specified in Section 4 (1) of the Tamil Nadu Acquisition of Land for Harijans Welfare Scheme Act, 1978.

The petitioner challenged the State Law in the High Court of Madras regarding the absolute power conferred to the District Collector to give his decision on the question of acquisition of land without enquiry. It was also contended that, 'no enquiry into the value of land was provided for under the Act. But the State's contention was that to give effect to the Directive Principles of State Policy mentioned under Article 46 of the Constitution, such acquisition of land was made. Having heard the contentions of both the petitioner and the respondent State, the High Court struck down the whole Act as unconstitutional as it did not enjoy the protection of Articles 31C or 31A and violative of Article 14, 19 and 300-A of the Constitution. Immediately an appeal was made to the Supreme Court by the State on the ground that the Act was protected by Article 31A. The Supreme Court upheld the whole Act except the provisions in Section 11 for the payment of compensation by installment. The Court observed that, after the amount has been determined, the prescribed authority shall tender payment of the amount to the persons entitled thereto and shall pay it to them in a lumpsum. It also observed that, the rest of Section 11 (1) is ultravires to the Constitution.

The Court rejected each of the contentions of the landowners with reasons. It also rejected the comparison of the State Act with the Land Acquisition Act (Central Act). The Court observed that, the power conferred to the District Collector was held to be reasonable and non-arbitrary. Besides, the computation of market value of the land under the State law was considered by the Court as unfair and unreasonable. This case is an important one where the Supreme Court upheld the validity of the State law as it was enacted to promote the economic interests of Scheduled Castes and Scheduled Tribes and other weaker sections of the society as provided under Article 46 of the Constitution.

It is clear from the above cases that, the State can make special provision for the advancement of any socially and educationally backward classes or Scheduled Castes and Scheduled Tribes in the form of reservation. But, the reservation made for the advancement of these people shall not eat away or cease the opportunities of the general categories. One of the measures initiated by the Government to give effect to the provision under Article 46 of the Constitution is the enactment of Scheduled Castes and Scheduled Tribes (Prevention of Atrocities) Act, 1989.

Reservation of Seats For Scheduled Castes and Scheduled Tribes in the House of the People and in the Legislative Assmeblies of the States

Article 330 Clause (1) states that, 'seats shall be reserved in the House of the people for:

(a) The Scheduled Castes;

(b) The Scheduled Tribes except the Scheduled Tribes in the autonomous districts of Assam; and

(c) The Scheduled Tribes in the autonomous districts of Assam'.

Clause (2) says that, 'the number of seats reserved in any State or Union Territory for the Scheduled Castes or the Scheduled Tribes under Clause (1) shall bear, as nearly as may be, the proportion to the total number of seats allotted to that State or Union Territory in the House of the people as the population of the Scheduled Castes in the State or Union Territory or of the Scheduled Tribes in the State or Union Territory or part of the State or Union Territory, as the case may be, in respect of which seats are so reserved, bears to the total population of the State or the Union Territory'.

Article 332 (1) states that, 'seats shall be reserved for the Scheduled Castes and the Scheduled Tribes, [except the Scheduled Tribes in the autonomous districts of Assam] in the Legislative Assembly of every state.

Clause (2) of the Article provides that, 'seats shall be reserved also for the autonomous districts in the Legislative Assembly of the State of Assam'.

Clause (3) says, 'the number of seats reserved for the Scheduled Castes or the Scheduled Tribes in the Legislative Assembly of any State under Clause (1) shall bear, as nearly as may be, the same proportion to the total number of seats in the Assembly as the population of the Scheduled Castes in the State or of the Scheduled Tribes in the State or part of the State, as the case may be, in respect of which seats are so reserved, bears to the total population of the State'.

The above two Articles i.e., 330 & 332, clearly indicate that minimum number of seats have been guaranteed to the Scheduled Castes and Scheduled Tribes in the Constitution. In addition to these seats, if the Scheduled Caste and Scheduled Tribe candidates obtain or capture seats in the election from the general constituency, there would be no repugnancy. Besides, the claim of eligibility for the reserved seats does not exclude the claim for the general seats. If seats are secured from the general unreserved constituencies, they are only additional seats to the guaranteed seats under Articles 330 & 332 of the Constitution. The very fact of guaranteeing seats for the Scheduled Castes and Scheduled Tribes under the Constitution shows that the framers of the Constitution have provided 'political equality' to the Scheduled Castes and Scheduled Tribes.

Claims of Scheduled Castes and Scheduled Tribes to Services and Posts

Article 335 says, 'the claims of the members of the Scheduled Castes and Scheduled Tribes shall be taken into consideration, consistently with the maintenance of efficiency of administration, in the making of appointments to services and posts in connection with the affairs of the Union or of a State'.

This Article clearly indicates that, any claim made either by the Scheduled Castes and Scheduled Tribes in making of appointments shall be considered by the State consistently with the maintenance of efficiency of administration. There is some overlapping between Article 335 and 16 (4) in as much as the reservation for 'Backwaıd Classes' in Article 16 (4) obviously includes reservation for members of the Scheduled Castes and Scheduled Tribes. The overlapping between the two provisions has been eliminated by the Supreme Court by holding that Article 335 operates as a limitation to the provision contained in Article 16 (4), though Article 16 (4) does not specifically refer to

Article 335 or raise any question of maintenance of efficiency of the administration. Therefore, a reservation for backward classes or Scheduled Castes and Scheduled Tribes will, thus, be struck down as violative of Article 14 and 16 (1), if it is unreasonably excessive.

But, in pursuance of the Constitutional provisions contained in Article 16 (4) and 335, instructions have been issued from time to time by the Government of India providing reservation in services for the members of the Scheduled Castes and Scheduled Tribes.

Special Officer for Scheduled Castes and Scheduled Tribes

The Constitution of India has made a provision for the establishment of a commission to look after the welfare of the members of the Scheduled Castes and Scheduled Tribes. Certain duties are imposed to the commission in protecting the interests of the people. Article 338 of the Constitution provides the following provisions;

1. There shall be a commission for the Scheduled Castes and Scheduled Tribes to be known as the 'National Commission for the Scheduled Castes and Scheduled Tribes'.
2. Subject to the provisions of any law made in this behalf by the Parliament, the Commission shall consist of a Chairperson, Vice-Chairperson and five other members and the conditions of service and tenure of office of the Chairperson, Vice-Chairperson and other members so appointed shall be such as the President may by rule determine.
3. The Chairperson, Vice-Chairperson and other members of the commission shall be appointed by the President by warrant under his hand and seal.
4. The commission shall have the power to regulate its own procedure.
5. It shall be the duty of the commission to;
   (a) Investigate and monitor all matters relating to the safeguards provided for the Scheduled Castes and Scheduled Tribes under the Constitution or under any order of the Government and to evaluate the working of such safeguards;

(b) Inquire into specific complaints with respect to the deprivation of rights and safeguards of the Scheduled Castes and Scheduled Tribes;

(c) Participate and advise on the planning process of socio-economic development of the Scheduled Castes and Scheduled Tribes and to evaluate the progress of their development under the Union and any State;

(d) Present to the President, annually and at such other times as the commission may deem fit, reports upon the working of those safeguards;

(e) Make in such reports recommendations as to the measures that should be taken by the Union or any State for the effective implementation of those safeguards and other measures for the protection, welfare and socio-economic development of the Scheduled Castes and Scheduled Tribes; and

(f) Discharge such other functions in relation to the protection, welfare and socio-economic development and advancement of the Scheduled Castes and Scheduled Tribes as the President may, subject to the provisions of any law made by the Parliament, by rule specify.

6. The President shall cause all such reports to be laid before each House of Parliament along with a memorandum explaining the action taken or proposed to be taken on the recommendations relating to the union and the reasons for the non-acceptance, if any, of any of such recommendations.

7. Where any such report, or any part thereof, relates to any other matter with which any State Government is concerned, a copy of such report shall be forwarded to the Governor of the State who shall cause it to be laid before the Legislature of the State along with a memorandum explaining the action taken or proposed to be taken on the recommendations relating to the State and the reasons for the non-acceptance, if any, of any of such recommendations.

8. The Commission shall while investigating any matter referred to in sub-clause (a) or (b) of Clause (5), have all the powers of

a Civil Court trying a suit and in particular in respect of the following matters, namely: -

(a) Summoning and enforcing the attendance of any person from any part of India and examining him on oath;

(b) Requiring the discovery and production of any document;

(c) Receiving evidence on affidavits;

(d) Requisitioning any public record or copy thereof from any Court or office;

(e) Issuing Commissions for the examination of witnesses and documents; and

(f) Any other matter, which the President may, by rule, determines.

9. The Union and State Governments shall consult the commission on all major policy matters affecting Scheduled Castes and Scheduled Tribes.

10. In this Article references to the Scheduled Castes and Scheduled Tribes shall be construed as including references to such other backward classes as the President may, on receipt of the report of the Commission appointed under Clause (1) of Article 340, by order specify and also to the Anglo-Indian community.

The Constitution (65th Amendment) Act 1990 has amended Article 338, wherein the Commissioner of Scheduled Castes and Scheduled Tribes was replaced by seven-member Commission and the functions of the Commission were enlarged. It is significant to note that another important institutional framework in relation to Article 338 has come into existence since 1968 in the form of Parliamentary Committee on the Welfare of Scheduled Castes and Scheduled Tribes. One of the objectives of the Committee is to consider the reports submitted by the Commissioner and to report as to the measures that should be taken by the Union Government in respect of matters within the purview of the Union Government including the Administration of the Union Territories. Besides, it is to be noted that, as per the amended provisions of Article 338, the Commission was reconstituted on 12th March 1992, which undertakes many measures for the welfare of the Scheduled Castes and Scheduled Tribes.

Control of Union Over Administration of Scheduled Areas and the Welfare of Scheduled Tribes

The Constitution has provided the following provisions for protecting the welfare of the Scheduled Tribes:

Article 339 (1) provides that, 'the President may at any time and shall, at the expiration of ten years from the commencement of this Constitution by order appoint a Commission to report on the administration of the Scheduled areas and the welfare of the Scheduled Tribes in the States. The order may define the composition, powers and procedures of the Commission and may contain such individual or ancillary provisions, as the President may consider necessary or desirable. Clause (2) of the above Article provides that, 'the executive power of the Union shall extend to the giving of directions to a State as to the drawing up and execution of schemes specified in the direction to be essential for the welfare of the Scheduled Tribes in the State.

In pursuance of the provisions of Article 339 of the Constitution, the Scheduled areas and the Scheduled Tribes Commission was appointed by the President on 28th April 1960, with Shri. U.N. Dhebar as the Chairman. The Commission submitted its report in 1961. In its report, it felt that, "Some of the safeguards for the tribals in the Constitution was originally only for ten years. In fixing this period, the Constitution has envisaged an effective follow-up programme, which would have obviated the need for their continuance. This hope has not materialised and the period has been extended but we are of the opinion that this has not been due to any deficiency in the Constitution itself, but it is the result of deficiency in performance".

Appointment of A Commission to Investigate the Conditions of Backward Classes

Article 340 of the Constitution provides that;

1. The President may by order appoint a Commission consisting of such persons as he thinks fit to investigate the conditions of socially and educationally backward classes within the territory of India and the difficulties under which they labour and to make recommendations as to the steps that should be taken by the Union or any State to remove such difficulties

and to improve their conditions and as to the grants that should be made for the purpose by the Union or any State and the conditions subject to which such grants should be made and the order appointing such Commission shall define the procedure to be followed by the Commission.

2. Clause (2) of the Article states that, 'A Commission so appointed shall investigate the matter referred to them and present to the President a report setting out the facts as found by them and making such recommendations as they think proper'.

3. Clause (3) says that, 'the President shall cause a copy of the report so presented together with a memorandum explaining the action taken thereon to be laid before each House of Parliament .

Pursuant to the power conferred under this Article, two Commissions were appointed by the President, one in 1953 under the Chairmanship of Kaka Kalelkar and the other in 1978 under the Chairmanship of B.P. Mandal. The first Commission submitted its report on the backwardness of the people relying upon 'caste' as the criterion, which was not accepted by the Government, as the Commission did not recognise the economic criterion. The second Commission also submitted its report, which was lying unattended till August 7th, 1990. The then Prime Minister V.P. Singh's Government accepted the recommendations made by the Mandal Commission which used multiple criterion for backwardness; among them caste is a predominant factor in which there was much opposition to this recommendations. Ultimately, a notification was issued on August 13th, 1990, for its implementation fixing 27% jobs reservation in Central services and public undertakings for the backward classes (Socially and Educationally).

This reservation of 27% of jobs to the backward classes was upheld by the Supreme Court in *Indra Sawhney V. Union of India.*[126] Subsequently, with a view to constitute a permanent statutory body, the National Commission for Backward Classes Act 1993, was passed by the Parliament and which came into force in the same year.

CONCLUSION

In the foregoing chapter, the special Constitutional provisions and measures provided for Scheduled Castes and Scheduled Tribes have been discussed. The framers of the Indian Constitution have incorporated the above provisions, for securing social justice to the depressed classes including Scheduled Castes and Scheduled Tribes. In the Preamble to the Constitution, it is provided that the State shall secure to the people of India Justice–social, economic and political, Liberty–of thought and expression, Equality–of status and of opportunity. To remove social evils like Untouchability from the society, the provision relating to the abolition of Untouchability is provided under Article 17 of the Constitution. To attain equality of all and to have equal opportunity, specific provisions are included under Article 14, 15, 16 and 29 (2) of the Constitution. It is expressly prohibited under these Articles that, on the grounds of caste, race, colour, religion, sex and language, no person shall be discriminated in providing admission to various colleges and public institutions, hotels, public places, wells etc. The same prohibition is also extended to employment providing either under State service or under the Union. A fundamental right like 'Right to life' is also guaranteed under Article 21 of the Constitution to protect life of a person from any authority or State. Therefore, no person's life or his personal liberty can be taken away except the procedure established by law. Here law means, law duly made by the Parliament.

Likewise, our Constitution-makers have provided reservation benefits to the vulnerable sections of the society to represent State Legislatures and Parliament. Therefore, certain quantam of seats are reserved for Scheduled Castes and Scheduled Tribes both in the State Legislatures as well as in the Parliament. This is a positive action of the Constitution-makers to bring these depressed classes including Scheduled Castes and Scheduled Tribes to the main stream of the society. Besides these provisions, the Parliament has also enacted a law i.e., Scheduled Castes and Scheduled Tribes (Prevention of Atrocities) Act, 1989, to regulate and to eradicate the 'problem of Untouchability'. Under this Act, several punishments are prescribed to remove Untouchability from the Hindu society.

Besides, the judicial responses on these provisions, which secure social, economic and political justice to the depressed classes including Scheduled Castes and Scheduled Tribes, are positive in protecting the interests of these people from their social problems. At the same time, the judiciary has fixed the quantum of reservation that can be made in favour of Scheduled Castes and Scheduled Tribes and backward classes, to 50%. The Supreme Court fixed this for the first time in *Balaji V. State of Mysore* in the year 1963. Again in Indra Sawhney, case the same Court observed that, reservation should not exceed 50%. This is because, in the garb of providing reservation to the backward classes including Scheduled Castes and Scheduled Tribes, the State shall not defeat the interest of the general category, otherwise the ideals enshrined in the Constitution would be defeated.

Through the above-mentioned provisions of the Constitution, it is possible to secure social, economic and political justice to all. At the same time, the State's action, in providing special benefits to the depressed classes in the form of reservation, can also be regulated by the judiciary and compel the State to act within the frame work of the Constitution to achieve social justice.

NOTES

1. According to Justice Gajendragadkar, "the concept of social justice thus takes within its sweep the objectives of removing all inequalities and affording equal opportunity to all citizens in social affairs as well as economic activities". [P.B. Gajendragadkar, *'Law Society and Social Justice'*, Asia Publishing House, 1965].
2. Dr. N.R. Madhav Menon – *"Social Justice and Social Process in India"* [Indian Academy of Social Sciences, India] 1988, p. 106.
3. Ibid., p. 8.
4. K.P.K. Shetty–*"Fundamental Rights and Socio-Economic Justice in the Indian Constitution"*, 1969, p. 154.
5. Granville Austin–*"Indian Constitution : Corner stone of a Nation"*, p. 26-28.
6. Dr. N.R. Madhav Menon, Opp. Cit., p. 140.
7. V.N. Shukla–*"Constitution of India"*, Eastern Book Company, Lucknow [1994], p. A-26.
8. Berubari Union & Exchange of Enclaves, R [AIR 1960 SC 845, 856].
9. Keshavananda Bharathi V. State of Kerala [1973] 4 SCC, p. 225.
10. The State's discrimination on grounds of race, religion and caste is prohibited generally by Article 15 (1) and specifically by Article 16

(2) [In respect of State employment], Article 23 (2) [Concerning compulsory public service], Article 29 (2) [In regard to State-run and State-aided educational institutions].

11. Article 15 (1) and 16 (2).
12. Dicey–'*Law of the Constitution*", 10th Edition, p. 193.
13. V.N. Shukla, Opp. Cit., p. 37.
14. Satish Chandra V. Union of India, AIR 1953 SC 250 and Kamala Gaind V. State of Punjab, 1990 Supp. SCC 800.
15. Jennings – "*Law of the Constitution*", p. 94.
16. "All India Sainik Schools Employees' Association V. Sainik Schools Society, AIR 1989 SC 88.
17. Dr. N.R. Madhav Menon [Ed.], Opp. Cit., p. 21.
18. Constitution of India, Article 330.
19. Article 332.
20. Article 15 (4).
21. Article 16 (4).
22. Dr. N.R. Madhav Menon [Ed.], Opp. Cit., p. 186.
23. D.N. Saraf – "*Social Policy, Law & Protection of Weaker Sections of Society*", [Eastern Book Company], 1986, p. 135.
24. AIR 1951 SC, [Similar decision was also given in B. Venkataramanna V. State of Madras, AIR 1950 SC].
25. This decision was pronounced on 9th April 1951 and the Constitution [First Amendment] Act was passed on June 18th 1951.
26. AIR 1963 SC 649.
27. AIR 1964 SC 1823.
28. AIR 1968 SC 1012.
29. AIR 1968 SC 1379.
30. AIR 1972 SC 1875.
31. AIR 1976 SC 2381 : (1976) 3 SCC 736.
32. Dr. B.R. Ambedkar in C.A.D., Vol. VII, pp. 701-2.
33. Supra Note [p. 23].
34. Ibid.
35. Ibid., p. 664.
36. AIR 1964 SC 179.
37. General Manager of S. Railway V. Rangachari, AIR 1962 SC.
38. Apparently, the three years reservations of 17½% of current appointments could add up to a reservation of 64.4%, since there were fewer new vacancies to be filled during the third year.

39. AIR 1964 SC 179 @ 187.
40. Ibid.
41. Ibid., p. 192.
42. Rangachari case.
43. Indra Sawhney V. Union of India, 1992 Supp. (3) SCC; AOR 1993 SC.
44. State of Kerala V. N.M. Thomas, AIR 1976 SC.
45. Thomas case impliedly overrules the 'Balaji and Devadasan cases'.
46. Dr. Paramananda Singh–"*Equality, reservation and Discrimination in India*" p. 36 [Deep & Deep Publications, New Delhi].
47. Ibid., p. 36.
48. AIR 1981 SC.
49. ABSK Sangh (Rly) followed Thomas case and again impliedly overruled Balaji and Devadasan cases.
50. 1985 Supp SCC, p. 714.
51. 1992 Supp (3) SCC 217 : AIR 1993, SC 477.
52. AIR 1988 SC 959 : (1988) 2 SCC 214.
53. Ibid., p. 1777.
54. Ibid., p. 960.
55. (1997) 2 SCC 332 : 1997 AIR SCW 3113.
56. Ibid., p. 332.
57. AIR 1998 SC 1767.
58. (1994) 3 SCC 1 : J.T. 1994 (2) SC 215.
59. (1995) 5 SCC 482.
60. M.K. Gandhi–"*Untouchability*" [Edited by Baratan Kumarappa] 1964.
61. According to B.R. Ambedkar, the word 'shop' is a place where its owner was prepared to offer his services to anybody who went there. Here it is used in the most comprehensive sense.
62. 'Places of public resort' includes a burial ground, where it was used wholly or partly in a special sense.
63. Constituent Assembly Debates, Vols. I-IV, p. 332-33.
64. See Chapter – 4.
65. Maneka Gandhi V. Union of India, AIR 1978 SC 597.
66. AIR 1950 SC 27.
67. AIR 1963 SC 1295.
68. AIR 1981 SC 746.
69. (1984) 3 SCC 161 : AIR 1984 SC 802.

70. (1982) 3 SCC 235 : AIR 1982 SC 1473.
71. (1985) 3 SCC 545 : AIR 1986 SC 180.
72. (1984) 3 SCC 243 : AIR 1984 SC 1099.
73. (1986) 2 SCC 68 : AIR 1986 SC 847.
74. Ibid., p. 74.
75. (1996) 2 SCC 549.
76. (1997) 11 SCC 121.
77. (1995) 3 SCC 42.
78. (1989) 4 SCC 286 : AIR 1989 SC 2039.
79. Ibid., p. 288.
79. (a) (1996) 4 SCC 645.
79. (b) (1996) 2 SCC 682.
80. (1992) 3 SCC 666 : AIR 1992 SC 1858.
81. (1993 1 SCC 645.
82. Ibid., p. 765.
83. AIR 1985 SC 652, Popularly known as 'Lime stone quarries' case.
83(a) (1987) 4 SCC 463.
83(b) (1996) 2 SCC 572: AIR 1996 SC 2992.
84. AIR 1984 SC 803.
85. Ibid.
86. Kendra Pahadiya V. State of Bihar, AIR 1981 SC 939.
87. Sunil Batra V. Delhi Administration, AIR 1978 SC 1675.
88. Bandhu Mukti Morcha V. Union of India, AIR 1984 SC 802; Neeraja Chaudhury V. State of Madhya Pradesh (1984) 3 SCC 243.
89. Sanjit Roy V. State of Rajasthan, AIR 1983 SC 328.
90. State of Himachal Pradesh V. Umed Ram (1986) 2 SCC 68 : AIR 1986 SC 847.
91. Sheela Barse V. State of Maharashtra, AIR 1983 SC 378.
92. Olga Tellis V. Bombay Municipal Corporation, AIR 1986 SC 180.
93. Anil Yadav V. State of Bihar (AIR 1982 SC 1008), which is popularly known as 'Bagalpur Blinding & Prisoners' case.
94. Opp. Cit., Note 123.
95. Constituent Assembly Debates, Vol. III, pp. 494–95.
96. CAD, Vol. II, p. 41.

97. Daily Rated Casual Labour V. Union of India, (1988) 1 SCC 122; Jaipal V. State of Haryana, (1988) 1 SCC 354; Federation of All India Customs & Central Excise Stenographers V. Union of India, (1988) 3 SCC 91.
98. K.L. Bhatia – "Dr. B. R. Ambedkar : Social Justice & the Indian Constitution", [Deep & deep Publications, New Delhi], p. 59.
99. Article 39 – A of the Constitution of India.
100. AIR 1979 SC 1369.
101. Ibid., p. 1380.
102. Sukh Das V. Union Territory of Arunachal Pradesh, AIR 1986 SC 928.
103. AIR 1981 SC 928; (1981) 2 SCR 408.
104. AIR 1986 SC 1322; (1986) 2 SCC 706.
105. Ibid., p. 1322.
106. Article 23 (1) of the Universal Declaration of Human Rights says, 'everyone has the right to just and favourable conditions of work'. Article 7 (b) of International Covenant on Economic, Social & Cultural Rights provides that 'the State parties to the Covenant recognise the right of everyone to the enjoyment of just & favourable conditions of work, which ensure safe and healthy working conditions'.

    Article 15 of African Charter of Human and Peoples' Right says, 'every individual shall have the right to work under equitable and satisfactory conditions'.
107. Article 10 (2) of the International Covenant on Economic, Social and Cultural Rights says, 'Special protection should be accorded to mothers during a reasonable period before and after childbirth. During such period, working mothers should be accorded paid leave or leave with adequate social security benefits'.
108. B. Shah V. Labour Court, Coimbatore, AIR 1978 SC 12.
109. AIR 1961 SC 895.
110. AIR 1958 SC 578.
111. Standard Vacuum Company, Opp. Cit., Note 142.
112. Article 25 (1) of UDHR says, ' everyone has the right to standard of living, adequate for health and well being of himself and of his family including food, clothing, housing and medical care and necessary social services and the right to security in the event of unemployment, sickness, disability, widowhood, old age or other lack of livelihood in circumstances beyond his control'.
113. Article 26 (1) of the Universal Declaration of Human Rights states that, "every one has the right to education. Education shall be free, atleast in the elementary and fundamental stages. Elementary

education shall be compulsory, technical and professional education shall be made generally available and higher education shall be equally accessible to all on the basis of merit".

114. Article 13 (2-A) of the International Covenant on economic, social and cultural rights provides that, "primary education shall be compulsory and available free to all. Clause (1) of the same Article recognises the right of everyone to education".

115. Opp. Cit., Note 113.

116. Opp. Cit., Note 114.

117. Menaka Gandhi V. Union of India.

118. Murali Krishna Public School Champapet V. Regional Director of School Education, Khairatabad.

119. AIR 1951 SC 226.

120. Jagwant Kaur V. State of Bombay [AIR 1952, Bombay].

121. Opp. Cit., Note 59.

122. Opp. Cit., Note 63.

123. Opp. Cit., Note 83.

124. Opp. Cit., Note 81.

125. AIR 1995 SC 2114.

126. Opp. Cit., Note 84.

4

UNTOUCHABILITY

"The root of the 'Untouchability' is the caste system; the root of the caste system is religion attached to Varna and ashram; and the root of varnashrama is Brahminical religion; and the root of the Brahminical religion is authoritarianism or Political power".

—B.R. Ambedkar

INTRODUCTION

One of the major facts of Hindu life is the existence of a system known as 'Untouchability'. The Constitution of India has abolished Untouchability and made its practice a penal offence. Legally therefore, 'Untouchability' is no longer a part of either Hindu or Indian life. Today the Harijans enjoy the same legal rights as the other caste people enjoy. They attend the same schools and colleges and are given special facilities in the matter of education. They are recruited to every branch of Public Service, Central and State Cabinets. They are given full freedom to practice any profession of their choice without any restrictions. Although the legal disabilities have vanished, yet their social disabilities have not been removed from such proclamation of 'abolition of Untouchability'. According to the doctrine of 'Chaturvarnya' or the four-fold division of society, the untouchables are outside the caste-system (Avarnas) and are called the fifth group (panchamas). They do not fall within the Hindu social order.

In many countries certain sections of the community suffer from social and economic disability. In the United States of America, a very advanced country, Negroes suffer such disabilities despite the Constitutional declaration of equality. In Africa 'the apartheid' singled out the black population of the continent for unfair discrimination that came to an end recently. Therefore, in India also the problem of 'Untouchability' has been in vogue in the Hindu social system since Vedic times. In the early Vedic literature, several names of castes occur that are spoken of in the smritis as antyajas. We have carmamna (a tanner of hides) in the Rig-Veda. The theory of the early smritis was that there were only four Varnas and there was no fifth Varna. But in modern times the so-called Untouchables are referred to as the 'panchamas', that is something against the smriti tradition.[1] Untouchability did not and does not arise by birth alone. It arises in various ways. In the first place, persons become out castes and untouchables by being guilty of certain acts that amount to grave sins. For instance, Manu prescribes that those who are guilty of Brahmana murder, theft of Brahman's gold or drinkers of spirituous liquors should be excommunicated, no one should dine with them or teach them, or officiate as priests for them, nor should marriage relationship be entered into with them and they should wander over the world excluded from all Vedic dharmas.[2] If they perform the proper 'prayashchitta' they are restored to caste and become touchable. In the second place, persons were treated as Untouchables simply through religious hatred and abhorrence because they belonged to a different sect or religion. For example, Apararka quotes verses from 'Brahmandapurana' on touching Baudhas, Pasupatas, Lokayatika and Brahmanas guilty of doing actions inconsistent with their caste; one should enter water with the clothes on and also on touching Shaivas and Atheists. Apararka quotes a verse of Vrddha-yajnavalkya that on touching Chandalas, Bhillas and Parasikas and persons guilty of mahapatakas one should bathe with the clothes on.

Thirdly, some persons, though not Untouchables ordinarily, became so, if they followed certain occupations, e.g., if a person touches a Brahmana who is 'devalaka' (i.e., has been doing worship to an image for money for three years) or who is a priest for the whole village, or a person who sells a soma plant, then he has to bathe with his clothes on. Fourthly, persons became Untouchables when in certain conditions e.g., a person if he touches even his wife in her monthly period or during the first ten days after delivery or if he touches a person during the period of mourning on the death of some relative or a person who has carried a corpse to the cemetery and has not yet bathed, he then has to take a bath with his clothes on. (Vide Manu V. 85) Fifthly, certain races such as mlecchas and persons from certain countries themselves were regarded as impure. Smritis say that persons following certain filthy, low and disapproved avocations were Untouchables. Besides, the underlying notions of Untouchability are religious and ceremonial purity and impurity. A man's nearest and dearest women relatives such as his own mother and wife or daughters are Untouchables to him during their monthly periods. As many professions and crafts were in ancient times hereditary, gradually the idea arose that a man who belonged to a caste pursuing certain filthy or abhorred avocations or crafts was by birth Untouchable. The only caste that is said by the most ancient Dharmasutras to be Untouchable by birth is that of Chandalas. Gautama says that the Chandala is the offspring of a Shudra from a Brahmana woman and that he is the most reprehensible among the pratilomas. Manu prescribes a bath for coming in bodily contact with a 'divakirti' (a chandala), Udakya (a woman in her monthly period), Patita (one outcasted for sin and crime), Sutika (a woman after delivery), a corpse (one who has touched a corpse). From this it is clear that the only antyaja who was 'asprishya' according to Manu was the Chandala. Gradually the spirit of exclusiveness and ideas of ritual purity were carried to extremes and more and more castes ultimately became Untouchables. According to some very orthodox writers of Smritis, they went to the extent of saying that on touching even a Shudra a 'dvijati' has to bathe.

As regards the public roads, Yajnavalkya says that they become pure by the rays of the sun and the moon and by wind even when they are trodden by Chandalas. Besides, the mud and water on public roads and on houses built of baked bricks, though they are touched by Chandalas are rendered pure by the mere blowing of wind over them. These rules clearly indicate that the smritis followed a reasonable rule about the public roads and do not countenance the restrictions maintained in some parts of south India especially in Malabar regarding the use of public roads by the Untouchables. Vishnu prescribes that if an Untouchable deliberately touched a man of the three higher castes he should be punished with beating, but Yajnavalkya prescribes that if a Chandala purposefully touches any one of the higher castes the Chandala should be fined one hundred panas.

Regarding the worshiping of Hindu deities is concerned; Untouchables were not completely excluded. When it is said that the Chandala is outside all dharma, the implication is that he is outside the Vedic rites a 'upanayana' and not that he cannot worship the Hindu deities, nor that he is not bound by the moral code. He could worship images of the 'avataras' of Vishnu. The Bhagavatapurana says that 'even the antyavasayins are purified by listening to the praises or names of Hari, by repeating the names of Hari and by contemplation on him. Yet the Untouchables could never see or touch the image of Vishnu enshrined in a temple of caste Hindus.

The institution of 'Untouchability' and tradition bound caste system divided the Hindus, wrapped their thinking and eroded the structure of the community. The Hindu scriptures interpolated the concept of Varna and legitimized the concept of 'chaturvarna' and gave it a divine origin. Those who did not appreciate the system-mostly indigenous people who had their own gods, religion and social system as well as those who opposed or violated this system were outcast and kept outside the pale of Hinduism. Later they were compelled to live outside the towns and villages and were treated as Untouchables. The idea that an impure person imparts pollution by his touch and even by his near approach to a member of the first three castes finds expression in the sutras. The people who were outcasts and forced to live outside the villages and towns were called as 'Chandalas'.

POST-VEDIC PERIOD

In the post Vedic times, society was clearly divided into four varnas. Each Varna was entrusted with well-defined functions. Among the four varnas, the first three varnas were 'dvijas' or the twice born, who were entitled to the wear sacred thread and to study Vedas, but the last varna i.e., Shudras were not assigned any of these rights. It is interesting to know that some of the Shudras were treated as Untouchables. The Varna system divided the society into four divisions, which gave rise to tension in the

Hindu society. The Kshatriyas, who acted as rulers, however, reacted strongly against the ritualistic domination of the Brahmins. Gradually the Hindu Varna system grew so strong that the social intercourse and inter marriage were prohibited. Society became strictly endogamous and was divided into watertight compartments. Those who violated the law of endogamy were ex-communicated and were forced to live outside the community. The Buddhist birth-stories i.e., Jatakas reveal the conditions of Chandalas who are considered as a despised group. They are described as occupying sites outside regular villages and towns, and sweeping was their hereditary occupation.[3]

By the close of the pre-Mauryan period rigidity had crept into the caste-system and inter-marriages were not encouraged but these were confined to higher classes alone. The chandalas were looked down upon and were doomed to miserable plight and lived outside the city. Besides, the Untouchables, who were also known as the panchamas (the fifth caste) or the antyajas (the last born) had been living outside the cities and towns for centuries and were not allowed to enter the cities or to have contact with the nobility and the upper caste people.

In the Gupta times, the chandalas were a neglected section also and have been described as living apart from the village settlement. The Chinese pilgrim Hsuan Tsang who came to India (629AD to 645 AD) gives an account of the conditions of the untouchables. By fifth century A.D. the Untouchables grew not only in numbers but had glaring disabilities. Whenever they entered the town the upper caste people kept themselves at a distance from them since the road was supposed to be polluted by them. The Untouchables used to announce their entry into the town by shouting loudly so that people might keep away from them.

MUSLIM PERIOD

Alberuni, writing in about 1020 A.D, grouped together 'Dom' and Chandala, as these two groups not reckoned among any caste or guild. They are occupied with dirty works, like scavenging, cleansing of villages and other services. In the beginning of the century the Hindus had developed a very complex social structure. Inter-marriages and inter-dining were strictly prohibited. The untouchables were made to live outside the towns and villages and they suffered from many social and economic disabilities, which made their lives miserable. In central Hindustan there was 'Untouchability' and chandalas were required to make their presence known by striking a piece of wood while entering the market place or the quarters inhabited by the upper caste people. This clearly shows that, during the Muslim rule, amongst the Hindus caste system was so rigid that both inter-marriage and inter-dinning were taboos. Because of rigid caste system, the Untouchables became a prey to the process of conversion started by the Muslims. Many low caste people, including the Untouchables embraced Islam and joined the invaders partly to avoid themselves from their persecution and partly in search of their freedom and liberty. Later, the Mughals came to India not only to conquer the country, but also to convert the Hindus to Islam. Islam has a proselytizing faith and its followers are zealous missionaries who look upon it to be their primary obligation to propagate the message of Muhammad. The Mughals were foreign conquerors and treated the Hindus as inferior people, and they were filled with conqueror's innate pride and had determined to maintain their separate identity in India. This was not tolerated by the Hinduism where it tried to defend itself by all means. It is believed that the caste-system was much more rigorous than in the previous periods, which enabled the Mughals to exploit this situation and its weaknesses. Consequently many lower caste Hindus, notably in Bengal and other parts, were converted to Islam to save themselves from the degradation and persecution of caste Hindus. Consequently 'Bhakti Movement' was started to consolidate all the groups irrespective of their religions. It is true that, under the patronage of Mughal administration Bhakti Movement gained its momentum. This movement was supported by a group of saints in different parts in India, e.g., Ramananda, Kabir, Tulsidas, Tukaram, Purandara Das and Basava. This 'Bhakti movement' was reformist in the sense that it attempted to correct some of the evils in Hinduism, particularly the practice of Untouchability without questioning the caste system. Later the reformists were initiated by caste Hindus and admitted them to the movements fold. This ultimately led to the dominance of the priestly class, the Brahmins, against whose orthodoxy the protests were initiated. When castes with different ritual ranks came to be associated with the movements, there developed a dual identity, a religious ideological identity with fellow participants of the movement and a socio-cultural identity with social collectiveness (castes) to which they traced their origin.[4] Consequently the first initial protest movement had got its ignition in the traditional Indian society to uplift the Harijan's social status. Again for the second time Bhakti movement's protest occurred against the social discrimination of the depressed classes. But this movement confined its attention to the philosophical realm without any proper socio-economic programme to uplift the Scheduled castes. In spite off this protest movement, the Scheduled Castes were debarred from worshiping in many Hindu temples, and use of the village wells. Besides, Untouchability was expressed in the maintenance of physical distance between Scheduled Castes and high castes and in extreme restrictions of commensal relationships between Untouchables and all others. During the rule of Marathas and Peshwas, it is recorded that, the Mahars and Mangs were not allowed within the gates of Poona after 3 P.M. and before 9 A.M. Because, before 9 A.M. and after 3 P.M. their bodies would cast too long a shadow, which falling on a number of the higher castes, especially Brahmins, defiled them. Thus the concept of 'Untouchability' was institutionalized. Besides, pollution and maintenance of social distance are specific forms of segregation and inequality started within the Indian caste system. Hinduism sanctifies this segregation through its theory of 'karma' and 'Dharma' and the cycle of rebirths.[5] But the generally accepted notion was that, the Untouchables were the aboriginal inhabitants who were conquered and enslaved by the Aryan invaders. They were known for performing all degrading tasks. They were alleged to have the characteristics of drunkenness, shamelessness, brutality, truthlessness, disgusting food practices and lack of personal honour. The ideas of Untouchability and unapproachability arose out of the ideas of ceremonial purity, which was first applied to the aboriginal Shudras in connection with the sacrificial ritual and late it was extended to other groups because of the theoretical impurity of certain occupations.[6]

In due course, the Varna system broke into hundreds of castes and sub-castes as a result of the operation of number of factors, like racial admixture, geographical expansion of the population, inter-regional isolation of the various parts of the country and growth of crafts which tended to become hereditary.[7] The result was the emergence of caste system, which is found in the Hindu society today. Although the Untouchables stood outside the pale of the Varna system, yet they formed an essential part of the caste system. Thus the concept of Untouchability is a strange idea of Indians. Those who believe in the theory of sanctity, based on the idea of 'touch', felt that more the sanctity more they are nearer to God. This shows that, if any one who touches the objects, which have no sanctity, is required to take bath or the ceremony of expiation to restore sanctity. A common man who is ignorant of the reason for the practice of Untouchability, which is sanctified by religion, believes that it would be a sin to violate the custom of practicing Untouchability. Thus the practice of Untouchability was not the result of a deliberate conspiracy to suppress the Untouchables or the Shudras, but it was the holding on to wrong beliefs about religious purity. In the traditional Hindu caste system, the Scheduled castes have been denied the social status as they are ritually far below the purity line. Besides, they fall below the Varna system, but surprisingly they are accommodated in the local Jati -system in the villages.

BRITISH PERIOD

India has developed a unique form of social stratification known as the caste system along with the cultural, linguistic and religious diversity. More significant than the caste system is the existence in the Indian society of social groups, which are identified as 'Untouchables'. Those social groups who controlled the economic resources and wielded political power became the privileged upper castes, and the others were treated as social outcastes, without access to the vital economic resources and bargaining power, they became the most exploited peripheral group in the Indian society.[8] The social customs denied the Untouchables of their right to seek higher social status and to pursue the occupations other than the hereditary ones. They were the poorest of the poor toiling in most unremunerative and often degrading occupations. Being predominantly rural, they have been mainly landless agricultural labourers and marginal sharecroppers and peasants, commonly indebted beyond redemption and held in varying degrees of 'bondage' in different parts of the country. Historically they have been completely bypassed by the controlling elite group. But the British rule awakened Harijans to the enquiry of certain social customs and religious traditions. One of the socio-religious traditions was the practice of Untouchability among the Hindus. With the advent of British, the upper castes joined hands with British and played a dominant role by completely discarding the Scheduled castes or the Untouchables. But surprisingly, the western education taught Indians the value of freedom and independence and dispelled from their minds the cringing, slavish mentality and freed them from the age-old superstitions and caste rituals. Due to the impact of western education three groups emerged with different plans of actions to ameliorate the bondage of Untouchability. The first group wanted to adhere to old society but wanted to reform by gradual process. The second group was revolutionary social reformers who wanted a complete transformation. The third group represented a revivalistic tendency. For many years, education was the monopoly of the Brahmins. It is the Christian's who opened the doors of education to the Untouchables. Consequently, many Untouchables embraced to Christianity and encouraged the other members of their families also to embrace Christianity. When the British conducted the census, the reports showed that the population of Muslims, Christians, and Sikhs was increasing and that of the Hindus was falling. This was due to large number of low castes embracing Christianity or Islam.

RENAISSANCE AND REFORMATION

After the publication of the census reports by the British, the Hindus became alert of their numerical strength. They thought that if they failed to regulate this, they would soon be reduced to a minority. Therefore in 1814, Raja Ram Mohan Roy founded the Atmiya Sabha. After 14 years he founded the Brahmo Samaj, which started to preach the gospel that unless religious evils were removed, the society could not develop. Consequently, the Samaj successfully attacked social evils like casteism and Untouchability. Later came the Arya Samaj in 1875 under the leadership of Swami Dayananda Saraswati, who decried casteism and Untouchability on the ground that the Vedas did not sanction them. The Arya

Samaj opened many schools and educated the masses. It created a feeling of self-confidence and self-reliance among the Hindus and undermined the prevailing notions of superiority of western races and culture. One important contribution of this Samaj was that it raised the social status of the Untouchables among the Hindus and was successful in preventing the Untouchables from leaving Hinduism and joining other religious groups. The Samaj started the purification (shuddhi) movement to reconvert those Untouchables who had accepted Islam and Christianity. But the sad thing was that even after they were received into the Hinduism, they were treated as Untouchables by the caste Hindus. Later, Ramakrishna mission was set up by Swami Vivekananda (1863-1902) in the memory of his Guru Ramakrishna Paramahamsa in 1896. Vivekananda said " Him I call a Mahatma whose heart bleeds for the poor, otherwise he is a Duratma. So long as millions live in hunger and ignorance, I hold every man a traitor who, while educated at their expenses, pays not the least heed to them". This gospel instilled in the hearts of millions of Untouchables a sense of brotherhood. He was the first Indian who described himself as socialist who declared that 'Shudras, who had all along been suppressed and depressed, must assert themselves and become the ruling force in the society'. Vivekananda's concern towards the Untouchables can be seen from his own words when he said " a time will come when there will be the rising of the Shudra class with their Shudrahood..... a time will come when the Shudras of every country with their inborn nature and habits will gain supremacy in every society". He thunders against priestcraft and superstition when he said, " priesthood is the bane of India, he declares and calls upon the common people to revolt against the tyranny of the priests".

Vivekananda further says with devastating sarcasm to the fact that ' the present religion of the Hindus is not in the Vedas, nor in the puranas, nor in Bhakti, nor in Mukti, but religion has entered the cooking pot'.[9] This shows that, during the phase of renaissance and reformation, the Prarthana Samaj, the Brahma Samaj and the Satyashodhak Samaj had started their work to ameliorate the conditions of the depressed classes including the Untouchables. The Prarthana Samaj and the Brahma Samaj did not believe in theism and had no faith in the caste system and the chaturvarna, which led to the emergence of the institution of Untouchability. Swami Dayananda brought out a collection of original Sanskrit texts called the 'satyartha prakash' to support widow marriage, to reject caste based on birth and the right of the Shudras to Vedic education. His mission instilled in the Hindus the ideas of toleration, unity and humanitarian approach towards the unfortunate Untouchables.[10] The Hindu social reform movements in the 19th century were urban and, through education and urbanization, some of the Untouchables moved from the lowest categories of rural society to the lowest strata of the urban society. With the growth of nationalism and the anti-British feelings towards the end of 19th Century, the problem of removal of Untouchability assumed political significance. Since the work of the missionaries was confined only to conversion, they did not contribute anything towards the removal of Untouchability.

INDEPENDENCE MOVEMENT

In the 19th century, the impact of western humanitarianism, liberal and rational ideas stirred several new Hindu reform movements, especially towards the cause of Untouchability. Jyotiba Phule from Pune began to advocate the very idea of asserting the worth of man irrespective of caste. He started a separate school for non-Brahmins in Pune in 1848 as a challenge to the Brahmins. And in 1852 he started "what one account flatly calls, the first school in India for Untouchables". Later he received financial assistance from the British authorities although he was ridiculed, insulted and ousted by reactionaries and relatives. Phule and his saintly wife nobly served the cause of the Untouchables and worked for their education and emancipation in Pune, the very center of orthodoxy. The problem of removing disabilities of the Untouchables gained momentum in the hands of the Satyashodhak Samaj under the leadership of Jyotiba Phule in 1873, a man from Mali caste. The Untouchables for the first time attacked directly the caste system under the guidance of this living spirit i.e., Phule. He requested the non- Brahmins not to engage any Brahmin priest to conduct their marriage rituals. Therefore he started to impart education to the Untouchables to end the practice of 'Untouchability'. Consequently, the Government of Bombay in 1856 took cognizance of the case of a Mahar boy who was refused admission to the government school at Dharwar. Ultimately in 1858 it was announced in a press note that "although the Governor-in-council does not contemplate the introduction of low-caste pupils into schools, the expenses of which are shared with Government by local contributors and patrons who object to such a measure, he reserves to himself the full right of refusing the support of Government to any partially aided school in which the benefits of education are withheld from any class of persons, on account of race or caste, and further resolves that all schools maintained at the sole cost of Government shall be open to all classes of its subjects without distinction.[11] Since the time of Jyotiba Phule in the Maratha region, all reformers who had felt the injustice of the situation had begun their campaign for educating the members of depressed classes.

Later, Sri. Narayana Guru [1854-1928], the disciple of Jyotiba Phule took the leadership of the Izhavas; an Untouchable group of Kerala. He also started to revolt against the caste system and gospelled the idea of one caste, one religion, one God and declared that the practice of Untouchability is a social crime against humanity and human values. He took drastic steps for the educational advancement of the Izhavas and sanskritized their way of life. With these he was able to transform the Izhavas from an Untouchable group in Kerala to 'backward caste' within a short period of 30 years.[12] Many schools and colleges were started throughout Kerala and many temples were built, and besides, he simplified rituals relating to marriage, worship and funerals. After Narayan Guru, the temple entry programme took a shape in the form of 1936 Kerala Temple Entry Act.

Later, the Indian National Congress was founded in Bombay in whose leaders felt that the Indian's socio – economic condition should be improved. Unfortunately, the Indian National Congress did not take any measures to eradicate social problems of the depressed classes. Consequently, after a long deliberation among Dewan Bahadur Ranganath Rao, Mr. M.G. Ranade, Mr. Narendra Nath Sen, and Mr. Janakinath Ghosal, it was decided to set up a separate organisation called the 'Indian National Social Conference' to deal with the Indian social economy.

When the organisation was established there were two schools of thought in the congress on the issues of social reform and political reform, one group argued in favour of social reform and other group argued in favour of political reform. In this conflict no substantial social reformation took place. Consequently, the depressed classes held a meeting under the chairmanship of Sri Narayan Chandravarkar on 11th November 1917. The chairman was authorized to request the Indian National Congress to pass a resolution declaring to the people of India the necessity of justice, and righteousness in removing all the disabilities imposed by religion and custom upon the depressed classes. Because these social disabilities were more vexatious and oppressive in nature, which prevented the depressed classes from admission to public schools, hospitals, courts of justice, public offices and the use of public wells. But the genesis of the congress resolution of 1917 on the Depressed Classes was not favourable. Dr. Ambedkar said "The congress did nothing...... It was a formal fulfillment of the conditions which the depressed classes had made for giving their support to the Congress–league scheme".[13] The problem of removal of Untouchability was being spread and discussed widely in the Indian Press and platform in 1917. The British laws gave depressed classes equal access to the law and formally discarded caste as a criterion for judgment in criminal, civil and commercial law.[14] They maintained the policy of non-interference in the social and religious customs.

When the Untouchables revolted against the upper castes, they were socially discarded and economically boycotted from the caste-Hindus for which no law or court did come forward to rescue the lives of the Untouchables.[15] This also prompted the Untouchables from separating themselves from the mainstream of Indian life. Mahatma Gandhiji's entry into Indian political scene in 1919 brought a total change in the working of the congress and its programmes. Gandhiji thought that first social inequalities should be removed to fight against the British rule. Besides he also felt the need for the removal of Untouchability, which would give the nation a new strength to attain Swaraj. He said "Swaraj is unattainable without the removal of the sin of Untouchability from the Hindu religion". He wanted to eradicate Untouchability by reviving Varnashrama in its pure form, which was devoid of the taint of birth, according to Gandhiji. Besides, he emphasized that the sin of Untouchability, the notion of defilement from which the Hindus should rid themselves of, then the Untouchables would be able to enjoy their civil rights such as access to roads, wells, public institutions in terms of equality.[16] According to Gandhiji, in order to achieve this, there should be a change of the attitudes of the caste Hindus. Gandhiji's inclination towards the eradication of Untouchability can be seen when he said, "I do not want to be reborn. But if I have to be reborn, I should be born as an Untouchable".[17] Gandhiji proposes two courses of actions for the removal of Untouchability. Firstly, educate the public opinion for securing to the Untouchables perfect freedom to enter ordinary temples and ordinary schools and to use common wells. Secondly, to erect model schools and temples and dig wells especially designed for the convenience of Untouchables but open to others, subject always to priority for Untouchables.[18] Under the leadership of Gandhiji, congress launched a special programme i.e., "the constructive programme of social amelioration". The main object of this programme was ' to organised the depressed classes for a better life, to improve their social, mental and moral conditions, to induce them to send their children to schools and to provide them many facilities which the other citizens enjoy.[19] This special programme was also accepted in the working committee of the congress in 1922. In the year 1923, the working committee passed a resolution at its meeting in Bombay and decided to request the All-India Hindu Mahasabha to take up the task of improving the conditions of the Untouchables and to remove the social evil like Untouchability from amidst the Hindu Community. Later the Hindu Mahasabha did not undertake this work properly, which resulted in the continuation of the problem of Untouchability. Although many programmes were undertaken to remove the social evil like 'Untouchability' from the Hindu community, yet it was not successfully eradicated. The progress of the Congress activities in removal of 'Untouchability' was very slow between 1924 to 1930. But on the contrary the Untouchables organized themselves to establish their rights in the form of Satyagraha. A Satyagraha was organised, at the Kalaram Temple situated in Nasik, a town in the Nasik district of the Bombay presidency, to establish the right of the Untouchables to enter Hindu Temples.

Another Satyagraha was organised, at Chowdar Tank situated in Mahad, the town in the Kolaba district of Bombay presidency, to establish their right to take water. These events show that irrespective of the quantum of support extended by the congress to the Untouchables, the members of the depressed classes continued their fight for securing their right to entry to public places, temples and wells.

Later, the British government held three Round Table Conferences to discuss the problems of the new constitution and a new type of government for India. The British government gave an opportunity to Ambedkar and Dewan Bahadur R. Srinivasan to represent the depressed classes in these conferences. This was the first time that Untouchables were allowed to represent not merely as separate element from the Hindus but also had the right to be consulted in the framing of a constitution of India. Ambedkar also felt the impossibility of the Untouchables' unity with the Hindus who treated them as a separate community vis-à-vis the British policy of administration. "The depressed classes were defined in terms of the religious concept of pollution as caste Hindus, contact with whom entails purification on the part of the high caste Hindus. But still the British did not construe pollution and purification as legitimate objects of government action. Because they had a long-standing policy of non-interference in social and religious practices, though there were many laws, which could be imposed against social disabilities, which were not strictly enforced. Therefore Ambedkar became disgusted over the attitudes of the British government towards the conditions of the Untouchables". He had no trust in the British sense of Justice. Therefore he decided to fight for a separate electorate for depressed classes that could protect the Untouchables from the dominance of upper caste Hindus. At one stage Ambedkar said "Lost rights are never gained again, by begging, and by appeal to the conscience of the usurpers, but by relentless struggle". Untouchability to him was such an abominable strain that it would not matter much even if some lives were sacrificed to remove it from the Hindu society.

The first session of the First Round Table Conference began on 12th November 1930, in which Mr. Mac-Donald made many important constitutional proposals. Among them one such proposal was that there should be full responsible governments in the provinces subject to the special responsibility and powers of the Governors of the provinces that are necessary to safeguard the interest of the minorities. But in the conference Ambedkar demanded for a separate electorate for the depressed classes. But the Hindu delegates said that they were prepared to accept the demand of reservation of seats for minorities but they insisted on a joint electorate. Finally, the conference was concluded with no solution being arrived at, with regard to the problem of communal representation.

When the Second Round Table Conference began on September 7, 1931, Gandhiji observed that, congress being the national party, which represented all sections of India including the depressed classes, should fight for the removal of Untouchability, as it was one of the party's political programmes. He advocated for joint electorate with reserved seats in the legislatures as he felt that separate electorates would split the Hindu religion and perpetuates the stigma. Consequently the rift between Ambedkar and Gandhiji, over the problem of separate electorate for depressed classes, became wider. Ambedkar insisted the British to provide separate electorate to the Untouchables, which could alone save them from the dominance of the upper caste Hindus. Ultimately, on August 17, 1932, the British Government announced the famous communal Award according to which the depressed classes were to have a number of special seats assigned to them in the provincial assemblies for a period of 20 years, where only the depressed classes could vote for such seats. Immediately Gandhiji refused to accept this Communal Award announced by British Government and took ' Epic Fast' against this award. The fact remains that; the Communal Award gave separate electorates not only for the Untouchables, but also for the Muslims, Sikhs, and Christians.

The Communal Award or Mac-Donald award para 9 of the text[20] says "all members of the depressed classes so entitled under the ordinary electoral qualifications will vote in a general constituency. In addition, since it is improbable that members of depressed classes would under present conditions secure adequate representation in the legislature by this means alone, it is provided that some special seats shall also be assigned to them. These seats will be filled by election from special constituencies in which only members of depressed classes residing in these areas will be entitled to vote. Members of depressed classes will thus be allowed two votes-one in a general constituency and one in a special constituency, while members outside them will vote in general constituency only. The separate depressed classes constituencies, however, are a temporary device designed to safeguard the community until its present social and educational disabilities have been, to some extent, made good, and His Majesty's Government intend that the new Constitution shall provide for their compulsory abolition after 20 years, if this has not previously been affected with the agreement of the parties concerned by the means afforded in the text of the Award itself".

Thus, the Award granted separate electorate to depressed classes along with the right to double-vote ignoring Gandhiji's opinion. On August 18, 1932 Gandhiji wrote a letter to the British Prime Minister, from Yaravada Jail, that ' his fast in the jail shall continue till the British Government on its own or under pressure of public opinion revise their decision and withdraw the scheme of communal electorates for the depressed classes. To this Mac-Donald replied that 'under the Government Scheme the depressed classes will remain part of Hindu community....... And that British Government has no intention of severing depressed classes form Hindu Community'.[21] Thus Ambedkar–Gandhiji confrontation, arising out of Gandhiji's threat to fast unto death had stirred up a serious controversy in every nook and corner of India. Later Ambedkar met Gandhiji at Yarawada Jail and found that his condition was becoming serious every minute. Having seen the condition of Gandhiji, Ambedkar consented to his proposal and an agreement was signed by Ambedkar and other caste-Hindu leaders i.e., M.M Malaviya, Sapru, Dr. Rajendra Prasad. This agreement is popularly known as the "Poona Pact".[22] According to this Pact, the depressed classes were to be allowed a separate electorate in the primaries but they were to vote in the joint electorates in the election itself. However, 18 percent of the seats in the Central and Provincial legislatures were reserved for the members of the depressed classes. But Ambedkar considered this as a betrayal of the Untouchables by Gandhiji. Ambedkar said that the Untouchables were worse off under the Prime Minister's Award.

When the seats reserved for Untouchables in the Provincial Legislatures were raised to 151 under the Poona Pact, congress captured 78 Scheduled Caste seats in the 1937 elections. In this connection Ambedkar observed that Poona Pact was in no way beneficial to the depressed classes because "if it increased the quota of seats for the Untouchables, it took away the right to the double vote.... this increase in seats can never be deemed to be a compensation for the loss of double vote. The second vote given by the Communal Award was a priceless privilege. Its value as a political weapon was beyond reckoning. The voting strength of the Untouchables in each constituency is 'one to ten'. With this voting strength free to be used in the election of caste Hindu candidates, the Untouchables would have been in a position to determine the issue of the General Election. No caste Hindu could have dared neglect the Untouchables in his constituency or be hostile to their interest".

In 1937, the congress government of Bombay passed the Bombay Harijan Temple Worship (Removal of Disabilities) Act, which allowed the trustees to admit the Harijans to the temples, even if the current Hindu customs debarred them. This enabled the Untouchables to enter the temples without any hesitation and fear.

The table given below shows the number of seats captured by Untouchables candidates who stood on the Congress ticket. When the Untouchables were elected on the congress seats, they were subjected to rigorous party discipline and were absolutely under the control of the party executive. They were not able to raise their voice against the disabilities, as they had no right to go against their party executive. Therefore, the basic mission of the Untouchables to ventilate these grievances through elected representatives remained a daydream. They began to think of establishing an independent organization to struggle for their cause.

Province	*Total seats reserved for Untouchables Under Govt. of India Act 1935.*	*Total seats captured by the Congress*
United Province	20	16
Madras	30	26
Bengal	30	06
Central Province	20	07
Bombay	15	04
Bihar	15	11
Punjab	08	-
Assam	07	04
Orissa	06	04
Total	151	78

Consequently a new organisation was formed by the name 'All India Scheduled Caste Federation' which was formally announced by Ambedkar at Nagpur in 1942. The Federation demanded for the guarantee of minimum representation in the legislature, executive and public services, and reasonable protections to the Untouchables in the future Constitution. Besides, the consciousness of the Harijans rose up as a result of the Gandhian movement and the work done by many voluntary organisations like Ramakrishna Mission, the Servants of India Society, the Harijan Sevak Sangh, the All India Scheduled Castes Federation, the Bharatiya Depressed Classes League etc. Ultimately, Ambedkar being the chairman of the Drafting Committee for the future Constitution of India managed to introduce a provision, for the removal of Untouchability and other safeguards to protect the interests of Untouchables in the Constitution of India. The relentless struggle of Ambedkar continued with his mission to make Scheduled Castes a political factor to reckon with. "The use of political means to change the conditions and status of the Scheduled Caste was first made by Ambedkar. Through his writings and speeches he emphasized the fact that political power was the key to all progress and that the Scheduled Castes could achieve salvation if they captured power by organizing themselves into a separate party. He believed that only when they achieved political power, the social and economic conditions of the Scheduled Castes and Scheduled Tribes be improved. Through Political action he wanted to force the hands of the Caste Hindus to ameliorate the conditions in which the Scheduled Castes and Scheduled Tribes were living".[23] The fact remains that, the contributions made by both Ambedkar and Gandhiji towards the upliftment and protection of Scheduled Castes can be understood as complementary to each other. Their profound contributions also shaped official policy in the subsequent years after independence.

CONSTITUTIONAL AND LEGAL PROVISIONS RELATING TO "ABOLITION OF UNTOUCHABILITY"

The framers of the Indian Constitution and social reformers wanted to eradicate the social evil like ' Untouchability' from the Hindu social order. As the problem of Untouchability was deep rooted in the Hindu social order, Untouchables were discriminated, degraded and denied various rights. Those at the top of the caste hierarchy denied many human rights to the so-called 'Untouchables'—except to live and serve the rest of the community as commanded by them. This custom of 'Untouchability' had not only thrown millions of Indian people into darkness but it had also eaten into the very foundation of the nation. Therefore, the Constitution-makers deliberately incorporated a separate provision, i.e. Article 17, into the chapter on 'Fundamental Rights' in part III of the constitution to completely eradicate this social evil and to establish an egalitarian society.

Following are some of the Fundamental Rights guaranteed under the Constitution of India for the abolition of ' Untouchability' and to remove all disabilities, which existed in the Hindu social order:

1. Article 15(1) prohibits 'the State from discriminating against any citizen on grounds only of religion, race, caste, sex, place of birth or any of them'. This right is available to the citizens against the State only.
2. Article 15(2) prohibits any restriction, disability or liability with regard to;
   (a) Access to shops, public restaurants, hotels and places of public entertainment; or
   (b) The use of wells, tanks, bathing ghats, roads and places of public resort maintained wholly or partly out of State funds or dedicated to the use of general public, on grounds only of religion, race, Caste etc. This right under Article 15 (2) is available to the citizens against any person. However a private well or tank does not come within the meaning of this clause.
3. Similarly, Article 16 (1) promotes equality of opportunity for all citizens in matters relating to public employment or appointment to any office under the State and Article 16 (2) prohibits any discrimination on grounds only of religion, race, caste etc. in respect of employment or office under the State.
4. Like wise, Article 17 of the Constitution states "Untouchability is abolished and its practice in any form is forbidden. The

enforcement of any disability arising out of 'Untouchability' shall be an offence punishable in accordance with law".

5. Besides, Article 23 (1) prohibits traffic in human beings and forced labour and thus aims at 'recognition and restoration of the dignity of man'.

6. Article 25 (1) guarantees the rights to religion to all persons, which includes the right to "freedom of conscience and right freely to profess, practice and propagate religion". But on the ground of religious freedom, no individual can lawfully defend 'Untouchability'.

   Article 25(2) removes the general obstacles which otherwise would have been so in providing social welfare and reform or the throwing open of Hindu religious institutions of public character to all classes and sections of Hindus. A Scheduled Caste Hindu has the right to worship in any temple in the same manner and to the same extent as any other non-Scheduled Caste Hindu.

   The High Court of Rajasthan made this point clear in the following two cases;

Surya Narayan Chaudhury V. State of Rajasthan

and

P.L. Mimroth V. State of Rajasthan

In the above two cases, the Scheduled Castes and Scheduled tribes were denied entry to the Nathdwara Hindu Temple despite Article 25 (2) (b) of the Constitution. Two writ petitions were filed in the High Court of Rajasthan under Article 226 of the Constitution. Chief Justice Verma and Justice Farooq Hassan made the following observations:

"It is tragic that on the eve of Gandhi Jayanthi we are debating a Harijan's right to enter a public temple for worship as an equal, and directions of the court should be needed for enforcement of this right to equality. All men are born equal and the classification between them thereafter is a man-made and artificial against the divine dictate. To present them as unequals before God is, therefore, an injustice and an insult to our Maker besides being contrary to the guarantee and mandate of equality in our Constitution as a basic human right. To name them 'Harijans' and then discriminate them for entry into a public temple to worship 'Hari' is not merely the violation of constitutional guarantee or an insult to them but sheer hypocrisy and insult to 'Hari' rendering their name a misnomer".

The above-learned Judges, after careful scrutiny, issued the following directions to the State of Rajasthan:

"Every devotee including a Harijan who wants to enter the Nathdwara temple for worship will be permitted by the authorities concerned to enter it in accordance with general practice and regulations of entry applicable to everyone else. The Harijans or members of any other weaker section of society will not be subjected to any additional restriction or condition, which does not apply to others. In other words, the entry of all devotees for worship into that temple would be regulated by the same conditions, which apply equally to everyone without any additional condition for entry being imposed on any Harijan devotee. It is further directed that the reported and much published practice of purification of Harijans alone before permitting them to enter the temple for worship by making them wear 'Anthimala', sprinkling them with 'Ganjala' and giving them 'Tulsidal' shall be discontinued forth with since this condition imposed on Harijan devotee alone is discriminatory. This practice violates the right of equality guaranteed to Harijans by Articles 14, 15 and 17 of the Constitution. The State Government must ensure discontinuance of this practice forthwith, if the same is still continuing. The State Government should also take strict measures to ensure that there is no further mockery of this constitutional guarantees and the offenders, if any, are promptly dealt with in accordance with law to prevent recurrence of any such incident in future".

7. Article 29(2) states that, " No citizen shall be denied admission into any educational institution maintained by the State or receiving aid out of State funds on grounds only of religion, race Caste, language or any of them".

8. Under Article 32, any citizen whose fundamental rights including the right against Untouchability under Article 17 are violated can move the Supreme Court directly by writ proceedings for the enforcement of the rights conferred by the Constitution. Public-spirited individuals, lawyers, social

workers, journalists and voluntary organizations can, on behalf of the Scheduled Caste, file Public Interest Litigation petitions in the Supreme Court under Article 32 or in the High Courts under Article 226 of the Constitution.

Although 'Untouchability' was abolished and its practice in any form was forbidden under Article 17 of the Constitution, yet for nearly six years there was no law to punish the offenders. In the year 1955, the Parliament passed the 'Untouchability Offences Act 1955' to make the practice of Untouchability a cognizable offence and to punish the practice of 'Untouchability' and enforcement of any disability arising out of this social evil. This Act came into operation in 1956 December. The Act provided punishment for enforcing religious and social disabilities in respect of access to any shop, public restaurant, hotel etc. refusing to admit a person to a hospital, refusing to sell goods and render services. The Act provided inadequate punishment for offences arising out of 'Untouchability', i.e., imprisonment upto six months, fine upto Rs. 500 or both. The Act also provided other punishments like, cancellation or suspension of licenses and suspension of government grants. In case, an offence committed in relation to a member of a Scheduled Caste, it could be presumed that it was committed on the ground of 'Untouchability' unless the contrary was proved. Besides, the offences committed under the Act are made cognizable and compoundable. The Act punished "not only the direct enforcement of disabilities but also indirect social support of Untouchability".[24]

Consequently, the Government of India appointed a committee under the chairmanship of Sri. L. Elaya Perumal in April 1965 to examine, interalia, the problems of Untouchability vis-à-vis the working of the Act, and to make recommendations to remove many loopholes in the Act. The committee submitted its recommendations providing penal provisions more rigid to punish those offenders. The committee also pointed out that there was inadequacy of the copies of the Act available in district offices and some cases were deliberately delayed to make Scheduled Castes and Scheduled Tribes to suffer and subject them to various hardships. On the basis of its recommendation, the Act was amended and renamed as 'Protection of Civil Rights Act, 1976.[25]

The Protection of Civil Rights Act defines the term 'Civil Rights' as any right accruing to a person by reason of the abolition of Untouchability by Article 17 of the Constitution. The consequence of abolition of Untouchability is the redemption of equal rights for all as guaranteed by Article 14 of the constitution. Following are the major offences and punishments contemplated under this Act;

(a) *Enforcing of religious disabilities:* Preventing any person from entering any place of public worship or from offering prayers or using the waters (on the ground of Untouchability) is punishable with imprisonment between one month and six months and fine between 100 to 500 rupees (Section 3).

(b) *Enforcing social disabilities:* Enforcing disability [on the ground of Untouchability] with regard to access to shop, hotel or places of public entertainment or the use of articles kept therein for public use or the access or use of any public conveyance, public residential premises and public conveniences etc., is punishable with same terms of imprisonment and fine as above. Enforcing any disability includes any discrimination on the ground of Untouchability.

(c) *Refusing to admit persons to hospitals:* Refusal of public hospital facilities and discrimination after admission [on the ground of Untouchability] are also punishable with the same punishments as above (Section 5).

(d) *Refusing to sell goods or render services:* If, on the ground of Untouchability, any one refuses to sell any goods or refuses to render services available to other persons in the ordinary course of business are also offences punishable under the Act (Section 6).

(e) *Insulting, abusing and obstructing behaviour:* Acts directed towards preventing persons from enjoying civil rights or boycotting or injuring them for having exercised any such right, encouraging people to practice Untouchability, insults or attempts to insult [on the ground of Untouchability] a member of the Scheduled Caste is punishable with same punishments as mentioned above. Encouraging the practice of Untouchability is said to include its practice as well as its justification on historical, religious or on any other ground (Section 7).

(f) *Unlawful compulsory Labour:* Compelling a person [on the ground of Untouchability] to do scavenging, sweeping, carcass removing or such other jobs is also punishable. Such acts are deemed to be enforcing a disability arising out of Untouchability (Section 7-A).

(g) *Abetment of offence:* Abetting of any offence under this Act is punishable.

(h) *Neglecting Investigation of offence by public Servants:* Public servants who are found willfully negligent in the investigation as abettors of the offences.

(i) *The Act has enhanced the punishment considerably:* For the first offence, the minimum punishment shall be imprisonment for one month and fine of Rs. 100 and the maximum imprisonment for six months and fine of Rs. 500. For the second offence, the minimum punishment shall be imprisonment for six months and fine of Rs. 200 and the maximum imprisonment for one year and Rs. 500. For the third and subsequent offences, the punishment may range from imprisonment for one year and fine of Rs. 1000 (Section 11).

(j) *The imposition of Fines by Government:* The State Governments have been empowered to impose collective fines on the inhabitants of any area where they are concerned in or abetting the commission of Untouchability offences.

The above provisions in the amended Act are remarkable and an improvement over the original Provisions. These Provisions enable to eradicate the social evils of Untouchability and discrimination from the Hindu society. But due to the changed circumstances, increased atrocities on Scheduled Castes and Scheduled Tribes and to provide more safety and security, the Parliament once again amended this Act and to incorporate some more new offences of atrocities against Scheduled Castes and Scheduled Tribes to safeguard the dignity and human rights of these people. Consequently, Parliament enacted a new law i.e., 'The Scheduled Castes and Scheduled Tribes [prevention of Atrocities] Act, 1989. This Act was indeed a bold step in the direction of meaningful implementation of the Constitutional Directives and to protect the rights of the Scheduled Castes and Scheduled Tribes through criminal sanctions.

Following are the atrocities, committed by a person who does not belong to Scheduled Caste and Scheduled Tribe, considered as punishable offences under Schedule Castes and Scheduled Tribes [Prevention of Atrocities] Act 1989;

1. Forcing a member of Scheduled Castes and Scheduled Tribes to drink or eat obnoxious substances or dumping waste in the premises or neighborhood with intention to cause insult or annoyance to him and forcibly removing clothes or parading naked a member of Scheduled Caste and Scheduled Tribe.
2. Forcing or compelling a Scheduled Caste and Scheduled Tribe to do beggar [forced labour] or bonded labour, wrongful occupation or cultivation of land belonging to Scheduled Castes and Scheduled Tribes, wrongful dispossession from land or interference with the enjoyment of rights over any land, premises or water and forcible causing of a Scheduled Caste and Scheduled Tribe to leave his house or village.
3. Preventing a Scheduled Caste and Scheduled Tribe person from voting or forcing him/her to vote for a particular candidate or vote in a manner prohibited by law.
4. Instituting a false suit or criminal proceeding against a Scheduled Caste and Scheduled Tribe person.
5. Giving false information to any public servant and thereby compelling him to use his power to cause injury, harm or harassment to a Scheduled Caste and Scheduled Tribe person.
6. Insulting or intimidating a Scheduled Caste and Scheduled Tribe person in public with the intention of humiliating that person.
7. Dishonoring or outraging the modesty of any woman belonging to a Scheduled Caste and Scheduled Tribe.
8. Polluting the water of a spring or reservoir ordinarily used by members of Scheduled Castes and Scheduled Tribes so as to make it unfit for use.
9. Using any custodial or dominant position to sexually exploit a woman belonging to Scheduled Castes and Scheduled Tribes.

10. Denying a Scheduled Caste and Scheduled Tribe person a customary right of passage to public resort or preventing him/her from using public places accessible to others.

Following are the punishments prescribed under the Act;

1. **Giving or fabricating false evidence:** Giving or fabricating false evidence intending or knowing it to be likely to lead to conviction of a Scheduled Caste and Scheduled Tribe person is an offence of atrocity. If such conviction of Scheduled Castes and Scheduled Tribes for a capital offence is made (i.e., punishable with death) then, such persons responsible for false evidence are liable to be punished with life imprisonment and with fine, If the person thus convicted is an innocent member of a Scheduled Caste and Scheduled Tribe, then the person who gives or fabricates the false evidence can be punished with death. If the false evidence is given or falsely made up against a Scheduled Caste and Scheduled Tribe person and thereby he is convicted for an offence other than capital offence and punishable with more than seven years of imprisonment, then the person who gave the false evidence can be punished with imprisonment of minimum of six months and maximum of seven years or more and with fine.
2. **Mischief by fire to property, house or temple of Scheduled Castes and Scheduled Tribes:** Committing mischief by fire with intention or knowledge to cause damage to property belonging to Scheduled Castes and Scheduled Tribes is punishable with imprisonment between six months and seven years and with fine. If any place of worship or residence or place for keeping the property of a member of Scheduled Castes and Scheduled Tribes is destroyed by committing mischief by fire or any explosive substance, the person causing the destruction can be punished with imprisonment for life and with fine.
3. **Committing serious crimes on account of the victim being a Scheduled Caste and Scheduled Tribe**: If a non-Scheduled Caste and Scheduled Tribe person commits any offence under the Indian Penal Code punishable with imprisonment for ten years or more against any Scheduled Caste and Scheduled Tribe person or his/her property, he can be punished with imprisonment for life and with fine.

4. **Causing disappearance of evidence against offenders guilty of atrocities:** A person having the knowledge that an offence under the Indian Penal Code has been committed against a Scheduled Caste / Scheduled Tribe person or his/her property and intentionally removes all the evidence to protect the offender from legal punishments or gives false information against the offence or the offender, can be punished with imprisonment provided for that offence.
5. **Public servants guilty of atrocities:** If a public servant commits any of the above offences, he shall be punishable with imprisonment ranging between one year and the maximum provided for that offence. A public servant willfully neglecting his duties under the Act is also punishable with imprisonment for a term between six months and one year [Section 3].
6. **Increased punishment in some cases:** If a person is convicted more than once for committing offences under this Act, he can be punished with minimum of one-year imprisonment. The Act also provides for the forfeiture of property, movable or immovable, used for the commission of the offence. Besides, during the pendency of the trail, the Court can order attachment of property which, on conviction, can be forfeited to the extent it is required for the purpose of realisation of any fine imposed.

Besides, under Section 21 of the Act, State Governments are required to take various measures to avoid any possible impediments in implementation of these Provisions. These include:

1. Giving legal aid to the victims of the atrocities.
2. Meeting the traveling and maintenance expenses of the witnesses and the victim during the investigation and trial of the case.
3. Providing facilities for the socio - economic rehabilitation of the victims of atrocities.
4. Appointing officers to supervise and to conduct prosecutions for committing offences under this Act.
5. Setting up of committees to assist the Government in formulating and implementing appropriate measures to prevent atrocities.

6. Provision for periodic surveys on the working of the Act with a view to identify measures for better implementation; and
7. Identifying areas where members of Scheduled Castes/ Scheduled Tribes are likely to be subjected to atrocities and adopting measures to ensure their safety.

These Provisions guarantee the minimum dignity and protection to the members of Scheduled Castes and Scheduled Tribes, which can be legitimately expected by every citizen from their Governments. In spite of all these Provisions enumerated under the Act, the performance of Untouchability in different forms is still in practice. The Supreme Court of India had an occasion to punish those persons who performed Untouchability against the members of Scheduled Castes and Scheduled Tribes in *State of Karnataka V. Appa Balu Ingale.*[26] In this case, the respondents were tried for the offences committed under Section 4 & 7 of the Protection of Civil Rights Act, 1976 and they were convicted and sentenced to undergo simple imprisonment for one month and a fine of Rs. 100. The charge against the respondents was that they restrained the complainant party by show of force from the ground that they were Untouchables. The prosecution produced four witnesses who were all Harijans. The trial Court and Appellate Court concurrently observed that, the charge against the respondents-accused was proved beyond reasonable doubts. But the High Court of Karnataka rejected the evidences of all the four witnesses who deposed to the actual incident as happened before their eyes on the following reasoning:

> "Thus, not only the evidence of these witnesses regarding the actual manner in which the accused obstructed and what words they uttered, is discrepant and not consistent, but what is not certain from the evidence is as to who among the accused persons obstructed to the accused. It cannot expect that all the accused would use the words simultaneously in a chorus in the manner the witnesses stated before the court. Therefore, it cannot be said with any amount of certainty, which among the accused was guilty of the offence. The evidence adduced on behalf of the prosecution was wholly insufficient to establish the charge of the offence, under Section 4 (iv) of the Act, leveled against them".[27]

But the Supreme Court observed that, the High Court fell into patent error in rejecting the prosecution evidence. Besides, the court said the charge against the respondents have been proved beyond doubt. The Supreme Court was convinced by all the four complainants when they said that the borewell in question was being drilled at a distance of about 15 feet from Harijan colony and water sprouted from the well on the date of the incident at about 9.30 P.M. At that time, many persons including the four complainants were present there. Two young girls of the Hindu community performed pooja. Thereafter, ten to fifteen Hindus took water from the well for performing pooja at the temple. They further said that, they along with five other persons, who were all Harijans, also brought pots for taking water from the well. At that time, the three respondents told the Harijans not to take water from the well, as they were 'Mahars' and that there was a separate well for them. The complainants further stated that, the three respondents further obstructed the Harijans from taking water saying that if the Harijans insist on taking water the result would be disastrous. Immediately one of the respondents told his men to bring a gun from his house and threatened the Harijans with dire consequences. The complainants further told the accused persons that Harijans have also right to take water from the well.

From this incident deposed by the complainants, the Supreme Court said, it did not find any infirmity in the evidence of the prosecution witnesses. The High Court lost sight of the fact that the social disability of the Harijan community was enforced on a threat of using a gun. It was proved beyond doubt that the complainants were stopped from taking water from the well on the ground that they were Untouchables. Therefore, the Supreme Court set aside the judgement of the High Court and restored the judgement of the Additional Session Judge, Belgaum, dated September 5, 1980. The Court, through Justice K. Ramaswamy, pointed out that the abolition of 'Untouchability' is the arch of the Constitution to make its preamble meaningful and to integrate the Dalits in the national mainstream.[28]

This shows that the Constitution makers deliberately included in the Constitution of India a Provision relating to the 'abolition of Untouchability' under Article 17. Besides, in order to protect the interests of Scheduled Castes and Scheduled Tribes and the commission of the offence of 'Untouchability' against them, the Parliament of India enacted various laws i.e., Scheduled Castes and Scheduled Tribes [Prevention of Atrocities] Act, 1989 with stringent Provisions to eradicate those offences with speedy trial.

The thrust of Article 17 and the Scheduled Castes and Scheduled Tribes [Prevention of Atrocities] Act, 1989 is to liberate the society from blind and ritualistic adherence and traditional beliefs, which lost all legal and moral base. The Act seeks to establish new ideal par with general public, absence of disabilities, restrictions or prohibitions on grounds of caste or religion, availability of opportunities and a sense of being a participant in the mainstream of national life. In this connection, Dr. Ambedkar's speech made in the Constituent Assembly on November 25, 1949, is worth remembering:

> "What we must do is not to be content with more political democracy. We must make our political democracy a social democracy as well. Political democracy cannot last unless there lies at the base of it a social democracy. What does social democracy mean? It means a way of life, which recognizes liberty, equality and fraternity as the principles of life. These principles – liberty, equality and fraternity – are not to be treated as separate items in a trinity. They form a union of trinity in the sense that to divorce from the other is to defeat the very purpose of democracy. Without equality, liberty would produce the supremacy of the few over the many. Equality without liberty would kill individual initiative. Without fraternity, liberty and equality would not become a natural course of things. It would require a constable to enforce them. We must begin by acknowledging the fact that there is complete absence of two things in Indian society. One of these is equality. On the social plane, we have in India a society based on the principle of graded inequality, which means elevation for some and degradation for others. On the economic plane, we have a society, in which there are some who have immense wealth as against many who live in utter poverty".

On 26th January 1950, we are going to enter into a life of contradictions. In politics, we will have equality and in social and economic life we will have inequality. In politics, we will be recognizing the principle of one man, one vote and one value. In our social and economic life, we shall, by reason of our social and economic structure, continue to deny the principle of one man, one value. How long shall we continue to deny equality in our social and economic life? If we continue to deny it for long, we will do so only by putting our political democracy in peril. We must remove this contradiction at the earliest possible moment or else those who suffer from inequality will blow up the structure of political democracy, which we have so laboriously built up.

The above Provisions are the most outstanding features of the Act. The Act covers almost all areas to punish those persons, who preach, practice and propagate Untouchability in any form. However excellent the Provisions are in the Act, they are conditioned by the effective implementation. Then only the problem of 'Untouchability' can be eradicated from the Hindu society from its root. Besides, by strictly adhering to these Provisions and punishing those people who violate them, an egalitarian society can be established. The legal abolition of Untouchability, no doubt, has given a new outlook towards life, but they are not given social status and dignity in the Hindu society. Many organizations like, People's Union for Civil Liberties, People's Union for Democratic Rights, Vigil India Movement Society for the promotion of equal Justice, Amnesty International are doing excellent work for protecting people's liberties by taking legal actions against the violations of human rights in various parts of the world. But if these organizations come forward to remove the social evil like Untouchability from the Hindu society, then the Scheduled Castes and Scheduled Tribes in this country will enjoy the liberties and freedom guaranteed under the Constitution.

CONCLUSION

From the above discussion, it is evident that, the problem of 'Untouchability', in the Hindu social order, is an ancient problem where the depressed classes including the Scheduled Castes and Scheduled Tribes [Untouchables] were subjected to many discriminatory and degrading practices. The social practice of 'Untouchability' spread so much so that disintegration started within the Hindu social order where the Untouchables started converting to various religions. At this point of time, many social reformers like Raja Ram Mohan Roy, Swami Vivekananda, Gandhiji and Ambedkar thought that, the Hindu social order could be saved only by providing some safety and security to the Untouchables in the Hindu Social Order. Therefore they contended that, Untouchables should be provided with liberties, freedom and right to enter public places 'including temple entry', which was denied to them since several centuries. At the time of drafting the Constitution for free India, they deliberately included several fundamental rights like 'Right to Equality, Freedom, Abolition of Untouchability, Right to life' and many other Provisions of social welfare to all the people of India including Scheduled Castes and Scheduled Tribes. With a view to enforce the Provision of 'Abolition of Untouchability' Parliament enacted number of Legislations i.e., 'Untouchability Offence Act, 1955, Protection of Civil Rights Act, 1976 and Scheduled Castes and Scheduled Tribes [Prevention of Atrocities] Act, 1989'. The above Legislations will certainly help the Untouchables [Scheduled Castes / Scheduled Tribes] to attain equality, to achieve social and economic justice, if they are properly implemented. Now the status of the Untouchables in the Hindu society is far better than what it was in the earlier days i.e., prior to the Constitution of India came into being.

NOTES

1. P.V. Kane–*"History of Dharmasastra"*, Bhandarkar Oriental Research Institute, Poona, 1941, p. 168.
2. Ibid., p. 168.
3. G.S. Ghurye – *"Caste and Race in India"*, p. 312–313.
4. Rebati Ballav Tripathy – *"Dalits : A sub-human Society"*, Ashish Publishing House, New Delhi, p. 10.
5. Ibid., p. 12.
6. Opp. Cit., Note 3.
7. Opp. Cit., Note 4.
8. Jose Kananaikil–*"Marginalisation of Scheduled Caste: A Sociological Interpretation in readings on Scheduled Castes"*, p. 79.
9. All the above quotations are from the Article "Vivekananda–The Apostle of Modernity", *The Sunday Statesman*, 25th September 1988, pp. 1-5.
10. J.R. Kamble–*"Rise and Awakening of Depressed Class in India"*, [National, New Delhi, 1979], pp. 38-39.
11. Opp. Cit., Note 3.
12. B. Kuppuswamy–*'Social change in India'*, [Vikas, New Delhi], p. 206.
13. B.R. Ambedkar–*"What Congress and Gandhi have done to the Untouchables"*, [Thacker, Bombay, 1946], p. 18.

14. Opp. Cit., Note 4.
15. Opp. Cit., Note 5.
16. Ibid., p. 25.
17. J.M. Mahar [Ed.]–"Gandhi & Ambedkar : A study of Leadership", in *"The Untouchables in Contemporary India"*, [The University of Arizona Press, Arizona, 1972], p. 72.
18. A.C. Pradhan–*"Emergence of Depressed Classes"* [Bookland International, Bhubaneshwar, 1986], p. 48.
19. Opp. Cit., Note 13.
20. The text of the 'Poona Pact' is put in the Appendix.
21. Bombay Chronicle – August 18th, 1932.
22. The text of the 'Poona Pact' is included in the Appendix.
23. Sachidananda–*"The Harijan Elite: A study of their status, mobility and role in Social transformation"*, [Thomas Press, Haryana, 1976], p. 6.
24. Marc Galenter–*"Law and Caste in Modern India"* [1963].
25. The protection of Civil Rights Act, 1976, is placed in the Appendix.
26. AIR 1993 SC.
27. Ibid., pp. 1127-28.
28. Ibid., p. 1134.

5

SOCIO–ECONOMIC CONDITIONS OF SC/ST–A CASE STUDY OF MYSORE DISTRICT

INTRODUCTION

India is predominantly an agricultural country and lives in villages. Industrial revolution of eighteenth century and early nineteenth century brought drastic changes in human life. Twentieth century has added more to human living, but majority of the Indian population is still living in object poverty. They are unable to fulfill their primary needs [Food, Clothing & Shelter] while they work hard from day to night.[1] India got freedom in 1947 from the Britishers, but the Scheduled Castes and Scheduled Tribes are still living in utter poverty and slavery conditions. In all walks of life, the upper caste groups exploit Scheduled Castes and Scheduled Tribes and they are under the domination of the caste Hindus even after 50 years of Independence. After independence, Indian National Government made several legislations, ordinances and policies from time to time to increase the income level as well as the socio-economic development of the weaker sections. But in practice, due to number of reasons, these policies and legislations hardly reach these people to elevate them from socio and economic disabilities.

For the purpose of studying socio, economic and political conditions and to find out how far Constitutional benefits are reaching the weaker sections, particularly the Scheduled Castes and Scheduled Tribes, three taluks in Mysore district have been selected i.e. T.N. Pura, Hunsur and Mysore. For empirical study, 600 respondents belonging to Scheduled Castes and Scheduled Tribes have been selected on random basis from the above three taluks. According to 1991 census, the total population of Mysore district is 31,55,800. Out of this, the population of Scheduled Castes and Scheduled Tribes is 5,82,489. Out of the total population of the district, Scheduled Castes and Scheduled Tribes constitute 15.22% and 3.23% respectively. Besides, Mysore district has been considered as the third largest district in the State of Karnataka, which is inhabited by more Scheduled Castes and Scheduled Tribes. The following table shows the population of the Scheduled Castes and Scheduled Tribes in the three taluks.

Sl.No.	*Name of the Taluks*	*Scheduled Castes*	*Scheduled Tribes*
1.	Hunsur	34,331	23,457
2.	Mysore	35,592	13,210
3.	T.N. Pura	59,097	5,124
	Total	1,29,020	41,791

Source: Handbook published by the Mysore District Welfare Department.

Besides, fifty officers, fifty leaders and twenty MLA's & MP's have been selected on random basis for extracting various information relating to the problems of Scheduled Castes and Scheduled Tribes. These officers, leaders and MLA's & MP's come within the jurisdiction of the above three taluks and they belong to Scheduled Castes and Scheduled Tribes. In order to get information from all the respondents, interview schedules and questionnaires were prepared and administered to them individually. Sincere attempts have been made to meet Dalit leaders, officers and MLA's & MP's to obtain relevant information on the socio, economic and political conditions of the Scheduled Castes and Scheduled Tribes. In addition to this, important Government departments like Mysore district Social Welfare Department, Scheduled Caste/Scheduled Tribe Development Corporation, Mysore Zilla Parishat, Department of Agriculture, Horticulture, Animal Husbandry, Sericulture have been consulted to obtain first hand information on various programmes launched by them for the economic development of the Scheduled Castes and Scheduled Tribes.

Following are the different developmental programmes launched by the above departments for the upliftment of Scheduled Castes and Scheduled Tribes.

DISTRICT SOCIAL WELFARE DEPARTMENT

The department has been launching various developmental programmes for the benefit of Scheduled Castes and Scheduled Tribes. For example;

(a) Academic Development Programme.

(b) Economic Development Programme.

(c) Social Development Programme.

(d) Special component planning programme.

(a) Academic Development Programme

For the purpose of inspiring the Scheduled Caste and Scheduled Tribe students, the department has under taken the following programmes.

(i) Cash Prizes:

For the purpose of developing the competitive spirit as well as to inspire the Scheduled Caste and Scheduled Tribe students to obtain maximum marks in their examinations compared to the other students, the department has been providing the following cash prizes to them, who secure first class with distinction in first attempt, in the following examination.

Details of the examination & cash prizes

(a) S.S.L.C.	Rs. 500.00
(b) P.U.C.	Rs. 750.00
(c) Degree	Rs. 1000.00
(d) Post Graduate degree	Rs. 1250.00
(e) Medical & Engineering Degree	Rs. 1500.00

In addition to the above prizes, the department of District Social Welfare provides a cash prize of Rs. 5000.00 to those Scheduled Caste and Scheduled Tribe students who obtain rank in the above-mentioned examinations.

(ii) Pre-Metric Hostels:

Among the various developmental programmes, educational development programme plays an important role. For the educational development of rural Scheduled Caste and Scheduled Tribe students as well as those students who are not able to study in the urban areas outside their homes, the department has been providing hostel facilities. The following table shows the expenditure, which is being incurred for each pre-metric student who is staying in the hostel.

Details of the Facilities Given for One Year

Sl. No.	*Details*	*Duration*	*Amount*
1.	Food (Meals expenditure)	1 year	Rs. 350
2.	Clothes (two pairs school uniforms)	1 year	Rs. 300
3.	Books	1 year	Rs. 100
4.	Hair cutting	1 year	Rs. 30
5.	News paper (For every hostel)	1 year	Rs. 500
6.	Medical expenses (For every hostel)	1 year	Rs. 1000
7.	Electricity & water charges (For every hostel)	1 year	Rs. 1000
8.	Bed & Blanket (For every Student)	3 Years	Rs. 300
9.	Utensils	1 year	Rs. 600
10.	Sports & equipments (For every hostel)	1 year	Rs. 1000
11.	Miscellaneous	1 year	Rs. 25

Source: Handbook published by the Department of Social Welfare, Government of Karnataka.

In addition to the above facilities, the department has been providing scholarships to the Scheduled Caste and Scheduled Tribe rural students, who are below the poverty line, to continue their education. The department also provides financial assistance to those Scheduled Caste and Scheduled Tribe hostels run by private individuals. Besides, many residential schools have been established in rural areas to inspire the Scheduled Caste and Scheduled Tribe children to join the schools. These children are provided with food, uniforms, books, pencils, pens & other basic amenities free of cost by the Government. In Mysore district, there are 41 residential schools for Scheduled Castes and Scheduled Tribes in which more than 3050 children are studying. In addition to this, there are 23 college hostels run by both Government and private persons in which 2375 students belonging to Scheduled

Castes and Scheduled Tribes are utilising the benefits provided by the Government.

(iii) Study Tour Expenses

The department of Social Welfare provides financial assistance to the students belonging to Scheduled Castes and Scheduled Tribes who are required to go for academic excursion if it is made as a part of college curriculum. For this purpose, a sum of Rs. 500 is provided to each of the students, who are studying in various institutions.

(iv) Book Bank Facilities:

The department of Social Welfare has also established Book Banks in Medical, Technical, Veterinary, Agriculture and Polytechnic colleges to assist Scheduled Caste and Scheduled Tribe students who are unable to purchase the prescribed texts. For this purpose, the department every year collects the list of required books from the above colleges and purchases the books. Having purchased, the same would be sent directly to those colleges for the benefit of Scheduled Caste and Scheduled Tribe students. The following table shows the amount earmarked for the purchase of required books & furniture.

Details of the Facilities Provided

Sl. No.	*Colleges*	*Duration*	*Amount*
1.	Engineering colleges (For each college)	5 years	Rs. 5000
2.	Veterinary/Medical colleges (For each College)	5 years	Rs. 5000
3.	Agriculture college (For each college)	5 years	Rs. 4500
4.	Polytechnic colleges (For each college)	5 years	Rs. 2400
5.	Almyrahs to keep books (For each college)	5 years	Rs. 2000

(v) Government of India Post-Metric Scholarships:

With a view to assist Scheduled Caste and Scheduled Tribe students who are studying in various colleges, the Government of India provides post-metric scholarships at the following rates:

Besides this, for the purpose of encouraging the Scheduled Caste and Scheduled Tribe students studying in various courses, the State Government also provides scholarships as per the following rates:

1.	Medical/Technical/Agriculture/ Veterinary/Horticulture courses	per student (per month)	Rs. 75.00
2.	Post Graduate Courses	– do –	Rs. 50.00
3.	Other general degree courses	– do –	Rs. 40.00

Sl. No.	*Colleges*	*Scholarship for hostel students (per month)*	*Scholarship for non-hostlers (per month)*
1.	Group 'A' Medical/Technical/Agriculture/ Veterinary/Fisheries/Homeopathy	Rs. 425.00	Rs. 190.00
2.	Group 'B' Diploma Courses: Technical/Medical/ Fisheries/Agriculture/other Post Graduate Courses	Rs. 290.00	Rs. 190.00
3.	Group 'C' Certificate Courses: Technical/Medical/ Fisheries/Agriculture/other Post Graduate Courses	Rs. 290.00	Rs. 190.00
4.	Group 'D' General degree courses: B.A./ B.Sc./ B.B.M./B.Com./M.A./M.Sc./M.Com./ M.B.A./Law etc.	Rs. 230.00	Rs. 120.00
5.	Group 'E' P.U.C. and other general courses	Rs. 150.00	Rs. 90.00

For the purpose of encouraging and inspiring those Scheduled Caste and Scheduled Tribe students who are doing research work in various Universities, the department of Social Welfare provides 'Student fellowship' to the extent of Rs. 8000.00 for M.Phil. students and Rs. 10,000.00 for Ph.D. students. This assistance is provided to meet the expenditure relating to collection of data, purchase of important books and completion of research work.

In addition to this, the department also provides engineering equipments including Calculators, T-squares, drawing boards to the Scheduled Caste and Scheduled Tribe students who are studying in various engineering colleges and polytechnics free of cost.

(b) Economic Development Programmes

In order to encourage the members of Scheduled Castes and Scheduled Tribes and to develop them economically, the department had launched various programmes.

(i) Woman's Tailoring Training Centres:

The department of Social Welfare has established five tailoring training centres in Mysore district for providing training to the unemployed Scheduled Caste and Scheduled Tribe women. For this purpose, hundred women are selected and given required training in tailoring. Those who successfully complete the training and pass the required examination would be given a tailoring machine free of cost to enable them to start tailoring profession and thereby to earn their livelihood.

(ii) Training programme for Law Graduates:

To encourage and to assist the unemployed Scheduled Caste and Scheduled Tribe Law graduates, the department of Social Welfare provides advocacy training to them. For this purpose, every year five law graduates would be selected and sent for training in the courts identified by the candidates. The training programme given will be for a period of four years during which they are provided a sum of Rs. 1000.00 per month as a stipend. The department also provides a sum of Rs. 5000.00 to each selected candidate for the purchase of required books and journals, which are useful for legal profession. These enable the Scheduled Caste and Scheduled Tribe unemployed law graduates to start their independent profession and earn their livelihood.

(iii) Self-Employment Training Programme:

Under this programme, the department of Social Welfare provides training to the unemployed young Scheduled Caste and Scheduled Tribe candidates in various fields like, Autorickshaw driving, light and heavy vehicle driving. The training will be given for a period of one month, during which a sum of Rs. 200.00 will be given as a stipend to each selected candidate. Those who successfully complete their training will be provided with licenses. The main object of this programme is to help the unemployed young Scheduled Caste and Scheduled Tribe candidates to take up independent jobs for their livelihood.

(iv) 'Navachetana' Programme:

This programme has been launched by the department of Social Welfare to assist the unemployed Scheduled Caste and Scheduled Tribe youths to take up self-employment on their own. Under this scheme, unemployed Scheduled Caste and Scheduled Tribe youths are selected and deputed to various public enterprises to undergo training in different professions for a period of one year. During this period the trainees will be given stipends and accommodation. Besides, the department will bear the entire expenditure incurred on this training programme. Following are the important public enterprises identified by the department for providing training to the Scheduled Caste and Scheduled Tribe candidates.

(a) C-DAC Training Institute
(b) Saint Johns Medical College
(c) Karnataka State Tourism Development Corporation
(d) Karnataka Land Army Corporation
(e) Karnataka Soaps and Detergents Corporation
(f) Karnataka Power Corporation
(g) Karnataka Electricity Board

(v) Nursery and Women Welfare Centres:

The department of Social Welfare has setup 85 women welfare centres in Mysore district exclusively for the children of Scheduled Castes and Scheduled Tribes. The department provides many facilities for these centres to look after the children who join these centres. The main object of this programme is to make the Scheduled Caste and Scheduled Tribe rural children between the age group of 3–5 to cultivate the habit of going to schools for learning. For this purpose, the department appoints one lady convener and an administrator to each of these centres. The task of the convener is to provide mid-day meal, sports equipments and to teach elementary knowledge to the children. The department is spending the following amount to each child in the welfare centres.

Details of Facilities Provided

1.	Mid-day meal (for each child)	per day	Rs. 1.00
2.	Two pairs of uniforms (for each child)	per year	Rs. 51.00
3.	For maintenance of cleanliness in the centre (for one centre)	per year	Rs. 150.00

Source: Handbook published by the Mysore district Social Welfare department.

(vi) Type writing & shorthand Training Programme:

The department of Social Welfare provides training programme in typing and shorthand to the Scheduled Caste and Scheduled Tribe youths in order to assist them to take up independent jobs as well as seek jobs in various institutions. Selected candidates are required to undergo 10 months training in different commercial institutions. During this period, the department provides stipends to all the trainees at the following rates:

(a) Type writing Training	per month	Rs. 50.00
(b) Shorthand Training	per month	Rs. 75.00
(c) Stenography Training	per month	Rs. 200.00

(c) Social Development Programmes

To eradicate social evils from the society, like 'Untouchability', 'Caste System', the department of Social Welfare has launched the following programmes;

(i) Incentive amount for the spouses of Inter-caste marriage:

For the purpose of encouraging the inter-caste marriage and to eradicate the social evil like 'Untouchability' from the Hindu society, the department of Social Welfare provides incentive amount to the spouses of inter-caste marriages. A sum of Rs. 25,000 (Twenty five thousand only) will be given to the spouses for their social security. Out of this amount, Rs. 12,500 is given in the form of National Savings Certificate and the remaining amount of Rs. 12,500 is given in the form of cash. To avail this facility, either of the spouses of inter-caste marriage must belong to Scheduled Caste or Scheduled Tribe community. Besides, such inter-caste marriage shall be registered in the Sub-Registrar's office in accordance with the Government regulations.

(ii) Financial assistance to Scheduled Castes and Scheduled Tribes who are subjected to atrocities:

Keeping in view of various atrocities committed against the members of Scheduled Castes and Scheduled Tribes by the upper castes or the non-Scheduled Castes and Scheduled Tribes, the department of Social Welfare provides compensatory amount to the aggrieved families ranging from Rs. 10,000 to Rs. 1,00,000. Following are the atrocities recognised under the Scheduled Castes and Scheduled Tribes (Prevention of Atrocities) Act 1989 and the range of compensatory amount provided by the department:

(i) *Murder:* Any member of the Scheduled Castes or Scheduled Tribes who is murdered by a non-Scheduled Caste and Scheduled Tribe, the family members of the deceased person will be paid a sum of Rs. 1,00,000 as compensation amount.

(ii) *For temporary handicap:* If a member of Scheduled Caste or Scheduled Tribe is temporarily handicapped by the members of other castes, such person will be given a compensatory amount of Rs. 2,500. If he is permanently handicapped, then a sum of Rs. 15,000 will be given to such aggrieved person by the department of Social Welfare. In addition to this amount, he will also be given a monthly pension of Rs. 250.

(iii) *Destruction of Property:* If any member of Scheduled Castes and Scheduled Tribes whose property or house is destroyed by the members of other castes, the aggrieved member will be given compensatory amount ranging from Rs. 10,000 to Rs. 20,000 or he will be provided with a site or a house, or one acre of cultivating land to ameliorate his economic conditions.

(iv) *Rape:* If a woman, belonging to Scheduled Caste or Scheduled Tribe, is subjected to rape, she will be paid a sum of Rs. 10,000 as a compensatory amount.

(v) *Death due to atrocities:* Under special circumstances, the Government provides employment to any one of the family members of the deceased person, whose death occurred due to the atrocities, committed against him by the caste Hindus or upper castes. Besides, the Government also provides free education to the children of the deceased person.

(iii) Untouchability Removal Camps:

The main object of this programme is to remove social evil like 'Untouchability' from the Hindu Society and to promote the feeling of oneness. For this purpose, the Government selects one village in each Legislative Constituency and spends a sum of Rs. 10,000 for conducting various programmes like seminars, workshops and camps to the members of the Scheduled Castes and Scheduled Tribes. Through these programmes, awareness is created on various facilities and benefits conferred by the Government as well as on the Constitutional rights and privileges for securing justice and equality. Besides, through these programmes, the members of Scheduled Castes and Scheduled Tribes are informed to utilise the facilities provided to them by the department of Social Welfare.

(iv) Legal Aid Programme:

In order to assist the members of Scheduled Castes and Scheduled Tribes, who are unable to approach the Law Courts, as they cannot afford to pay Court fees and Lawyer's fees, the Government has established 'Legal Aid Cell' in each district to provide legal assistance in Civil, Criminal and Land acquisition cases. The entire Court fee and other expenditure will be borne by the Government. The primary object of this programme is to help the Scheduled Castes and Scheduled Tribes to face the litigations in the Law Courts for getting justice.

(d) Special Component Programme

This is one of the important programmes launched by the department of Social Welfare to uplift the Scheduled Caste and Scheduled Tribe families who are living below the poverty line in various rural areas. Under this programme, every year, Zilla Panchayat chooses 78 villages, in which, the eligible beneficiaries are selected by the village councils and provides them various facilities through different departments. Following are the departments through which different facilities are provided to the members of Scheduled Castes and Scheduled Tribes;

(i) Zilla Panchayat:

Under the special component programme, Zilla Panchayat has taken up several works for the upliftment of Scheduled Castes and

Scheduled Tribes. The department provides pumpsets, drinking water facilities and borewells to the members of Scheduled Castes and Scheduled Tribes who are living in rural areas. In many villages, there is no drinking water facility. For the purpose of providing enough drinking water, many wells have been dug and tube wells have been provided. The main object of this programme is to provide drinking water facilities to the colonies of Scheduled Castes and Scheduled Tribes.

(ii) Department of Agriculture:

Under the special component programme, the department of Agriculture provides good quality of seeds & fertilizers to the Scheduled Caste and Scheduled Tribe farmers free of cost. It also provides financial assistance to purchase diesel pumpsets for lifting water from the tanks. For the purpose of storing water, financial assistance is also given to the Scheduled Caste and Scheduled Tribe farmers to construct concrete tanks. A sum of Rs. 12,900 (i.e., 60% of the total cost) is also provided to each beneficiary to dig open well in his land for the purpose of cultivation.

(iii) Department of Horticulture:

Under this special component programme, the department provides intensive training in Horticulture to the selected candidates who belong to Scheduled Castes and Scheduled Tribes. The duration of the training programme will be for a period of 10 months. During this period, the trainees will be paid a sum of Rs. 300 as monthly stipend along with required uniforms, plates, glasses and blankets. Besides, the department provides financial assistance to the Scheduled Castes and Scheduled Tribes to develop coconut trees and fruit gardens if they have half acre and one acre land respectively. The financial assistance provided to the Scheduled Caste and Scheduled Tribe rural youths varies in its range from Rs. 1000 to Rs. 2000 every year. National Bank for Agriculture and Rural Development (NABARD) has also come forward to provide 50% of financial assistance to the Scheduled Castes and Scheduled Tribes who raise loan for the development of Horticulture. At present NABARD is providing loan to the Horticulture department for the development of Coconut, Almond, Cardamom, Pepper, Beetle leaves, Grapes, Mango, Guava,

Pomegranate, Pineapple, Ginger, Rose etc. In addition to this, the department provides sprinkler sets on reduced rates to the members of Scheduled Castes and Scheduled Tribes who have vegetable and fruit gardens.[2]

(iv) Department of Women & Welfare:

Under the special component programme, the department of women & welfare provides nutritious food to the Scheduled Caste and Scheduled Tribe pregnant women as well as to the children, below the age of 3 years through 'Anganavadi Centres'. The main object of this programme is to provide nutritious food to the pregnant women to protect their health. This is because, many pregnant women, who belong to Scheduled Castes and Scheduled Tribes, do not take nutritious food during pregnancy period due to poverty and ignorance. Consequently, when a child is born, it suffers from many handicaps.

(v) Department of Animal Husbandry:

Under the special component programme, the department of Animal Husbandry has launched various programmes in accordance with the NABARD's regulations for the development of hybrid cows, buffaloes, sheep and pigs. Following are the important programmes undertaken by the department;

(i) *Supply of Hybrid cows:* Under this scheme, the department spends a sum of Rs. 21,460 for each beneficiary. Out of this amount, 60% of the amount is given in the form of financial assistance and the remaining 40% is given in the form of loan. This amount covers one pair of cow, construction of a cowshed, cattle feed and fodder for the cows. Every year, more than 500 beneficiaries are benefited from this scheme. The main object of this scheme is to assist the unemployed Scheduled Caste and Scheduled Tribe youths to take up self-employment and to earn their livelihood.

(ii) *Supply of good breed buffaloes:* Under this scheme, the Karnataka Milk Federation provides to each Scheduled Caste and Scheduled Tribe beneficiary a pair of buffalo and a shed. The department of Animal Husbandry also provides a sum of Rs. 18,000 to each beneficiary, which includes maintenance

expenditure, fodder for the buffaloes, construction of a shed and purchase of one pair of buffaloes. The department also conducts a training programme to the beneficiaries to know more about the rearing of buffaloes.

(iii) *Supply of Sheep:* Under this scheme, the department provides 20 female sheep and one male sheep to each Scheduled Caste and Scheduled Tribe beneficiary. A sum of Rs. 9,800 is given to each beneficiary, which includes insurance, maintenance, fodder, construction of a shed, purchase of sheep and rearing. This scheme enables the beneficiaries to improve their economic conditions.

(iv) *Development of Milking cows:* The Karnataka Milk Production Unit has established nearly 6,000 co-operative milk centres all over the State. The object of these units is to provide milking cows to rural people in general and Scheduled Castes and Scheduled Tribes in particular on loan basis. Each unit provides 60% financial assistance to the Scheduled Caste and Scheduled Tribe farmers to purchase one pair of milking cows. This amount covers construction of a shed, fodder for the cows, maintenance and insurance. Besides, the department of Animal Husbandry also provides financial assistance to Scheduled Caste and Scheduled Tribe farmers as well as the unemployed youth to purchase milking cows. This enables them to start their own profession and to earn money by selling milk. In due course, they can improve their economic conditions.

(vi) Department of Sericulture:

Under the special component programmes, the department of Sericulture provides financial assistance to the Scheduled Castes and Scheduled Tribes who take up sericulture. Nearly four thousand Scheduled Caste and Scheduled Tribe families are depending on this sericulture for their livelihood. For the purpose of assisting the members of Scheduled Castes and Scheduled Tribes and to develop the sericulture, the department has launched various programmes. Following are some of the programmes undertaken by the department;

(i) *Community Development centres:* The department has set up many centres in each Taluk to provide silkworm eggs to the

Scheduled Caste and Scheduled Tribe farmers free of cost. The centre also provides technical advice to the farmers to develop silkworms on a scientific basis. Each beneficiary would be given basic facility for the improvement of silkworm eggs.

(ii) *Financial Assistance:* The department provides financial assistance to the Scheduled Caste and Scheduled Tribe farmers for the construction of houses for silkworm rearing. As silkworms are very delicate and often react to the fluctuating atmosphere, they are to be kept in a proper atmosphere. Besides, financial assistance to the extent of 60% would be provided for growing mulberry leaves as well as to dig borewells in their land to use this water for sericulture. The department also provides basic facilities like baskets, fertilizers and required equipments free of cost. Both the State Government as well as Central Government provide financial assistance under 'Special Aid Scheme'. All these benefits are provided to the Scheduled Caste and Scheduled Tribe farmers to enable them to improve their economic conditions.

SCHEDULED CASTE AND SCHEDULED TRIBE DEVELOPMENT CORPORATION [SCSTDC]

Another important Government department, which is exclusively meant for the economic development of Scheduled Castes and Scheduled Tribes, is the 'SC/ST Development Corporation'. This corporation was established in 1975 with an object of providing financial assistance to the members of Scheduled Castes and Scheduled Tribes for their all round development. The corporation has launched a number of programmes for the economic development of Scheduled Castes and Scheduled Tribes. Among them, the important are;

1. Self-Employment planning.
2. Land ownership planning.
3. Training programmes.
4. Personal Irrigation Tube Well programme.
5. Rehabilitation programme for 'Devadasis'.
6. Rehabilitation programme for 'Paurakarmikaru'.
7. Enterpreneurship Development programme.
8. Free pumpset programme.

9. Ganga Welfare programme
10. Financial Assistance for Hawkers.

Self-Employment Planning

Under this programme, the corporation provides financial assistance to the unemployed Scheduled Caste and Scheduled Tribe youths to establish their own avocation. Financial assistance to the extent of Rs 35,000 would be provided to the selected candidates for weaving, to start automobile shops, petty shops, cycle shops, to purchase typewriters, Autorickshaws etc. The ceiling limit of Rs. 35,000 is not applicable to the purchase of Autorickshaws. Under this scheme, the corporation provides 50% amount and the remaining 50% amount will be provided to the beneficiaries by any Nationalized Banks or through any financial institutions.

Land Ownership Planning

This planning has been in vogue since 1990-91. The primary object of this scheme is to identify those Scheduled Caste and Scheduled Tribe farmers who have no land for cultivation. The corporation provides a sum of Rs. 30,000 as financial assistance to each beneficiary to purchase land for cultivation. Out of this amount, 50% will be given as loan amount and 50% will be in the form of financial assistance. When the land is purchased, it shall be registered in the name of the female member of the beneficiary and the same will be lent to the beneficiary on lease for a period of 10 years. With an annual interest of 5%, the beneficiary shall return the loan amount to the corporation within the stipulated period of 10 years. After the completion of the loan amount, the beneficiary will become the owner of the land. The main object of this scheme is to assist the Scheduled Caste and Scheduled Tribe farmers to improve their economic Status and to earn independently.

Training Programme

The corporation conducts training programme for the Scheduled Caste and Scheduled Tribe farmers in the field of cultivation. During this training, farmers would be informed about the manner of cultivation, method of ploughing the land, using the seeds, fertilizers and other pesticides. They are also informed about the scientific method of cultivation, which brings more yield and good quality of crops. Whatever the expenditure incurred on this training programme will be borne by the corporation itself. This type of training enables the farmers to cultivate their land scientifically get more production.

Personal Irrigation Tube well Programme

Under this programme, the corporation provides financial assistance of Rs. 30,000 to each Scheduled Caste and Scheduled Tribe beneficiary to dig tube well in their land. Out of this amount, the corporation will provide 50% and the remaining amount will be provided through banks, as loan amount. The primary object of this programme is to assist the Scheduled Caste and Scheduled Tribe farmers to have tube wells in their lands for cultivation where there is no irrigation facility. This enables the farmers to cultivate more and more without depending on rain.

Rehabilitation Programme for 'Devadasis'

The purpose of this programme is to assist the 'Devadasis' who belong to Scheduled Castes and Scheduled Tribes. The corporation provides various facilities to Devadasis like self-employment programme, training programmes in various fields. In order to utilise these benefits, the Devadasis should be identified and recognised by the women and child welfare department. Besides, when the Devadasis give up their profession, they are rehabilitated by the Government to lead a decent and dignified life in the society.

Rehabilitation Programme for 'Paurakarmikas'

Under this programme, the corporation identifies the members of Scheduled Caste and Scheduled Tribe who are working as 'Paurakarmikas' and provides alternative jobs. The Government considers the nature of work done by the Scheduled Caste and Scheduled Tribe 'Paurakarmikas' as inhuman, degrading and unhealthy. Therefore the Government has undertaken several rehabilitation programmes to rehabilitate them by providing alternative jobs for their livelihood. The corporation also provides training to these 'Paurakarmikas' in different fields to take up self-employment for their livelihood. For this purpose, the corporation provides 50% financial assistance or a maximum of Rs. 10,000. It also provides 15% margin money in the form of loan and the remaining amount will be given through Bank loan. From this programme, every year more than two thousand Scheduled Caste and Scheduled Tribe 'Paurakarmikas' receive benefits. This is an important programme as it provides alternative jobs to the Paurakarmikas to lead a dignified life along with the caste Hindus.

Entrepreneurship Development Programme

Under this programme, the corporation selects unemployed Scheduled Caste and Scheduled Tribe youths and provides training in different fields like handicrafts, weaving, motor vehicle driving [including both small and heavy motor vehicles] and Computer education. During the training period, stipend will be given to all the trainees and the entire expenditure of such training will be borne by the corporation. After successful training, financial assistance is given to them to start their own profession by purchasing the required materials. The corporation provides a sum of Rs. 50,000 as loan to each successful candidate in the training to undertake business activities in which he is trained. Out of this amount, 75% will be provided by the Bank and the remaining amount, i.e., the corporation provides 25%. More than 500 Scheduled Caste and Scheduled Tribe unemployed youths are receiving benefits from this programme every year.

Free Pumpset Programme

Under this programme, the corporation provides free pumpsets to Scheduled Caste and Scheduled Tribe small farmers who have already dug wells in their own lands. This facility is provided to lift water from the well and the same shall be utilised for their land. To avail this facility, the small and poor Scheduled Caste and Scheduled Tribe farmers are to be identified by the corporation. The object of this programme is to enable the small and poor farmers to cultivate their land and grow more and more, so that they can achieve economic stability.

Ganga Welfare Programme

Under this programme, the corporation provides irrigation facilities to the Scheduled Caste and Scheduled Tribe small farmers who have bloc land. The land identified by the corporation should be in one place. Under this scheme, the irrigation facility include tube well, pumpsets, electricity, pump house and pipe line. Besides, all these facilities are provided free of cost. For the first five years, the corporation will take the entire responsibility to monitor the programme. After the completion of five years, from the commencement of the programme, the responsibility to monitor this will be entrusted to co-operative society formed by the beneficiaries. Besides, the corporation provides intensive training to the beneficiaries for cultivating their land scientifically to grow more and more crops.

Financial Assistance for Hawkers

The corporation also provides financial assistance to Hawkers to carry on their business. With a view to assist those Scheduled Castes and Scheduled Tribes, who are interested to carry on small business in the streets, the corporation provides a sum of Rs. 10,000. It also provides loan through various Banks and financial institutions. This is to enable the poor hawkers to earn their livelihood.

MYSORE ZILLA PARISHATH

Another important Government department, which has launched number of programmes for the development of Scheduled Castes and Scheduled Tribes, is 'Mysore Zilla Parishath'. Following are the important programmes undertaken by the Zilla Parishath;

1. Housing Programme
2. Vocational Employment Programme
3. Training Programmes
4. Loan disbursement Programmes

Housing Programme

For the purpose of providing houses to the poor and houseless Scheduled Castes and Scheduled Tribes, the department constructs houses under various schemes like Ashraya Yojana, Ambedkar Yojana, Indira Awaj Yojana and Integrated Tribal Development Yojana. Under 'Ashraya Yojana' scheme, the department constructs houses in 20" x 30" dimension. Out of the total constructed houses, 31.5% houses will be provided to the poor Scheduled Castes and

Scheduled Tribe free of cost. Whereas, the houses constructed under 'Ambedkar Yojana' scheme, 100% houses would be provided only to the poor Scheduled Castes and Scheduled Tribes free of cost. Likewise, 66% of houses will be provided to the poor Scheduled Castes and Scheduled Tribes under Indira Awaj Yojana, whereas 100% houses would be provided to poor Scheduled Tribes free of cost under 'Integrated Tribal Development Yojana'. The total cost of each house constructed under these schemes would be Rs. 20,000. It is observed that from these schemes, many poor and homeless Scheduled Castes and Scheduled Tribes have been benefited to a greater extent.

Vocational Employment Programme

As the Indian farmers gamble with rain for cultivation, they are left without any employment for many months in a year. In order to make them engage in their work throughout the year, the Central Government has launched two important programmes namely, Jawahar Rozgar Yojana and Employment Assurance Yojana. Under these two programmes, the department provides vocational employment to all agricultural labourers including Scheduled Castes and Scheduled Tribes.

Jawahar Rozgar Yojana & Employment Assurance Yojana

Under these two schemes, the department of Zilla Parishath provides vocational employment to the agricultural labourers only for 100 days in a year. This is because of the fact that, agricultural labourers will not get work in their lands throughout the year. In a year, they will be engaged for nearly six to seven months in cultivation and the rest of the days, they will be left without any work. In order to engage themselves during this period, the department provides financial assistance to undertake the development of forests, improvement of agricultural lands and gardens. For this purpose, 60% of amount will be given to the beneficiaries to meet labour charges and remaining 40% of the amount is provided for the purchase of the materials. The main object of this programme is to make the agricultural labourers in general and Scheduled Castes and Scheduled Tribes in particular, to engage themselves in various developmental works and earn money whenever they have no work in their agricultural lands.

Training Programme

The department of Zilla Parishath also conducts various training programmes for the unemployed Scheduled Caste and Scheduled Tribe youths to train them in different professions. Following are the important training programmes provided to the unemployed Scheduled Caste and Scheduled Tribe beneficiaries;

(a) Computer Training Programme

(b) Diary Development Training

(c) Typewriting Training

(d) Coaching classes for Scheduled Caste and Scheduled Tribe students who appear for IAS, IPS, IFS, Bank examinations.

The main object of these training programmes is to assist the unemployed Scheduled Caste and Scheduled Tribe youths to acquire knowledge in various fields, so that they can start their own independent profession for earning their livelihood.

Loan Facilities

The department of Zilla Parishath also provides loan facility to those Scheduled Caste and Scheduled Tribe candidates who successfully complete their training programmes. Following are the items for which loan is sanctioned by the Zilla Parishath;

(a) Xerox machines

(b) To establish telephone booths

(c) Typewriters

(d) Computers

(e) Irrigation pumpsets

Every year, the department selects unemployed Scheduled Caste and Scheduled Tribe youths and provides them financial assistance to purchase the above items. Out of the total sanctioned amount, the Zilla Parishath provides 60% amount as subsidy amount and the remaining 40% amount will be provided by the Banks as loan amount. The beneficiaries are required to repay only the 40% Bank loan amount and not the subsidy amount. This type of loan facility will help the poor Scheduled Castes and Scheduled Tribes to improve their economic conditions and to earn their livelihood.

DETAILS OF THE CONDITIONS OF THE SC/ST RESPONDENTS

The following tables reveal the various responses given by the Scheduled Caste and Scheduled Tribe respondents, who belong to three taluks of Mysore district, i.e., T.N. Pura, Hunsur and Mysore, in respect of their socio-economic and political conditions. The total number of Scheduled Caste and Scheduled Tribe respondents selected from the above three taluks for empirical study are six hundred.

Table 1
Caste of the Respondents

Sl.No.	Caste	Number	Percentage
1.	Scheduled Caste	462	77%
2.	Scheduled Tribe	138	23%
	Total	600	100%

As seen from the above table, it is evident that, out of the 600 respondents, 462 respondents belong to Scheduled Caste i.e., 77% and 138 respondents belong to Scheduled Tribe, i.e., 23%. These facts show that majority of the respondents are from Scheduled Caste community.

Table 2
Age of the Respondents

Sl.No.	Age Group	Number	Percentage
1.	30 – 40 years	60	10.00%
2.	41 – 50 years	250	41.66%
3.	51 – 60 years	240	40.00%
4.	60 years & above	50	08.33%
	Total	600	100%

As seen from table 2, 40% of the respondents, i.e., 240 respondents, belong to the age group of 51–60 years, respondents of the age group between 4–50 constitute 41.66%, i.e., 250 respondents. We find only 10%, i.e., 60 respondents, are in the age group of 30–40 years, while 8.33% belong to the age group of 60 years and above, i.e., 50 respondents.

Table 3
Occupations of the Respondents

Sl.No.	*Occupation*	*Number*	*Percentage*
1.	Agricultural labourers *	206	34.33%
2.	Cultivators [Own Land] **	116	19.33%
3.	Small business men	55	09.16%
4.	Services	83	13.83%
5.	Agricultural labourers & Cultivators	140	23.33%
	Total	600	100%

* Agricultural labourers are those working for wages in other's land.
** Cultivators are those working in their own land.

The table 3 shows the different occupational groups of Scheduled Caste and Scheduled Tribe respondents. Agricultural labourers constitute 34.33%, i.e., 206 respondents. Only 9.16% i.e., 55 respondents, belong to small business group. Cultivators constitute 19.33%, i.e., 116 respondents, while the agricultural labourers and cultivators together constitute 23.33%, i.e., 140 respondents. Lastly, the salaried class i.e., service [including Government & Private employees] constitute 13.83% i.e., 83 respondents. From these facts, it is evident that 206 respondents are completely depending upon agriculture for their livelihood, as they have no other jobs, whereas 116 respondents cultivate lands belonging to them and earn money for their livelihood. Only 83 respondents are in service who get salary. These respondents are working either in Government departments or in Private establishments. But 140 respondents have engaged in cultivating both their own lands and the others. As they have hardly half or one acre of land for cultivation, which is not adequate for their livelihood, they go and work in other's land. Only 55 respondents are engaged in small business like running teashops, sale of clothes, petty shops etc., as they have no adequate money to start big business. To meet their family expenditure, majority of the respondents depend on agriculture. Besides, as majority of them are illiterates, they cannot get jobs either in Government departments or in Private institutions.

From the above table, it is clear that, 12.5% respondents earn less than Rs. 5,000 per annum, whereas 25.5% respondents are placed in the income between Rs. 5,001 & Rs. 10,000. Majority of

Table 4
Income Positions of the Respondents

Sl.No.	*Income level [Annual]*	*Number*	*Percentage*
1.	Less than Rs. 5000	75	12.50%
2.	Rs. 5001 to Rs. 10,000	153	25.50%
3.	Rs. 10,001 to Rs. 15,000	189	31.50%
4.	Rs. 15,001 to Rs. 20,000	108	18.00%
5.	Rs. 20,001 to Rs. 30,000	48	08.00%
6.	Rs. 30,000 and above	27	04.50%
	Total	600	100%

the respondents i.e., 31.5%, belong to the income between Rs. 10,001 and Rs. 15,000. As many as 108 respondents i.e., 18%, belong to the income category of Rs. 15,001 & Rs. 20,000. Only 8% of respondents, i.e., 48 respondents, are in the income group between Rs. 20,001 and Rs. 30,000, whereas negligible percent of 4.5 respondents earn more than Rs. 30,000 in a year. From these facts, it is evident that only 27 respondents out of the 600 are able to earn more than Rs. 30,000 in a year. Their economic conditions are better than the rest of the category. Besides, the majority of the respondents earn between Rs. 5,000 to Rs. 15,000 in a year, which is inadequate for their family maintenance. Therefore, they are considered as poor and economically backward to meet their basic needs like food, clothing and shelter.

Table 5
Educational level of the Respondents

Sl.No.	*Educational Level*	*Number*	*Percentage*
1.	Illiterate	328	54.66%
2.	Primary [I - IV Std.]	82	13.66%
3.	Middle School [V – VII Std.]	51	08.50%
4.	Metric [VIII – X Std.]	67	11.16%
5.	Degree & above	72	12.00%
	Total	600	100%

As seen from table 5, it is evident that, majority of the respondents, i.e., 54.66%, are illiterates. Out of the 600 respondents, only 82 of them, i.e., 13.66%, have passed primary school education, whereas 51 respondents, i.e., 8.5%, have passed middle school education, 67 respondents, i.e., 11.16%, have passed metric examination. Only 12% of the respondents have passed degree and above education. These facts show that, the educational level of Scheduled Castes and Scheduled Tribes is very low as they are suffering from various disabilities like poverty, discrimination, inequality and inhuman treatment in their villages. Besides, lack of educational background and lack of inspiration from their parents are also responsible for the low level of education of the respondents.

Table 6
Assets owned by the Respondents

Sl.No.	*Land [both wet & dry]*	*Number*	*Percentage*
1.	Landless	206	34.33%
2.	Less than 2 Acres	232	38.66%
3.	Between 2 Acres to 5 Acres	126	21.00%
4.	Above 5 Acres	36	06.00%
	Total	600	100%

The above table shows the land holding status of the respondents. As seen above, it is clear that, only 36 respondents, i.e., 6%, possess above 5 acres of land [both wet & dry], 21%, i.e., 126 respondents have possessed land between 2 acres to 5 acres and 38.66%, i.e., 232 respondents have got land less than 2 acres. Besides, 206 out of 600 respondents have no land to cultivate. These facts show that the Scheduled Castes and Scheduled Tribes are not economically sound and stable as only 6% of them have land above 5 acres. Majority of them are landless labourers who work in the agricultural lands belonging to others. It is observed that, those who have land less than 2 acres are also suffering from economic constraints, as their income is inadequate to maintain their families.

Table 7
Assets [moveable] of the Respondents

Sl.No.	*Number possessed*	*Number*	*Percentage*
1.	**Cows:** One pair	176	29.33%
2.	Two pairs	112	18.66%
3.	More than two pairs	52	08.66%
4.	No cows	260	43.33%
	Total	600	100%

The rearing of domestic animals like sheep, goats, bullocks, cows contribute to the income of the respondents. As seen from the table 7, majority of the respondents, i.e., 43.33%, have no cows for their use, only 176 respondents, i.e., 29.33%, have one pair of cows and only 8.66%, i.e., 52 respondents, have got more than two pairs of cows. As the Scheduled Caste and Scheduled Tribe respondents are predominantly agricultural labourers having little land, they naturally depend on the rearing of cattles not only for agricultural purposes but also for milk production. Even though the Government provides financial assistance to purchase cows, they have no place to rear them. Therefore, majority of the respondents, i.e., 260 out of 600 respondents, have no cows at their disposal. It is observed that, due to the lack of enough place to rear cows, many respondents do not possess them. Consequently, their economic status is affected. Besides, those who have two pairs or more are earning a sum of Rs. 3,000 to 4,000 per month, which is sufficient to maintain their families in their villages.

Table 8
Assets [moveable] of the Respondents

Sl. No.	*Number possessed*	*Number*	*Percentage*
1.	**Sheep**: One pair	34	05.60%
2.	More than 4 less than 10	192	32.00%
3.	More than 10 sheep	237	39.50%
4.	No sheep	137	22.83%
	Total	600	100%

The above table indicates that, as many as 237 respondents out of 600, i.e., 39.50%, have more than 10 sheep and 34 respondents have only two sheep. Besides, 137 respondents, i.e., 22.83%, have no sheep at their disposal but 32% of respondents have more than 4 and less than 10 sheep. These informations show that more respondents have possessed more than 10 sheep. Rearing of sheep is much easier than cattle rearing. It is also observed that, many respondents derive more income through the sale of sheep as each sheep costs more than Rs. 500. Those who do not possess sheep are of the opinion that, as they have no place in their home to rear them, they do not like to rear sheep.

Table 9
Assets [moveable] of the Respondents

Sl. No.	*Number possessed*	*Number*	*Percentage*
1.	Bullocks: One pair	186	31.00%
2.	Two pairs	87	14.50%
3.	More than two pairs	32	05.33%
4.	No Bullocks	295	49.16%
	Total	600	100%

As seen from the table, it is evident that, majority of the respondents, 295 out of 600, i.e., 49.16%, have no bullocks, as they are unable to buy them. 87 out of 600 respondents, i.e., 14.5%, have possessed two pairs of bullocks and only 5.33% of respondents have more than two pairs of bullocks. Whereas, 186 out of 600 respondents, i.e., 31%, have possessed one pair of bullocks. These facts show that, only less number of respondents, i.e., 5.33%, are able to possess more than 2 pairs of bullocks for cultivating their land, as they are, to some extent, economically sound enough to purchase bullocks. Those who do not have bullocks are required to hire them for cultivation. The reasons given by the majority are; firstly, they are economically poor to purchase bullocks as each pair costs more than Rs. 8,000. Secondly, even if they purchase, they have no place to keep them in their houses.

Table 10
Crops Grown by the Respondents

Do you grow?	*Positive response*	*Number*	*Percentage*
Paddy	182	600	30.33%
Ragi & Jowar	110	600	18.33%
Sunflower	42	600	07.00%
Groundnut	60	600	10.00%

The above table indicates the various crops grown by the respondents in their lands. As seen from the table, majority of the respondents, i.e., 182 out of 600 respondents [30.33%] grow paddy in their land as they have irrigation facilities. It is observed that, these respondents have wet land ranging from one acre to four acres in which they grow paddy two times in a year. In one acre of wet land, approximately, they grow paddy ranging from 18 to 20 bags.[3] In a year, each of these respondents grow paddy to the extent of 60 to 65 bags.

As many as 110 respondents, i.e., 18.33%, grow both Ragi and Jowar in their dry land. Each of these respondents possesses dry land ranging from one acre to three acres. In one acre of dry land, they grow 15 to 18 bags of Ragi and Jowar (alternatively). Most of these respondents belonging to Mysore and Hunsur taluks, where there is no irrigation facility, are required to depend on the rain for cultivation in their land. In a year, each respondent grows paddy and Ragi (alternatively) to the extent of 30 to 35 bags.

Out of 600 respondents, only 42, i.e., 7%, grow sunflower in their land. In each acre of land, they grow sunflower ranging from 10 to 12 bags. It is observed that, some of these respondents have pumpsets in their land and some of them have to depend on rain. Each respondent, approximately, grows sunflower to the extent of 30 to 35 bags in a year.

Only 60 respondents out of 600, i.e., 10%, grow groundnuts in their land. It is observed that all these respondents are depending on rain to grow groundnut. In each acre of land, they grow groundnut ranging from 15 to 20 bags.

Table 11

Sl. No.	*Do you remain?*	*Positive response*	*Number*	*Percentage*
1.	Below poverty line	412	600	68.60%
2.	Semi-starved	121	600	20.16%
3.	Adequately fed	67	600	11.16%

ECONOMIC DISABILITIES

The above table shows the living standard of the Scheduled Castes and Scheduled Tribes. Majority of the respondents are living below the poverty line. 412 out of 600, i.e., 68.6% respondents, are living below the poverty line. They are not getting one square meal a day, which shows their utter poverty and penury. It is observed that, these respondents are living in huts or in tiled houses, 20.16% respondents, i.e., 121 out of 600 are living in a semi-starved condition, where they get one meal a day. But only 67 out of 600, i.e., 11.16% respondents, are getting adequate food. These facts show that majority of the Scheduled Castes and Scheduled Tribes' economic status is very poor, as they have no adequate assets. Naturally their health also deteriorates, as they cannot take nutritious food as well as required medicines.

Table 12

Sl.No.	*Means of subsistence of the Respondents*	*Positive response*	*Number*	*Percentage*
1.	Working as landless labourers	206	600	34.33%
2.	Cultivating own land	256	600	42.66%
3.	Small business (Petty shops, Tea shops, sale of cloths, etc.)	55	600	09.16%
4.	Service	83	600	13.83%

As seen from the above table, it is clear that, 206 out of 600, i.e., 34.33% respondents, are required to work as agricultural labourers in other's land for their subsistence, whereas 42.66% respondents, i.e., 256 out of 600, work in their own land for their subsistence. Whatever little acres of land they have, they cultivate for their livelihood. As many as 83 out of 600 respondents, i.e., 13.83%, are in service (either in Government institutions or in private) and getting salary. They have no land for cultivation but they are completely depending on their jobs for subsistence. 55 out of 600 respondents, i.e., 9.16%, are depending on their small business for subsistence. Out of the amount they earn from their business (which includes petty shops, teashops, sale of clothes etc.) they lead their life. As they have no land of their own, their subsistence depends on their earning from the business.

Table 13
Loan Position of the Respondents

Sl.No.	*Do you raise loan ?*	*Positive response*	*Number*	*Percentage*
1.	Agriculturist	462	600	77.00%
2.	Employees [Government/Private]	83	600	13.83%
3.	Businessmen	55	600	09.16%

The above table shows the loan position of the respondents. One common factor, which is found in the above table, is that, all category of respondents raise loan from different sources. Majority of the respondents are agriculturists, 462 out 600 respondents, i.e., 77%, who raise loan for their agricultural work. As they have no other source, they have to depend on loan for this purpose. 13.83% respondents who are in different services are also interested to raise loans, as their income from salary is very less to maintain their families. It is observed that in each family, there are more than 5 members in which only one person works. As they are required to depend solely on the salary, often they raise loan in Banks and other financial institutions. Besides, 55 out of 600 respondents, i.e., 9.16%, are small businessmen who do not have land to earn money. They have to depend on their own business for their livelihood. As business requires capital, they are required to raise loan to carry on their business as well as look after their family. Therefore, it is clear that, all the respondents raise loan either for cultivation of land or for the business or for the maintenance of their families.

Table 14

Sl. No.	*From whom do you raise loan ?*	*Positive response*	*Number*	*Percentage*
1.	Village money lenders	384	600	64.00%
2.	Nationalized Banks	72	600	12.00%
3.	Agricultural Banks	105	600	17.50%
4.	Co-operative Societies	39	600	06.50%

From the above table, it is evident that, different respondents raise loan from different institutions. Majority of the respondents, i.e., 384 out of 600 (64%) seek loan from village moneylenders. These respondents are of the opinion that getting loan from village moneylenders is easier than seeking loan from financial institutions. Because, no formalities are essential to seek loan from them unlike the Banks and other financial institutions. As many as 105 respondents, i.e., 17.5%, raise loan from agricultural Banks, whereas, 72 respondents, i.e., 12%, seek loan from Nationalised Banks. Only 39 respondents, i.e., 6.5%, seek loan from Co-operative Societies. From these facts, it is clear that, raising loan from village moneylenders is more convenient and easy. Besides, simple terms of borrowing, easy accessibility, immediate payment and accommodative nature of the village moneylenders at the time of repayment have influenced the Scheduled Caste and Scheduled Tribe respondents to raise loan from them. But what hurts them is the high rate of interest charged by the moneylenders. The respondents who seek loan from various financial institutions are often subject to many hardships by the Bank authorities. Because, normally financial institutions compel the loan seekers to pledge assets (either moveable or immovable) as security for lending loan. But it is unfortunate that, Scheduled Castes and Scheduled Tribes have little assets to pledge. By and large, various financial institutions have no meaning for the Scheduled Caste and Scheduled Tribe respondents as the very nature of their transactions deter them from approaching banks.[4] Therefore, majority of the respondents seek loan from the village moneylenders on faith and confidence as they have possessed little property for their livelihood.

Table 15

Sl. No.	*Rate of interest paid by the respondents/month*	*Response*	*Number*	*Percentage*
1.	1% to 2%	45	600	07.50%
2.	3% to 4%	184	600	30.66%
3.	5% to 10%	371	600	61.83%
4.	Above 10%	–	600	–

The above table indicates different rates of interests paid by different respondents for their loan. 371 out of 600 respondents, i.e. 61.83%, pay interest towards their loan from 5% to 10%. Most of the respondents belonging to this category pay more interest to the village moneylenders as they get loan easily from them. As many as 184 respondents, i.e., 30.66%, pay interest towards their loan amount ranging from 3% to 4%, whereas, only 7.5% respondents, i.e., 45 out of 600, pay interest to their loan amount from 1% to 2%. Majority of these respondents are those who seek loan from various financial institutions like Co-operative Societies, Nationalised Banks and Agricultural Banks, because the rate of interest charged by the financial institution is less than the interest charged by the village moneylenders. From the above table it is clear that, none of the respondents is paying interest above 10%. This is because of the respondents' utter poverty and their inability to pay over and above 10% interest to the loan amount.

As seen from the table, 270 out of 600 respondents, i.e., 45%, are of the opinion that, they raise loan for the purpose of cultivation of paddy, ragi, jowar and sunflower. 127 out of 600, i.e., 21.16%

Table 16

Sl.No.	*Purpose for which loan is raised*	*Response*	*Number*	*Percentage*
1.	Consumption	82	600	13.66%
2.	Agricultural development	270	600	45.00%
3.	Festivals	112	600	18.66%
4.	Marriages/Death ceremonies	127	600	21.16%
5.	Personal use	09	600	01.50%

respondents, are of the opinion that, they seek loan for conducting marriages & other ceremonies in the village, whereas 18.66% respondents, i.e., 112 out of 600, seek loan for celebrating village festivals. But 82 respondents out of 600 say that they raise loan for consumption purpose. Only 1.5% respondents, i.e., 9 out of 600, borrow loan for their personal enjoyment. During the course of interview with the respondents, it is observed that, only 45% of respondents actually utilise their loan amount for cultivation purpose. But the rest, use the loan amount for other purposes including celebration of village festivals, conducting their son's or daughter's marriage, or for personal enjoyment. Many a time, the loan raised for agricultural development from various financial institutions is used for their social purposes. This is one of the reasons why majority of the Scheduled Castes and Scheduled Tribes are still economically very poor.

SOCIAL DISABILITIES

The Scheduled Castes and Scheduled Tribes are still encountering many social disabilities in their villages. This has been observed during the survey made in the three taluks i.e., T.N. Pura, Hunsur, Mysore.

Table 17

Sl.No.	*Are you discriminated in respect of?*	*Positive Response*	*Number*	*Percentage*
1.	Wage rate	118	600	19.66%
2.	Interest rate	97	600	16.16%
3.	Providing loan	107	600	17.83%
4.	Providing employment in agricultural land	278	600	46.33%

The above table indicates the discriminatory treatment of the caste Hindus over Scheduled Castes and Scheduled Tribes in respect of wage rate, interest rate, while providing loan and employment. 118 out of 600 respondents are of the opinion that, while fixing wage rate, they are often discriminated by the landlords of the upper castes. 16.16% respondents are discriminated by the village moneylenders while fixing interest rate for their loan, whereas as many as 278 out of 600 respondents, i.e., 46.33%, say that, the landlords while providing employment in their lands, they are discriminated. It is observed during the survey that, the majority of the upper caste landlords give first preference to their own community people while providing employment in their lands. The same discriminatory treatment is found when the moneylenders provide loan to the Scheduled Castes and Scheduled Tribes. 17.83%, i.e., 107 respondents, express their view that, the moneylenders provide more loan to their people than the Scheduled Castes and Scheduled Tribes. From these facts, it is evident that both the landlords and moneylenders follow discriminatory treatment towards the Scheduled Castes and Scheduled Tribes in the villages.

Table 18

Sl.No.	*From where do you bring drinking water ?*	*Response*	*Number*	*Percentage*
1.	Village public Tank	110	600	18.33%
2.	Village Public Wells	82	600	13.66%
3.	Tube well of your own street	278	600	46.33%
4.	River	130	600	21.66%

As seen from the above table, it is evident that, majority of the Scheduled Castes and Scheduled Tribes, i.e., 46.33%, bring drinking water from the village tube well of their street because, it is very near to them to fetch water. As many as 130 out of 600 respondents, i.e., 21.66%, bring their drinking water from near by river, as they are prevented from taking water from village tube well. As many as 110 out of 600 respondents, i.e., 18.33%, take water from village public tank. But, only 82 out of 600 respondents, i.e., 13.66%, are allowed to take water from village public well. It is observed that, there would be frequent conflict between the Scheduled Castes,

Scheduled Tribes and caste Hindus over the drinking water issue. Recently, in Byrapura, one of the villages in Hunsur taluk, it so happened that the tube well in Harijan keri stopped functioning. Consequently, the Harijans have little choice but to beg for drinking water from the upper castes. But these Harijans were not allowed to take water from the bore well belonging to the upper castes' street.[5] Conflict started between these two groups, which was ultimately resolved through the intervention of the police. These facts clearly show that, even today, in many villages, Harijans are being discriminated and prevented from taking water from tube wells and village public wells.

The above table shows the extent of equal status enjoyed by the Scheduled Castes and Scheduled Tribes in their villages in respect of various matters vis-à-vis caste Hindus. 118 out of 600 respondents, i.e., 19.66%, enjoy equal status with the caste Hindus in worshipping gods in various villages. But the rest of them are prevented from entering into the village temples for worshipping god. It is observed that, those Scheduled Castes and Scheduled Tribes who are clean and cultured are allowed to worship the gods in village temples. The caste Hindus think that, if the Harijans are allowed, the temples would be polluted, as, majority of the temples in various villages are maintained by the caste Hindus.

Table 19

Sl. No.	*Do you enjoy equal status in?*	*Positive Response*	*Number*	*Percentage*
1.	Worship in village temples	118	600	19.66%
2.	Taking Tea/Coffee/Snacks from the village Tea shops	212	600	35.33%
3.	Serving food in the common plates and glasses	202	600	33.66%
4.	Village meeting and its decision making process	163	600	27.16%
5.	Village community feasts	217	600	36.16%
6.	Marriage with non-Harijans or caste Hindus	–	600	–
7.	Schools	151	600	25.16%
8.	Barber Service	132	600	22.00%
9.	Priest Service (in marriage/death/festive occasions)	58	600	09.66%
10.	Getting groceries from grocery shops	371	600	61.83%

As the concept of pollution centres around water and food, as many as 65% respondents are not allowed to take tea or coffee from the village teashops maintained by the caste Hindus. That means, only 212 out of 600 respondents i.e., 35%, are enjoying equal status with the caste Hindus in taking tea, coffee or snacks from the shops maintained by the upper castes. In many village hotels, separate glasses and plates are kept exclusively for Harijans to use when they visit hotels for taking food. As seen from the above table, only 202 out of 600 respondents, i.e., 33%, are allowed to use common plates and glasses to take food in the village hotels. But the rest of them, i.e., 67%, are prevented from using common plates. These respondents are required to bring their own plates and glasses to take food, coffee or tea from the hotels. It is also observed that, these respondents are served with coffee, tea or food outside the hotels, because, many shop keepers and hoteliers still believe in the practice of 'Untouchability'.[6]

On many occasions, village affairs are managed by the caste Hindus through informal Panchayat, where Harijans are not represented. Several times they are not invited also to take part in the decision making process. Whenever they are invited, they are required to sit outside the meeting place, or sit at a distance but not allowed to take part in the decision making process of the informal Panchayat. This is evident from the fact that, only 163 out of 600 respondents, i.e., 27.16%, enjoy equal status in the village meeting and decision making process with the caste Hindus.

It has been observed in many villages that, whenever village feasts are arranged, majority of the Scheduled Castes and Scheduled Tribes are served food at a distance from the temple premises. This is evident from the above table, where only 217 out of 600 respondents, i.e., 36.16%, are allowed to enjoy equal status in village feasts along with the upper castes, whereas, the rest of the respondents, i.e., 64%, are not allowed to enjoy equal status in village feasts like 'Mari festival', marriages etc.

So far as inter-caste marriages are concerned, none of the respondents enjoys equal status with the caste Hindus. It is observed that, when a Harijan boy loves a girl who belongs to upper caste, he will be banished from that village or he will be beaten. In one or two cases, as informed by few of the respondents, both Harijan boy and upper caste girl have eloped and married, but never returned to their village with an apprehension that either they would be socially boycotted or they would be beaten by the caste Hindus.

In respect of barber services, only 132 out of 600 respondents, i.e., 22%, enjoy equal status in the villages. But the remaining respondents are discriminated while they approach a barber for hair cutting and shaving. It is observed that, in several villages, Harijans are kept outside the barbershops and their hair is cut. Therefore, it is clear that, the members of Scheduled Castes and Scheduled Tribes are discriminated in barber's services also. Sometimes the Harijans try to find out barbers from their own caste.

Another important area in which discrimination is found in the villages is in priestly services. Only 58 respondents out of 600, i.e., 9.66%, are allowed to utilise priestly services for marriages and other ceremonies. The remaining 90% of the respondents, i.e., 542, do not enjoy equal status in priestly services with the upper castes. As priestly services are normally provided by the caste Hindus, majority of the Harijans are deprived of this service. Therefore, whenever the Harijans celebrate marriage ceremony or any other ceremony, they have to find out a priest from their own community.

So far as grocery shops are concerned, more than 61% respondents enjoy equal status with the upper castes while purchasing grocery from village shops. The remaining 39%, i.e., 229 respondents, are discriminated by the village shopkeepers while selling many household things. It is informed that, whenever both a Harijan and an upper caste visit a shop, the Harijan must make way for the upper caste to purchase first. In many villages, the shopkeepers themselves insist the Harijans to allow first the upper castes to buy articles, and then only, they are allowed to purchase the groceries. These facts clearly show that, even in grocery shops, in villages, Scheduled Castes and Scheduled Tribes are discriminated. It has also been informed that, as majority of Harijans are depending on the caste Hindus for loan and employment, individually they cannot protest against them when they are discriminated. Besides, their social and economic disabilities like, low status, poverty and illiteracy prevent them from protesting against the upper castes.

As many as 151 out of 600 respondents, i.e., 25.16%, are of the opinion that their children in schools enjoy equal status with the other children who belong to upper castes. But majority of the respondents express their view that, frequently their children are subject to discrimination, humiliation and ill-treatment either by the school teachers or by the other children. It is observed that, even today in many schools in villages, Harijan's children are not allowed to drink water from the tumbler kept for upper caste's children. If the Harijan boy or girl drinks water from the tumbler, he/she would be severely punished. The children of the Scheduled Caste and Scheduled Tribe are asked to sit in the backbenches who are often neglected by the teachers. Several times they are treated harshly and looked down upon.[7] Patwardhan, an eminent sociologist, observes that, social environment, poverty and stigma in schools are the major obstacles for the Untouchable's education.[8]

POLITICAL PARTICIPATION AND AWARENESS OF GOVERNMENTAL POLICIES

In a democratic politics, the creative role of the people is important to bring about social changes in the society. Therefore, politics acts as a powerful means to eradicate social and economic deprivation. Through exercising franchise, individuals could bring such Government, which would protect their interests and bring about social reformation.

Table 20

Sl. No.	*Do you vote in the following general elections?*	*Positive Response*	*Number*	*Percentage*
1.	Parliament	418	600	69.66%
2.	Vidhana Sabha	418	600	69.66%
3.	Zilla Parishath	512	600	85.33%
4.	Taluk Panchayat	600	600	100%
5.	Village Council	600	600	100%

As seen from the table 20, it is evident that, 69.66% respondents exercise their vote both in Parliament and Vidhana Sabha elections. The rest of the respondents i.e., 31%, do not vote, as they are not interested in it. It is observed that, they do not trust their representatives as they never visit villages and hear their grievances. They express that, once they are elected they would always stay either in Bangalore or in New Delhi, without bothering about their problems. It is also informed that, political parties become very active on the eve of the elections. Besides, each general election brings politicians to many villages with assurances and promises. Once they get elected, they visit villages only after five years. As many as 512 out of 600 respondents, i.e., 85.33%, vote for Zilla Parishath elections. These respondents feel that, the elected members of Zilla Parishath are easily accessible for them to solve their problems, whereas, 100% respondents vote both in Taluk Panchayat and Village Council elections, as the elected persons to these bodies are available either in their Taluk or in their villages. This enables the respondents to approach them whenever they get problems. Moreover, these respondents consider their problems and find out solutions for them.

Table 21

Sl. No.		*Response*	*Number*	*Percentage*
1.	Are you a member of any political party ?	123	600	20.50%
2.	Do your representatives visit your village and solve your problems ?	86	600	14.33%

The above table reveals the attitude of the elected representatives towards their voters and the respondents' involvement in political parties. 123 out of 600 respondents, i.e., 20.50%, belong to different political parties. Among these respondents, most of them have knowledge of politics. But majority of the respondents, i.e. 80%, are not members of any political

Table 22

Sl. No.	*Have you contested in the following elections ?*	*Positive Response*	*Number*	*Percentage*
1.	Parliament	12	600	02.00%
2.	Vidhana Sabha	36	600	06.00%
3.	Zilla Parishath	62	600	10.33%
4.	Taluk Panchayat	68	600	11.33%
5.	Village Council	82	600	13.66%

parties. According to these respondents, poverty, ignorance, nonsupport and their caste have prevented them from becoming a member of a political party. Besides, political parties are only for rich people and not for them.

As seen from the table, only 12 out of 600 respondents, i.e., 2%, have contested for Parliament elections, whereas 6% of the respondents have contested for Vidhana Sabha elections. As many as 62 out of 600 respondents, i.e., 10.33%, have contested for Zilla Parishath election and 11.33% respondents have contested for Taluk Panchayat elections. 82 out of 600 respondents, i.e., 13.66%, are of the opinion that they have contested in the village Council elections. From the above facts it is clear that, the percentage of respondents who have contested for Parliament and Vidhana Sabha elections is less than the percentage of respondents who have contested for Zilla Parishath, Taluk Panchayat and Village Council elections. The reasons given by these respondents are;

1. They have no economic resource at their disposal.
2. They do not get support from the other who belong to upper castes.
3. They are educationally and socially backward to contest in general elections, which require not only money power but also muscle power.

But from the above table it is observed that, the members of Scheduled Castes and Scheduled Tribes prefer to contest in village Council, Taluk Panchayat and Zilla Parishath elections than the Parliamentary and Assembly elections, which require huge money. Besides, some respondents are of the opinion that even though they have got awareness of elections yet they are unable to contest and compete with the others. From this, it is evident that, the socio-

Table 23

Sl. No.	*What steps do you take to remove social disabilities?*	*Positive Response*	*Number*	*Percentage*
1.	Complain to: Police Station	22	600	03.66%
2.	Law Courts	–	600	–
3.	Village Panchayat	278	600	46.33%
4.	Associations / Organisations	176	600	29.33%
5.	Political representatives	124	600	20.66%

economic disabilities of the Scheduled Castes and Scheduled Tribes result in low participation in the political system.

The above table reveals the various steps taken by the respondents to overcome from their social disabilities. Majority of the respondents are of the opinion that, even today they are often exposed to many social disabilities in villages. For example, they are being subjected to humiliation, injustice and unequal treatment by the caste Hindus. Whenever they are exposed to these disabilities, they take recourse to any of the authorities mentioned in the above table. 22 out of 600 respondents, i.e., 3.66%, are of the opinion that, whenever they are confronted with any social disabilities in their village, they give complaint to the police station, where as, 20.66% respondents approach their political representatives and ask them to solve their problems. As many as 176 respondents, i.e., 29.33%, are neither interested to meet their political representatives nor village Panchayat but they approach associations to rectify their social problems. They are of the opinion that, they do not trust them, as they give false assurances and promises. As village Panchayats are dominated by the caste Hindus or upper castes, there also, they do not get justice. But majority of the respondents, i.e., 46.33%, approach village Panchayat to get their social problems solved. They think that village Panchayat is represented by number of people where they need not spend money for solving their problems. They express their view that, it is more convenient and conducive for them to bring their social problems before the village Panchayat, as its members are easily accessible in the village. Whereas, none of the respondents approach Law Courts for the removal of their social disabilities. From these facts it is evident that, only negligible percent of respondents, i.e. 3.66%, approach police station for solving their social problems. But the remaining respondents, i.e., 97%, do not approach police as it is expensive and they have no faith in the police officials. Besides, it is also observed that, whenever they are socially discriminated, humiliated or tortured by the upper castes, it is futile to give complaint against them, as the police do not take action against them. Therefore, majority of the respondents gives complaint to the village Panchayat whenever social disabilities like Untouchability, humiliation, discrimination and unequal treatment are confronted by them.

Table 24
Form of Protest

Sl. No.	*What form of protest would you adopt to remove your social problems ?*	*Response*	*Number*	*Percentage*
1.	Hunger strike	122	600	20.00%
2.	Public meeting	122	600	20.00%
3.	Holding peaceful march	96	600	16.00%
4.	No protest	382	600	63.66%

Apart from the methods mentioned in the above table, the respondents also undertake various steps to protest against their social disabilities. As seen from the table, 122 out of 600 respondents, i.e., 20%, are of the view that, whenever they are socially discriminated, humiliated and treated unequally, they undertake 'hunger strike' and 'public meeting' against such people for the removal of their disabilities. For this purpose, the respondents seek assistance from social activists who belong to various associations. It is informed that, on one occasion, some respondents were prevented from taking water in the village tube well. Consequently, with the help of social activists, they protested against the upper castes through hunger strike and public meetings and ultimately the caste Hindus agreed to share water with the respondents. Only 16% of the respondents hold peaceful march protesting against the attitude of the caste Hindus whenever they are discriminated. But majority of the respondents, i.e., 382 out of 600 respondents, (i.e., 63.66%) are of the opinion that they do not resort to any of these methods. Because, these methods would not solve the problems of the respondents rather it aggravates the communal hatred between them and the upper castes. From the above table it is clear that, the Scheduled Castes and Scheduled Tribes have little awareness of their rights and privileges. But what prevented them from claiming equal status and other benefits is their poverty, illiteracy, insecurity in the villages and dependence on the upper castes for their jobs and loans.

From the above table, it is evident that only 56 out of 600 respondents, i.e., 9.33%, are aware of the 'Untouchability offence Act and SC/ST (Prevention of Atrocities) Act. But majority of the respondents, i.e., 91%, have no awareness about these enactments,

Table 25

Sl. No.	Are you aware of ?	Positive Response	Number	Percentage
1.	Untouchability offence Act, 1955, or Protection of Civil Rights Act, 1976	56	600	09.33%
2.	SC/ST (Prevention of Atrocities) Act, 1989	56	600	09.33%

which protect the interests of the Scheduled Castes and Scheduled Tribes. Illiteracy, poor educational family background and inadequate opportunities are the main reasons for their ignorance about these enactments. Besides, these respondents have no awareness about the fact that 'Untouchability' has been abolished and any such performance would be punishable under the Indian Constitution.

Table 26

Sl. No.		Positive Response	Number	Percentage
1.	Do you know that there is reservation for SC/ST's in legislatives, public services and in public education	218	600	36.33%

When the respondents were interviewed, 218 out of 600 respondents, i.e., 36.33%, expressed their views affirmatively. But the remaining 64% respondents are not aware of reservation policies as guaranteed under the Constitution of India. They have no knowledge about reservation provided in public employment and public education. It is observed that, due to inadequate knowledge about the reservation they do not claim these benefits.

The above table indicates the respondent's awareness on various Government programmes for their Socio-economic developments. As seen from the table, 17.33% of the respondents expressed their view that, they have some knowledge of IRDP (Integrated Rural Development Programme) and Jawahar Rozgar Yojane as they are getting benefits from these programmes,

Table 27

Sl. No.	*Are you aware of the following Government programmes?*	*Positive Response*	*Number*	*Percentage*
1.	I.R.D.P.	107	600	17.33%
2.	Jawahar Rozgar Yojane	107	600	17.33%
3.	Employment Assurance Scheme	177	600	29.50%
4.	Ashraya Scheme	118	600	19.66%
5.	Bhagya Jyoti Scheme	118	600	19.66%
6.	Ambedkar Vasati Yojane	198	600	33.00%

whereas, rest of the respondents, i.e., 83%, have no knowledge about these programmes. Regarding the Employment Assurance Scheme, only 177 out of 600 respondents, i.e., 29.5%, are aware of this programme. Many of these respondents have got vocational employment by the Government for the forest development and dairy development. As many as 118 respondents, i.e., 19.66%, are aware of 'Ashraya Scheme and Bhagya Jyoti Scheme', because, under these schemes, many of these respondents have received the benefit of electricity and houses. But 198 out of 600 respondents, i.e., 33%, are of the opinion that, they are aware of 'Ambedkar Vasati Yojane', which provides houses to Scheduled Castes and Scheduled Tribes free of cost. It is observed that, under this scheme, many Scheduled Castes and Scheduled Tribes have received benefits from the Government. These facts show that majority of the respondents are not aware of all the developmental programmes launched by the Government. They are of the opinion that, unless they are informed about these schemes, they are not in a position to have knowledge of them.

Table 28

Sl. No.	*Whether various develop–mental programmes of the Government are being ?*	*Positive Response*	*Number*	*Percentage*
1.	Benefited	218	600	36.33%
2.	Partly benefited	104	600	17.33%
3.	Not benefited	278	600	46.33%

As seen from the table, it is clear that, 218 out of 600 respondents, i.e., 36.33%, are of the opinion that, they have fully benefited by the various developmental programmes launched by the Government, whereas, 17.33% respondents expressed their view that, they have been partly benefited. The reasons given by them are;

1. Due to the middlemen, they are not able to get full benefits of the schemes.
2. They are not aware of many programmes launched by the Government.
3. The imposition of various restrictions by the Government restricts them from utilising the benefits utilising the benefits fully.

But as many as 278 respondents out of 600, are of the view that they have not been benefited from any of the Government programmes, because, many times due to middlemen, as well as, the attitude of the banks, they do not get benefits rather they are frustrated they are made to go from pillar to post. Therefore, they feel that these schemes launched by the Government are useful only to those who are having influence, knowledge and money.

For the purpose of obtaining first hand information on the Governmental development programmes and their actual implementation, 50 Scheduled Caste and Scheduled Tribe officers, 50 Dalith leaders and 20 Scheduled Caste and Scheduled Tribe MLA's & MP's have been interviewed. They have expressed their own opinions on various programmes of the Government and their usefulness. The following table shows their different responses and opinions.

Table 29

Sl. No.	*Do you think that PCR Act and SC/ST (Prevention of Atrocities) Act are strictly being implemented?*	*Positive Response*	*Number*	*Percentage*
1.	SC/ST officers	11	50	22.00%
2.	SC/ST Dalith leaders	08	50	16.00%
3.	SC/ST MLA's & MP's	15	20	75.00%

As seen from the table, it is evident that, 11 officers out of 50, i.e., 22%, are of the opinion that the enactments like 'Protection of Civil Rights Act and SC/ST (Prevention of Atrocities) Act' are strictly being implemented by the Government, whereas, only 16% of Dalith leaders say Government is implementing the above legislations for the protection of Scheduled Castes and Scheduled Tribes. But the rest of the respondents, i.e., 84%, say that there is no actual implementation of these enactments. They said, most of the enforcement officers are caste Hindus who are not interested to implement them seriously. 15 respondents (MLA's & MP's) out of 20, i.e., 75%, express their view that, these legislations are being implemented by the Government for the purpose of protecting the interests of Scheduled Castes and Scheduled Tribes. These facts clearly show that, except the opinions of MLA's and MP's, the majority of the other respondents are of the view that these legislations are not being properly implemented by the enforcement agencies. It is observed that, whenever a Scheduled Caste or a Scheduled Tribe member gives a complaint to a police station against the atrocities done by the upper castes, the police officers would not accept the complaints. Therefore, many Scheduled Caste and Scheduled Tribe members think that it is futile to approach the police station. The police officers never enforce the provisions of PCR Act or SC/ST (Prevention of Atrocities) Act against the wrong doers. It is observed that, out of 25 complaints given to the police officers by the Harijans, one or two complaints were considered and action was taken against the wrong doer. But 75% of the MLA's & MP's say that, the enforcement officers would respond to the complaints given by the Scheduled Castes and Scheduled Tribes, as it is their obligation to safeguard their interests.

Table 30

Sl. No.	*Whether adequate welfare programmes are being launched by the Govt.?*	*Positive Response*	*Number*	*Percentage*
1.	SC/ST officers	23	50	46.00%
2.	SC/ST Dalith leaders	18	50	36.00%
3.	SC/ST MLA's & MP's	12	20	60.00%

The above table shows that, 23 out of 50 officers, i.e., 46%, express their opinion that Government's welfare programmes to Scheduled Castes and Scheduled Tribes are useful and adequate for their development, whereas, rest of the officers, i.e., 54%, say that the various development programmes launched by the Government are insufficient and inadequate for them. Majority of the MLA's and MP's, i.e., 12 out of 20 (60%) are of the opinion that, the Government launches fruitful and enough development programmes for the members of Scheduled Castes and Scheduled Tribes. They express their regret that, at the implementation level many social and economic development programmes are at failure. But 36% of the Dalith leaders are of the view that, Government sincerely undertakes many programmes for the upliftment of Scheduled Castes and Scheduled Tribes. But majority of the leaders, i.e., 64%, said, enough programmes are not being launched. They are of the opinion that, among many programmes which are launched, only few programmes will be actually implemented by the Government, because, many officers who are incharge of these programmes are not interested to implement them fully for the benefit of Harijans. From these facts, we can say that although Government is launching many developmental programmes for the upliftment of Scheduled Castes and Scheduled Tribes, yet, all of them are not implemented because of the indifferent attitude of the officers who are incharge of these programmes. It is also observed that, in several departments, the 'fund' reserved for welfare programmes are not being fully utilised by the officers concerned. As soon as the financial year is over, the same 'fund' would be returned to the Government along with a report saying that the fund has not been utilised by the Scheduled Castes and Scheduled Tribes. Majority of the respondents in all the three categories (i.e., Officers, Dalith leaders and MLA's & MP's) are of the opinion that 'Scheduled Castes and Scheduled Tribes reserved fund' is sometimes diverted to some other programmes to defeat the interests of the Harijans.

Table 31

Sl. No.	*Do you think that 'Reservation Policy' is strictly implemented in public services & public education ?*	*Positive Response*	*Number*	*Percentage*
1.	SC/ST Officers	16	50	32.00%
2.	SC/ST Dalith leaders	08	50	16.00%
3.	SC/ST MLA's & MP's	12	20	60.00%

In respect of the actual implementation of 'Reservation Policy' in public services and public education, the officers, leaders and MLA's & MP's have expressed their different opinions as shown in the above table.16 out of 50 officers, i.e., 32%, are of the opinion that, there is a strict implementation of 'reservation policy' in all levels including public service and public education. But the majority of the officers, i.e., 68%, say there is no actual implementation of reservation policy in public services and public education. They are of the view that, in many departments, the reserved posts are still vacant as the concerned officers do not appoint them. Rather they send false report to the Government saying that, suitable candidates are not available for the vacant reserved posts.

As many as 60% of the MLA's & MP's express their view that, 'reservation policy' is strictly implemented in public services and public education. Because of the reservation policy, today, there are many Class I & Class II officers working in various services. They are of the view that, in many branches of education, important positions are held by the Harijans because of 'reservation policy' provided in the Constitution of India. But the remaining 40% of the MLA's & MP's express their negative opinion.

Only 16% of the Dalith leaders, i.e., 8 out of 50, express their view that, the Government is strictly implementing 'reservation policy', both in public services and public education. But majority of them, i.e., 84% leaders, are of the opinion that, there is no actual implementation of 'reservation policy' in public service and public education. According to them, even though there are many unfilled

Table 32

Sl. No.	*What reasons do you attribute for not fully implementing the 'reservation policy' by the Government? (Multiple reasons from all these categories of respondents)*	*Positive Response*	*Number*	*Percentage*
1.	Negligence of the Government officers	80	120	66.66%
2.	Interference	22	120	18.33%
3.	Misuse of funds	22	120	18.33%
4.	Non utilization by the SC/ST's	18	120	15.00%

reserved posts in various departments, the Government is not showing interest to fill these posts. It is observed that, in many private educational institutions, where they are receiving grants, many reserved posts are still vacant. The managements of these institutions are not interested to fill the reserved posts even though they receive grants periodically from the Government. Therefore, majority of these leaders have no faith in the Government, as 'reservation policy' is not properly implemented.

The above table indicates the different responses provided by the officers, leaders and MLA's & MP's (all together) regarding the reasons for not fully implementing the 'reservation policy'. As many as 80 respondents (i.e., 66.66%) are of the opinion that the negligent attitude of the concerned officers is the sole reason for non-implementation of 'reservation policy' in various fields. But 18.33% of the respondents say that, it is due to the interference from politicians as well as misuse of funds by the officers who are incharge of various developmental programmes; the 'reservation policy' is not properly being implemented. Whereas, 18 respondents out of 120, i.e., 15%, express their views that, many reservation beneficiaries or Scheduled Castes and Scheduled Tribes are not fully utilising these reservation benefits. Many times, it is observed that, they never bother about the various developmental programmes launched by the Government. They are under the notion that, such developmental programmes are meant only for

Table 33

Sl. No.	*Even after 50 years of Independence, socio-economic disabilities of SC/ST have not been fully removed. What reasons do you attribute to this ? (Multiple response from all the three categories)*	*Positive Response*	*Number*	*Percentage*
1.	Lack of interest from the Government	38	120	31.66%
2.	Governmental benefits are not reaching the needy	94	120	78.33%
3.	Beneficiaries are not utilising the benefits properly	64	120	53.33%
4.	Majority of the SC/ST's are still ignorant of developmental programmes	46	120	38.33%
5.	Middlemen are misusing the benefits before they reach the needy	82	120	68.33%

rich people within their caste. As they can easily manipulate the officers and get benefits from these programmes. Therefore, several schemes are left without being implemented by the Government.

The above table reveals the reasons why even after 50 years of Independence, socio-economic disabilities of SC/ST's have not been removed completely. 38 out of 120 respondents, i.e., 31.66%, are of the view that due to lack of Government interest, the socio-economic disabilities of Harijans have not been fully removed. As many as 94 out of 120 respondents, i.e., 78.33%, say that the various Government programmes, which provide benefits to the Scheduled Castes and Scheduled Tribes, are not properly reaching them. It is observed that, the really needy people are deprived of these benefits as their benefits are snatched away by the rich people among the Harijans. But 64 respondents out 120, i.e., 53.33%, are of the view that, whatever the benefits provided by the Government to Scheduled Castes and Scheduled Tribes are not properly utilised by them. These respondents observe that when loan is sanctioned to Harijans, many of them use the amount for other purposes. Therefore, they are still suffering from socio-economic disabilities. Besides, 38.33% respondents say that, due to illiteracy and ignorance of Scheduled Castes and Scheduled Tribes, many developmental programmes are not being properly utilised by them. Many times, these people are not aware of various programmes launched by the Government for their development. 82 respondents, i.e., 68.33%, are of the view that, due to the interference of middlemen, the Harijans do not get benefits provided by the Government through various programmes.

Table 34

Sl. No.	*What steps do you propose to remove various disabilities of SC/ST's completely?*	*Positive Response*	*Number*	*Percentage*
1.	Income Criterion	32	120	26.66%
2.	Employment Criterion	32	120	26.66%
3.	Onetime reservation Criterion	78	120	65.00%
4.	Accountability Criterion	10	120	08.33%

The above table shows the various steps proposed by Scheduled Caste and Scheduled Tribe officers, Dalith leaders and

MLA's & MP's for the complete removal of the disabilities of Harijans. 26.66% respondents, i.e., 32 out of 120, propose that, while providing reservation benefits to Scheduled Castes and Scheduled Tribes, the Government should consider income as well as employment criterion. Those Scheduled Castes and Scheduled Tribes, whose income is more than Rs. 1 Lakh, shall not be provided 'reservation benefits'. Likewise, if a member of Scheduled Caste and Scheduled Tribe is in Class I post either in Central service or in State service, his children shall not be provided any reservation benefit. Only 10 out of 120 respondents, i.e., 8.33%, propose that, once a benefit is obtained by any Scheduled Caste and Scheduled Tribe, they should utilise that benefit, if they misuse it for any other purpose they shall be made accountable to the Government. As many as 65% of the respondents, i.e., 78 out of 120, are of the opinion that, if Government fixes 'onetime reservation Criterion', then the reservation benefits will percolate down to the needy and the real targeted people and thereby remove many disabilities of the Scheduled Castes and Scheduled Tribes. From these facts it is evident that, all the respondents are of the opinion that if the above-mentioned criteria are strictly adhered by the Government while providing reservation benefits, within a short period, the disabilities of the Harijans can be removed completely.

CONCLUSION

The empirical study of the foregoing chapter reveals that, the Scheduled Castes and Scheduled Tribes in many villages remain in utter poverty, illiteracy and ignorant of various Governmental programmes launched for their development. Many of them are under employed and economically dependent on the caste Hindus. From the study of socio-economic disabilities of Scheduled Castes and Scheduled Tribes in many villages, it has been observed that, the majority of the Harijans are landless agricultural labourers who are frequently discriminated by the caste Hindus in providing living wages and required loan. The study also shows the discriminatory treatment of the upper castes towards the Scheduled Castes and Scheduled Tribes in respect of temple entry, priestly service, village community feasts and marriages in many villages even today. Besides, the political participation of the Scheduled Castes and Scheduled Tribes is also very low, as elections require huge finance. Therefore, majority of the Scheduled Castes and Scheduled Tribes are unable to contest for elections and participate in the decision making process in various levels. Only a small number of Scheduled Caste and Scheduled Tribe population contest for general elections who are having better economic status and political consciousness. In many villages, majority of the Harijans bring their complaints to village Panchayat, political representatives and non-Governmental organisations. But they never prefer to approach either police stations or Law Courts as they are expensive and out of their reach. Despite the fact that there are number of enactments which protect and safeguard the interests of the Scheduled Castes and Scheduled Tribes, yet they have become dead legislations as they are not being properly enforced by the Government officers. This is also the view expressed by many Scheduled Caste and Scheduled Tribe officers, leaders and MLA's & MP's. Majority of them said, there are number of developmental programmes launched by the Government, but they are not being properly implemented so as to reach the needy people. Consequently, majority of the Scheduled Castes and Scheduled Tribes have no faith and confidence in the administration as they think that these Constitutional benefits are available only to those who can bribe the officials and not to the needy people.

Besides, whenever the Harijans are discriminated in their villages, according to the study report, majority of them do not protest against the upper castes discriminations as they are not going to be employed as labourers and prevented from seeking loan. This shows that, even today, the Scheduled Castes and Scheduled Tribes are afraid of the upper castes in their villages as they depend on them for many things. From these facts, it is evident that, the socio, economic and political disabilities of the Scheduled Castes and Scheduled Tribes are still in existence, which prevents them from acquiring equal status with the caste Hindus.

NOTES

1. S. Omprakash–*"Development of the weaker sections"*, Problems, Policies and Issues, p. 27.
2. Handbook, published by Zilla Panchayat, Mysore, p. 30.

3. One bag is equal to 100kg.
4. C. Parvathamma – *"Scheduled Castes and Scheduled Tribes: A Socio-economic survey"*, [Ashish Publications, New Delhi, 1984], pp. 280-281.
5. *"The New Indian Express"*, published from Bangalore, dated Sept. 1st, 1999.
6. Opp. Cit., Note 5.
7. S. Mallik–*"Social Integration of Scheduled Castes"*, Abhinav Publications, New Delhi, 1979, p. 160.
8. S. Patwardhan–*"Change among Indian Harijans": Maharashtra–'A case study'*, Orient Longman, New Delhi, 1973, pp. 99-102.

6

CONCLUSION

The present study is aimed at understanding the plight of those who have been incessantly subjected to injustice, inequality, humiliation, caste based discrimination and degradation by the upper castes since ancient times. The existence of varnashrama dharma is an evidence for the division of the society into four orders and the prevalence of caste system in the Hindu social order. Throughout the Vedic period the stratification of society into four orders was maintained, where each order was conferred with specific functions to be performed. For example, Brahmanas were required to perform sacrificial ceremonies and rituals, which occupied the highest status in the Hindu society. Kshatriyas were placed in the second order of the society whose services were used for war purposes, and were regarded as warriors or protectors of the State. Likewise Vaishyas were placed in the third order of social status who were considered as traders and businessmen. Lastly, the Shudras were placed in the last order of the Hindu society, who were considered as manual labourers and doing all menial jobs in the society. This shows that the society was stratified and different groups were assigned different status in the hierarchical way. In this hierarchy, Shudras were placed in the last order of the society, who were not allowed to study the Veda and Upanishads and were prevented from hearing Vedic recitations. These closely show that the recitation of Veda and Upanishads were confined only to Brahmanas, as a result, the Shudras were kept outside the reach of these Holy Scriptures. Shudras were totally neglected and deprived of some privileges and were subjected to punishment under certain circumstances. For example, if a Shudra hears recitation of Vedas, his ears would be filled with molten tin or lac; if he recites Veda, his tongue would be cut off; if he remembers any Vedic verses, he would be dismembered. This would show that such a cruel and barbaric punishment was being given to Shudras in ancient period. Besides, they were incessantly prevented from participating in any ritual ceremonies and sacrifices. This rigid stratification of society and denial of ritual ceremonies to them became more prominent especially, in the post-Vedic period.

But, during the British period, the rigidity of caste system was diluted to some extent when British Courts administered a uniform criminal law. The Courts in three presidency towns discouraged the practice of priesthood as a monopoly of Brahmins, which shows that Courts took cognizance of discriminatory treatment and discouraged such practices. For the purpose of allowing the Untouchables to join educational institutions, the Government of Bombay issued a notification in 1923 to all the institutions to admit children belonging to depressed classes; otherwise they would be deprived of grants to their institutions. This, of course, marked a significant event in the British regime in allowing the children of the depressed classes to join any educational institutions of their choice and sit with the children of caste Hindus. Subsequently, the Statute passed, in 1925, by the Madras Government which threw open all public streets, roads, offices, public resort, public tank to all people including the Untouchables was for a significant development in providing status to Untouchables, during the British rule; consequently, Untouchables were allowed to enter Hindu temples to worship gods and goddesses of their choice. These facts clearly reveal that, the conditions of the depressed classes including the Untouchables were deplorable during the Vedic period. But their conditions were improved to some extent only during the British regime as they brought uniformity in criminal law and encouraged the Untouchables to enter and to worship in Hindu temples and to have access to public places, offices and resorts. But the fact remains that, Britishers were not interested to eradicate caste system from the Hindu society, rather they had confined themselves in business, of trade and commerce. Consequently, the practice of Untouchability was not completely eradicated from the Hindu society, even though some of the Hindu temples and public places were thrown open to the Untouchables also.

The role of Bhakti Movement in eradicating the practice of Untouchability is of paramount importance. Bhakti Movement was started by Ramananda, Kabir, Tulsidas, Tukaram, Purandara Das and Basava. Their main objective was to secure some rights to the Untouchables and to the depressed classes and to strengthen the Hindu religion. This movement fought against the social discrimination of the depressed classes but confined itself to its philosophical ideologies rather than actual socio-economic welfare programmes. Despite the honest attempts made by the Bhakti Movement, the practice of 'Untouchability' was not fully eradicated from the Hindu society; rather Untouchables were debarred from entering into Hindu temples to worship gods. Consequently, Brahmo Samaj was founded which started to impact the gospel of removing all religious evils like casteism and practice of Untouchability. Besides, Arya Samaj was also founded under the leadership of Swami Dayananda Saraswati, which opened many schools and gave education to all people including the Untouchables. These two samajas endeavoured to teach philosophical ideologies for removing social evils, but in practice, their impact was not significant in the removal of Untouchability as they confine themselves only for imparting philosophy rather than removing social evils like caste systems and Untouchability. But the real reformation of caste system started with the establishment of separate schools for Untouchables by Jyotiba Phule, with the financial assistance of British Government. Under the leadership of Phule, the Untouchables, for the first time, started to attack the caste system directly and assert their identity in the Hindu society. Phule started to impart education to all Untouchables and the depressed classes of people to eradicate 'Untouchability' from the Hindu society. This was a significant contribution of Phule where he educated the Untouchables and made them to fight against injustice, inequality and degradation done by the caste Hindus.

Equally, the contribution of the Constitution makers like Gandhiji, Nehru and Ambedkar was also significant in protecting and securing the interests of the Untouchables or the Scheduled Castes and the Scheduled Tribes. Gandhiji's words, for removing the practice of Untouchability from the Hindu society, are noteworthy. He said, "Swaraj is unattainable without the removal of the sin of 'Untouchability' from the Hindu religion". Gandhiji also stressed that, the Untouchables would also enjoy their civil rights like access to roads, wells, public institutions, public employment etc., provided the Hindu society removes the social evil like 'Untouchability'. In the first Round Table Conference, many Constitutional proposals were made to safeguard the interests of the depressed classes including the Scheduled Castes and the Scheduled Tribes. Ambedkar who was the champion of the depressed classes insisted for a separate electorate for the Untouchables, which enables them to protect themselves from the dominance of the caste Hindus and to capture political power. But it was not materialised even though, the British Government, in 1932, announced the famous Communal Award wherein the depressed classes could only vote for such seats reserved for them in the Provincial Legislatures. This was due to Gandhiji's insistence for the revocation of Communal Award. If the Communal Award had been accepted and implemented then, the Untouchables would have become politically independent and would not have faced social and economic disabilities as they are facing today.

Inspite of this major set back, the Constituent Assembly took cognizance of the conditions of the Untouchables and endeavoured to incorporate some of the provisions to the future Constitution of India which provide equal status and opportunity to all including the Scheduled Castes and the Scheduled Tribes. In this connection, the Constituent Assembly formulated the 'Bill of Rights', which secure social justice ad equality to all people. For example, Right to equality,[1] Prohibition of discrimination on the grounds of religion, caste, race, sex or place of birth,[2] equality of opportunity in matters of public employment,[3] Abolition of Untouchability,[4] Right to life,[5] Right not to be denied admission to any citizen in any educational institution, maintained by the State or receiving aid out of State funds on grounds of only religion, race, caste,[6] Right to Constitution Remedies.[7] The very object of guaranteeing these rights to all people including the Scheduled Castes and the Scheduled Tribes is to provide social justice and to establish an egalitarian society. In relation to these guaranteed rights, the contribution of judiciary in protecting the interest and welfare of the Scheduled Castes and the Scheduled Tribes and the interpretation of these provisions of paramount importance so far as the 'reservation policy' is concerned, the Supreme Court of India, from Balaji to Madhav's case, has been insisting that the reservation contemplated in Article 15 (4) and 16 (4) to Scheduled Castes and the Scheduled Tribes and backward classes in educational institutions as well as in public employment should not exceed 50%. Although the 50% rule fixed by the Supreme Court in Balaji's case was relevant at the time of its decision, yet it is irrelevant today, as there is a substantial increase in the Scheduled Castes and Scheduled Tribes and backward class population in India. But in an extraordinary circumstance, the Court has opined that, some concession may be extended to the Scheduled Castes and the Scheduled Tribes for promoting them to higher posts. For example, in *N.M. Thomas V. State of Kerala,*[8] Justice Krishna Iyer said, 'temporary exemption of Scheduled Caste and Scheduled Tribe employees from passing departmental examination for promoting them to higher posts is valid and justified to secure them social justice'. The Supreme Court has also observed that, under extraordinary circumstances, this 50% rule may be slightly relaxed to secure social justice to the Scheduled Castes and Scheduled Tribes and the backward classes when they are not adequately represented in the services of the Union and the States. The fact remains that even tough Articles 15 (4) and 16 (4) speak about the protective discrimination, yet reservation is restricted to below 50%. But as long as socio-economic and political justice are not properly provided to the backward classes including the Scheduled Castes and the Scheduled Tribes, so long the reservation even if it exceeds 50% can be justified. Because, the goal of the Preamble to the Constitution of India is to provide socio and economic justice to those depressed classed who were deprived and denied certain privileges form ancient time and make them to be equal with the rest of the society. Therefore, it can be observed that, the 50% rule fixed by the Supreme Court is not reasonable and practicable as the population of Scheduled Castes and the Scheduled Tribes and the backward classes is also rapidly increasing. Therefore, there is a need to revise this 50% rule as long as these deprived sections of the society do not attain socio and economic justice as enumerated in the Constitution. Besides, the 50% rule was fixed by the Judiciary as early as 1963 in Balaji's case taking into consideration the then prevailed situations and circumstances. But the Courts are still following the same 50% rule despite the population of Scheduled Castes and Scheduled Tribes and backward classes has enormously been increased, situations and circumstances have been substantially changed.

Besides, in order to secure social justice to the Scheduled Castes and the Scheduled Tribes, the concept of carry-forward rule has to be strictly followed, so that unfilled reserved posts in a particular year may be filled in the subsequent years when the candidates from Scheduled Caste and Scheduled Tribe community are available. But unfortunately, the Supreme Court, in *T. Devadasan V. Union of India,*[9] struck down such 'carry forward rule' adopted by the Union Government as it exceeded 50% rule. In this connection, the observation made by Justice Krishna Iyer in Akhil Bharatiya Shoshit Karamchari Sangh (Rly.) is noteworthy. When he said, "In no year Scheduled Caste and Scheduled Tribe candidates be actually appointed to substantially more than 50% of the promotional posts. Some excess will not affect as mathematical precision is difficult in human affairs, but substantial excess will void the selection".

Justice Chinnappa Reddy also observed that, '50% rule laid down by the Supreme Court is only for the guidance of the judges and they need not be bound by it'. Again in **Indra Sawhney** V. **Union of India**, the Supreme Court has observed that, 'the carry forward rule is valid only when it does not exceed 50% rule'. But it seems to be unjustifiable and impracticable as 50% rule does not secure social justice to the backward classes including the Scheduled Castes and the Scheduled Tribes as Articles 15 (4) and 16 (4) have not fixed such quantum of reservation.

Another important aspect, which is required to be noted, is the concept of 'creamy layer' propounded by the Supreme Court in **Indra Sawhney's case**. This concept of creamy layer is an innovative judicial principle through which the forward people among the backward classes can be prevented from utilising the reservation benefits conferred in the Constitution. The very object of reservation policy is to uplift those people who are both socially and educationally backward or the Scheduled Castes and the Scheduled Tribes. But even after 50 years of Independence, with all the Governmental welfare programmes, the Scheduled Castes and Scheduled Tribes socio-economic conditions have not been improved. This is because, the forward class among the Scheduled Castes and the Scheduled Tribes are eating away the reservation benefits which are conferred to the really needy people or the targeted section of the society. In this connection, the concept of 'creamy layer' shall be extended even to the Scheduled Castes and the Scheduled Tribes, so that the Constitutionally guaranteed benefits, to these sections of the people, would reach them. This slowly removes the various social and economic disabilities, which are being faced by the Scheduled Castes and Scheduled Tribes. In due course, the elite or the creamy layer within the Scheduled Castes and the Scheduled Tribes community can be completely eliminated from the purview of the reservation benefits and provide social justice to the needy people as required under the Constitution.

The Judicial responses on the reservation policy, equality and the protection of the interests of the Scheduled Castes and Scheduled Tribes are laudable and praiseworthy. This can be seen form Balaji to Madhav's case. The provisions of 'Abolition of Untouchability' in Article 17 of the Constitution is also an important one as it secures equality of the status and opportunity to all the Scheduled Castes and Scheduled Tribes and bring about social justice to them. The decision of the Supreme Court in **State of Karnataka** *V.* **Appa Balu Ingale** is also laudable as it protected the interests of the Scheduled Castes and Scheduled Tribes and curbed the practice of Untouchability in any form. The various enactments[10] made by the Parliament to punish those persons who perform Untouchability in any form is also praiseworthy.

Even though the Constitution of India has guaranteed equality of Status to all Scheduled Castes and Scheduled Tribes, yet in many villages, unequal treatment, discrimination and atrocities are being done to them only on the ground of caste. Even today in many villages, the Scheduled Castes and Scheduled Tribes are not allowed to enjoy equal status with the caste Hindus. For example, Scheduled Castes and Scheduled Tribes are not allowed to enter Hindu temples for worshipping gods, shops, wells and bathing ghats. This shows that social discrimination is still in practice more in the rural area than in the urban areas. Therefore, we can say that Constitutional provisions are good enough to secure social justice to Scheduled Castes and Scheduled Tribes, but their implementation by the public servants is at failure. For instance, performance of Untouchability in any form is legally abolished, but still in many places practice of Untouchability is in vogue.

Besides, the Constitution-makers have also imposed some social obligations on the State to perform for the attainment of social and economic justice. Mere achieving of social justice will not bring equality of status and opportunity, unless it is followed by economic justice. For example, State shall promote with special care the educational and economic interests of the weaker sections of the people and in particular, the Scheduled Castes and the Scheduled Tribes and shall protect them from social injustice and all forms of exploitation.[11] The primary object of incorporating Directive Principles of State Policies to the Constitution of India is to secure social and economic justice to all people including Scheduled Castes and the Scheduled Tribes. Under these principles, the State has been launching number of socio-economic welfare programmes to uplift and to develop the vulnerable sections of the society including the Scheduled Castes and the Scheduled Tribes. For example, free hostel facilities, scholarships, various training programmes in different fields, loan facilities for purchasing agricultural implements, cows, sheep etc., providing houses free of cost under Ashraya and Ambedkar schemes, providing vocational employment to Scheduled Castes and the Scheduled Tribes farmers, free legal aid are some of the important programmes undertaken by the State.

It is evident from the empirical study that Government has been spending crores of rupees by undertaking various welfare programmes for the benefit of Scheduled Castes and the Scheduled Tribes. As the majority of the Scheduled Castes and the Scheduled Tribes are illiterate and ignorant of various Governmental programmes, they are not utilising them properly. The study reveals that whatever the benefits are being given by the State to these people, are actually not reaching them. Rather, these benefits are cornered by the elite section of the people among the Scheduled Caste and the Scheduled Tribe community depriving the needy persons. On the other hand, those Scheduled Castes and the Scheduled Tribes who receive benefit from various welfare programmes are not utilising them properly rather these benefits are being misused by them. For example, when loan is provided to the Scheduled Castes and the Scheduled Tribes for the purchase of cows or sheep or for the purchase of agricultural implements, they spend part of the money for purchase of cows or sheep, but bulk of the amount is utilised for their social ceremonies like marriage, festivals and various ceremonies. This is also one of the reasons why their socio-economic conditions have not been improved so far even though Government spends crores of rupees for their development. Besides, the intervention of middlemen or the brokers, in receiving loan and other benefits by the Scheduled Caste and Scheduled Tribe farmers and unemployed youths, has also deprived the Scheduled Castes and the Scheduled Tribes from getting full reservation benefits. Because, 50% of the loan amount sanctioned for Scheduled Castes and the Scheduled Tribes would be appropriated by these middlemen. Consequently, the remaining loan amount would be spent for their social purposes. This is also one of the reasons why, even though the Government is providing loan facilities to the Scheduled Castes and the Scheduled Tribes, their socio-economic conditions have not been fully improved.

The present study also reveals that, majority of the Scheduled Castes and the Scheduled Tribes are agricultural labourers, who are depending on their land lords for their livelihood, they work from morning till evening in other fields for money. If their landlords or upper castes do any atrocities to them they cannot protest against them as they depend on the caste Hindus for their livelihood. It is also evident from the study that, only 25 to 30% of the Scheduled Castes and the Scheduled Tribes are allowed to enjoy their equal status with the upper castes, but the remaining 70% of them are prevented from enjoying equal status in worshiping gods in temples, taking coffee and tea in village shops, hotels, attending feast, participating in village ceremonies, as indicated in table 3.3 of chapter 5. These facts clearly show that, even after 50 years of Independence and the Constitutional protections conferred, the conditions of the Scheduled Castes and the Scheduled Tribes are still deplorable, as even today, they are subjected to discrimination, humiliation and injustice by the upper castes.

So far as their political participation is concerned, only 5 to 10% of the Scheduled Castes and the Scheduled Tribes are able to contest for general elections, as they are economically strong to face elections. But the remaining 90% of the Scheduled Castes and the Scheduled Tribes are unable to contest for election due to their economic disabilities. The observation of the Scheduled Caste and the Scheduled Tribe officers, leaders and politicians was that, even though members from Scheduled Caste and Scheduled Tribe community contest for elections, they are not supported by the upper castes. Because of these facts, the majority of Scheduled Castes and Scheduled Tribes are reluctant to contest for general elections. Consequently, they cannot revolt against the injustice, inequality, and humiliation done to them by the upper castes. Therefore, the Government should provide as many benefits as possible to the Scheduled Castes and the Scheduled Tribes to overcome from their socio-economic disabilities and to improve their economic standard to face the challenges in their lives.

PROPOSALS AND SUGGESTIONS

Following are the suggestions and proposals made by the researcher for the complete development of the Scheduled Castes and the Scheduled Tribes;

1. The State shall undertake such welfare measures, which would really help the Scheduled Castes and the Scheduled Tribes to improve their socio-economic and political conditions.
2. As far as possible, State should provide benefits directly to the targeted people without permitting the middlemen to intervene in this regard.
3. While providing loan facilities to the Scheduled Castes and the Scheduled Tribes for undertaking self-employment and for purchasing of various agricultural materials, an undertaking should be taken from the beneficiaries stating that, 'the loan amount would be utilised only for such purpose for which it is sanctioned, otherwise, they are liable for punishment'.
4. The Government should relax the procedures for obtaining loan from various financial institutions so that, the Scheduled Caste and the Scheduled Tribe beneficiaries would get the entire loan amount without the intervention of the middlemen or brokers.

5. The State should make the officers liable when the amount reserved for Scheduled Castes and Scheduled Tribes development is not fully utilised by them for the development of Scheduled Castes and the Scheduled Tribes. Because, in many departments, officers who are in-charge of this reserved fund are not utilising for Scheduled Castes and the Scheduled Tribes development, rather the same money is being misused or returned to the Government.
6. The Government shall constitute a vigilance committee, which shall supervise and scrutinise various welfare programmes undertaken by different departments. This committee should consist of 4 members including the Commissioner who is of the cadre of IAS. Among the other three members, one should be a senior most politician who is known for integrity, honesty and social work. Another member should be from Judiciary, who should be a retired Judge of a High Court. The third member should be from a University, who should be a retired professor known for uprightness, good character and conduct and who has expertise in sociology and law. This vigilance commission should be empowered to investigate the actual implementation of the governmental welfare programmes and their actual utilisation by the beneficiaries. It is also to be empowered with some Quasi-Judicial power to penalise those officers and beneficiaries who misuse these benefits and privileges conferred by the State consistent with the Constitutional mandates.
7. The Government shall conduct periodic peace-meetings and other cultural programmes in various villages, allowing all sections of the society to participate in these programmes so that, it enables all people cutting across the caste barriers, to assemble and enjoy together the various cultural programmes, thereby a good atmosphere and environment can be created and unity and oneness can be brought among them.
8. The Government shall follow one-time reservation policy for the development of all Scheduled Castes and Scheduled Tribes. That is, once a candidate from Scheduled Caste and Scheduled Tribe community receives reservation benefit both in public education and employment, shall not be allowed again to claim reservation. If this policy is strictly adopted by

the State, in due course, substantial number of Scheduled Castes and Scheduled Tribes will get reservation benefits and thereby they can improve their socio-economic conditions.

9. The Government shall extend the 'creamy layer' concept even to the Scheduled Castes and Scheduled tribes. The essence of this concept is that, the forward people among the backward classes shall not be allowed to receive reservation benefits. If this is strictly adhered to, then the really needy people within the Scheduled Caste and Scheduled Tribe community would get reservation benefits and very soon they can overcome their socio and economic disabilities. For this purpose, economic criterion should be adopted by the State.

10. In order to eradicate caste system from the society, the Government shall punish those individuals who practice Untouchability and instigate others to perpetuate caste prejudices not only in public places but also in private places. Then only we can establish an egalitarian society as contemplated in the Preamble to the Constitution of India.

11. The State shall provide free and compulsory education for children belonging to Scheduled Castes and Scheduled Tribes upto matriculation as contemplated in the Constitution.[12] For this purpose, residential schools shall be established and all facilities are to be provided to them so that, when they complete their matriculation, they will be in a position to compete with the other children more effectively and efficiently not only in education but also in Government services. In due course, many of them do not require any governmental benefits given under the reservation policy.

12. The Government shall keep a vigil over the actual utilisation of benefits by the beneficiaries provided under various social welfare programmes. Once the beneficiaries' misuses the benefits conferred to him, then the Government shall not provide him again any benefits under the reservation policy. This compels the beneficiaries to utilise the given benefits properly for the purpose for which it is provided. Thereby he can improve his economic condition and overcome from his social disabilities.

If the above proposals are strictly followed by the State over a period of time, the ideals of the Preamble to the Constitution of India can be achieved, i.e., equality of status and opportunity, justice–social, economic and political. Therefore, there is an immediate need for the Government to follow these proposals and suggestions to establish a casteless and classless society as required by the Constitution of India.

NOTES

1. Article 14 of the Constitution.
2. Article 15 of the Constitution.
3. Article 16 of the Constitution.
4. Article 17 of the Constitution.
5. Article 21 of the Constitution.
6. Article 29 (2) of the Constitution.
7. Article 32 & 226 of the Constitution.
8. Opp. Cit., Note 77.
9. Opp. Cit., Note 69.
10. Untouchability Offences Act, 1955 – "Scheduled Castes and Scheduled Tribes (Prevention of Atrocities) Act, 1989 & Rules 1995.
11. Article 46 of the Constitution of India.
12. Article 45 of the Constitution of India.

BIBLIOGRAPHY

Ahuja, Ram–*"Indian Social System"* Rawat Publications, New Delhi.

Ambedkar, B.R.(1979), "Annihilation of Caste" in *Dr. Babasaheb Ambedkar: Writings and Speeches,* Vol. I, Government of Maharashtra, Bombay.

Ambedkar, B.R.(1979), "States and Minorities: What are their rights and how to secure them in the Constitution free India" in *Dr. Babasaheb Ambedkar: Writings and Speeches,* Vol. I, Government of Maharashtra, Bombay.

Ambedkar, B.R (1987), "Philosophy of Hinduism" in *Dr. Babasaheb Ambedkar: Writings and Speeches,* Vol. III, Government of Maharashtra, Bombay.

Ambedkar, B.R.(1987), "The Hindu Social Order: Its essential principles" in *Dr. Babasaheb Ambedkar: Writings and Speeches,* Vol. III, Government of Maharashtra, Bombay.

Ambedkar, B.R.(1989), "What is to be an Untouchable" in *Dr. Babasaheb Ambedkar: Writings and Speeches,* Vol. V, Government of Maharashtra, Bombay.

Ambedkar, B.R.(1990), "The Untouchables : Who are they and why they became Untouchables" in *Dr. Babasaheb Ambedkar: Writings and Speeches,* Vol. VII, Government of Maharashtra, Bombay.

Ambedkar, B.R.(1990), "Who were the Shudras?: How they came to be the Fourth Varna in the Indo-Aryan Society" in *Dr. Babasaheb Ambedkar: Writings and Speeches,* Vol VII, Government of Maharashtra, Bombay.

Austin, Granville–*"Indian Constitution : Corner Stone of a Nation".*

Bains, B.N.(1994), *"Reservation Policy and Anti-Reservationists"*, B.R. Publishing Corporation. Delhi.

Berreman, G.D.(1960), "Castes in India and the United States", *American Journal of Sociology.*

Berreman, G.D.(1979), *"Caste and other Inequalities"*, Folklore Institute, Meerut.

Beteille, A.(1965),"*Caste, class and Power*", University of California Press, Madras.

Beteille, Andre (1977), "*Inequality among men*", Oxford University Press, Delhi.

Chakravarthy, Anand (1983), "Some aspects of inequality in rural India: A Sociological perspective" in *Andre Beteille (Ed), Equality and Inequality: Theory and Practice*, Oxford University Press, Delhi.

Chousalkar, Ashok S.(1990), "*Indian Idea of Politically resistance"– Aurobindo, Tilak, Gandhi and Ambedkar*, (Delhi Publications).

Dahrendorf, R. (1969), "On the origin of inequality among men" in *Andre Beteille (Ed), Social Inequality*, Penguin Books.

D' Souza, V.S.(1980), "*Educational Inequalities among Scheduled Castes: A Case Study in the Punjab University*", Chandigarh.

Deliege, Robert–"At the threshold of Untouchability: Pallars and Valaiyars in a Tamil village" in *C.J. Fuller (Ed) Caste Today*, Oxford University Press, Delhi.

Dicey–"*Law of the Constitution*", 10th Edition.

Dubois, Abbe J.A. (1959), "*Hindu manners, Customs and Ceremonies*" Clarendon, Oxford.

Dushkin, Lelah (1972), "Scheduled Castes Politics" in *J.M. Mahar (Ed), The Untouchables on Contemporary India*, Arizona University Press, Arizona.

Jennings –"*Laws of the Constitution*".

Gajendragadkar, P.B.(1965), "*Law, Society and Social Justice*" (Asia Publishing House).

Galanter, Marc (1991), "*Competing Equalities*", Oxford University Press, Delhi.

Ghurye, G.S.(1961), "*Caste, Class and Occupation*", Popular Book Depot, Bombay.

Ghurye, G.S.(1932), "*Caste and Race in India*", London: Kegan Paul, Trench, Trubner & Co.

Gokhale, Jayashree (1993), "*From Concession to Confrontation: The Politics of an Indian Untouchable Community*", Popular Prakashan, Bombay.

Goyal, B.R.(1981), "*Educating Harijans*", Academic Press, Gurgoan.

Gupta, S.K.(1985), "*The Scheduled Caste in Modern Indian Politics: Their Emergence as a Political Power*", Munshiram Manohar Lal, Delhi.

Hanumanthan, K.R. (1979), "*Untouchability*", Koodal, Madurai.

Hutton, J.H. (1946), "*Caste in India*", Cambridge University Press, Cambridge.

Illaiah, Kancha (1996), *"Why I am not a Hindu"*, Samya, Calcutta.

Issacs, Harold R.(1965), *"India's Ex-Untouchables"*, Asia, Bombay

Jogdand, P.G. (1991), *"Dalit Movement in Maharashtra"*, Kanak, New Delhi.

John Rawls (1985), *"A Theory of Justice"*, Oxford University Press.

Joshi, B.R. (Ed) (1986), *"Untouchable Voices of the Dalit Liberation Movement"*, Select Book Service Syndicate, New Delhi.

Kamble, J.R. (1979), *"Rise and Awakening of Depressed Classes in India"*, National, New Delhi.

Kamble, N.D. (1982), *"The Scheduled Castes"* Ashish, New Delhi.

Kapadia, Karin (1996), *"Siva and Her Sisters: Gender, Caste and Class in Rural South India"* Oxford University Press, Delhi.

Khan, M.A.(1980), *"Scheduled Castes and Their Status in India"* Uppal, New Delhi.

Kothari, Rajni (1970), *"Caste in Indian Politics"* Orient Longman, New Delhi.

Lynch, O.M. (1969), *"The politics of Untouchability"* Columbia University Press, New York.

Majumdar, R.C. (1989), *"The History and Culture of the Indian People: Struggle for Freedom"*, Bharatiya Vidya Bhavan, Bombay.

Menon, Madhav Dr. N.R. (1988), *"Social Justice and Social Process in India"* (Indian Academy of Social Sciences, India).

Moffatt, Michael (1979), *"An Untouchable Community in South India: Structure and Consensus"*, Princeton University Press, Princeton.

Moon, Vasant (1982), *"Dr. Babasaheb Ambedkar : Writings and Speeches"*, Vol. II, Education Department, Maharashtra.

Murgar, L. (1991), *"Dalit panther Movement in Maharashtra"*, Popular Prakashan, Bombay.

Narayanan, R.P. (1986), "Reservation in Politics and the Scheduled Castes Elite" in *Vimal P. Shah and Binod C. Agarwal (Ed) Reservation: Policy, Programme and Issues,* Rawat, Jaipur.

Natarajan, S. (1962), *"A Century of Social Reform in India"*–Asia Publishing House, Bombay.

Omvedit, Gail–*"Dalit and Democratic Revolution: Dr. Ambedkar and Dalit Movementsion Colonial India"*, Sage, New Delhi.

Paranjpe, A.C. (1970), *"Caste, Prejudice and the Individual"*, Lalvani, Bombay.

Parvathamma, C. (1984), *"Scheduled Castes and Scheduled Tribes"*, Ashish, New Delhi.

Parvathamma, C. (1987), *"Scheduled Castes : At the Cross Roads"*, Ashish, New Delhi.

Patil, V.T. (1995), *"Studies in Ambedkar"* (Devika Publications, New Delhi).

Patwardhan, S. (1973), *"Change among India's Harijans: Maharashtra–A Case Study"*, Orient Longman, New Delhi.

Pradhan, Atul Chandra (1986), *"The Emergence of the Depressed Classes"*, Bookland International, Bhubaneshwar.

Rajashekaraiah, A.M. (1989), *"B.R. Ambedkar: The Quest for Social Justice"* (Publishing House, New Delhi).

Ram, Nandu–"Law and the Atrocities on the Weaker Sections in India" in *R.G. Singh (Ed)–The Depressed Classes of India: Problems and Perspectives*, B.R. Publishing Corporation, New Delhi.

Rangari, A.D. (1984), *"Indian Caste System and Education"*, Deep and Deep Publications, New Delhi.

Sachindanand (1977), *"The Harijan Elite: A Study of their Status, Networks Mobility and Role in Social Transformation"*, Thomson, Faridabad.

Sanyal S. and Roy Burman, B.K. (1970), *"Social Mobility Movements Among Scheduled Castes and Scheduled Tribes of India"*, Government of India Publications, New Delhi.

Saraf, D.N. (1986), *"Social Policy, Law & Protection of Weaker Sections of Society"* (Eastern Book Company).

Seth, V.N. (1987), "Caste System and Status Change: A Study of Harijan Protest in Banda" in *Satish K. Sharma (Ed) Reform, Protest and Social change*, Ashish, New Delhi.

Shah, Ghanshyam (1986), "Protective Discrimination, Equality and Political will" in *Vimal P. Shah and Binod C. Agarwal (Eds)–Reservation: Policy, Programmes and Issues*, Rawat Publications, Jaipur.

Sharma, K.L. (1999), *"Social Inequality in India ; Profiles of Caste, Class & Social Mobility"*, New Delhi.

Sharma, K.L. (1997), *"Social Stratification and Mobility"*, Rawat Publications, New Delhi.

Shetty, K.P.K. (1969), *"Fundamental Rights and Socio-economic Justice in the Indian Constitution"*.

Shukla, V.N. (1994), *"Constitution of India"*, Eastern Book Company, Lucknow.

Singh, K.S. (1993), *"The Scheduled Castes: People of India, Anthropological Survey of India"*, Vol. II, Oxford University Press, Delhi.

Singh, M.(1985), "End of Untouchability–A Legal way ?" in *P.N. Pimpley and S.K. Sharma (Eds)–Struggle for Status*, B.R. Publishing Corporation, New Delhi.

Singh, Paramananda Dr.–*"Equality, Reservation and Discrimination in India"*, Deep and Deep Publications, New Delhi.

Singh, Yogendra (1969), "Social structure and Panchayats" in *M.V. Mathur and Iqbal Narain (Eds)–Panchayat Raj, Planning and Democracy*, Asia Publishing House, Bombay.

Srinivas, M.N. (1987), *"The Dominant Cast and Other Essays"*, Oxford University Press, New Delhi, 1987.

Srinivas, M.N. (1962), "Caste in India" in his *'Caste in Modern India and other Essays'*, Popular Prakashan, Bombay.

Taylor, Carl (1965), *"India's Roots in Democracy"*, Orient Longman, Bombay.

Thurston, E. (1909), *"Castes and Tribes of Southern India"*, Government Press, Madras.

Venugopal, P.–*"Social Justice and Reservation"*, Emerald Publishers, Madras.

APPENDICES

APPENDIX 1

THE SCHEDULED CASTES AND THE SCHEDULED TRIBES (PREVENTION OF ATROCITIES) ACT, 1989

[No. 33 of 1989]

[11th September 1989]

Received the assent of the president on September 11th, 1989, and published in the Gazette of India, Extra, Part–II, section 1, dated 12th September, 1989, Sl. No. 39.

An Act to prevent the commission of offences of atrocities against the members of the Scheduled Castes and Scheduled Tribes, to provide Special Courts for the trial of such offences and for the relief and rehabilitation of the victims of such offences and for matters connected therewith or incidental thereto.

Be it enacted by Parliament in the Fortieth Year of the Republic of India as follows :

CHAPTER - I

Preliminary

1. Short title, extend, and commencement

(1) This Act may be called the Scheduled Castes and the Scheduled Tribes (Prevention of Atrocities) Act, 1989.

(2) It extends to the whole of India except the State of Jammu and Kashmir.

(3) It shall come into force on such date as the Central Government may, be notification in the Official Gazette, appoint.[1]

2. Definition

(1) In this Act, unless, the context otherwise requires:

(a) *"atrocity"* means an offence punishable under Section 3;

(b) *"Code"* means the Code of Criminal Procedure, 1973 (2 of 1974);

(c) *"Scheduled Castes and Scheduled Tribes"* shall have the meanings assigned to them respectively under Clause (24) and (25) of Article 366 of the Constitution.

S.C. & S.T. (Prevention of Atrocities) Act, 1989

(a) *"Special Court"* means a Court of Sessions specified as a Special Court in Section 14;

(b) *"Special public Prosecutor"* means a Public Prosecutor specified as 'Special Public Prosecutor' or an advocate referred to in Section 15;

(c) Words and expressions used but not defined in this Act, and defined in the Code or the Indian Penal Code (45 of 1860) shall have the meanings assigned to them respectively in the Code, or as the case maybe, in the Indian Penal Code.

(2) Any reference in this Act to any enactment or any provision thereof shall, in relation to an area in which such enactment or such provision is not in force, be construed as a reference to the corresponding law, if any, force in that area.

CHAPTER - II

Offences of Atrocities

3. Punishments for Offences of Atrocities

(1) Whoever, not being a member of a Scheduled Caste or a Scheduled Tribe;

(i) forces a member of a Scheduled Caste or a Scheduled tribe to drink or eat any inedible or obnoxious substances;

(ii) acts with intent to cause injury, insult or annoyance to any member of a Scheduled Caste, or a scheduled Tribe by dumping excreta, waste matter, carcasses or any other obnoxious substance in his premises or neighbourhood;

(iii) forcibly remove clothes from the person of a member of a Scheduled Caste or a Scheduled Tribe or parades him naked or with painted face or body or commits any similar act which is derogatory to human dignity;

(iv) wrongfully occupies or cultivate any land owned by, or allotted to, or notified by any competent authority to be allotted to, a member of a Scheduled Caste or a Scheduled Tribe or gets the land allotted in him transferred;

(v) wrongfully dispossesses a member of a Scheduled Caste or a Scheduled Tribe from his land or premises or interferes with the employment of his rights over any land, premises or water;

(vi) compels or entices a member of a Scheduled Caste or a Scheduled Tribe to do 'begging' or other similar forms of forced or bonded labour other than any, compulsory service for public purpose imposed by Government;

(vii) forces or intimidates a member of a Scheduled Caste or a Scheduled Tribe not to vote or to vote to a particular candidate or to vote in a manner other than that provided by law;

(viii) institutes false, malicious or vexatious suit or criminal or legal procedures against a member of a Scheduled Caste or a Scheduled Tribe;

(ix) gives any false or frivolous information to any public servant and thereby causes such public servant to use his lawful power to the injury or annoyance of a member of a Scheduled Caste or a Scheduled Tribe;

(x) intentionally insults or intimidates with intent to humiliate a member of a Scheduled Caste or a Scheduled Tribe in any place within the public view;

(xi) assaults or uses force to any woman belonging to Scheduled Caste or a Scheduled Tribe with intent to dishonour or outrage her modesty;

(xii) being in a position to dominate the will of a woman belonging to a Scheduled Caste or a Scheduled Tribe and uses that position to exploit her sexually to which she would not have otherwise agreed;

(xiii) corrupts or fouls the water of any spring, reservoir or any other source ordinarily used by the members of the Scheduled Caste or the Scheduled Tribe so as to render it less fit for the purpose for which it is ordinarily used;

(xiv) denies a member of a Scheduled Caste or a Scheduled Tribe any customary right of passage to a place of public resort or obstructs such member so as to prevent him from using or having access to a place of public resort to which the members of public or any section thereof have a right to use or access to;

(xv) forces or causes a member of a Scheduled Caste or a Scheduled Tribe to leave his house, village or other place of residence; shall be punishable with imprisonment for term which shall not be less than six months but which may extend to five years and with fine.

(2) Whoever, not being a member of a Scheduled Caste or a Scheduled Tribe:

(i) gives or fabricates false evidence intending thereby to cause, or knowing it to be likely that he will thereby cause, any member of a Scheduled Caste or a Scheduled Tribe to be convicted of an offence which is capital by the law for the time being in force shall be punished with imprisonment for life and with fine; and if an innocent member of a Scheduled Caste or a Scheduled Tribe be convicted and executed in consequence of such false or fabricated evidence, the person who gives or fabricates such false evidence, shall be punished with death;

(ii) gives or fabricates false evidence intending thereby to cause, or knowing it to be likely that he will thereby cause, any member of a Scheduled Caste or a Scheduled Tribe to be convicted of an offence which is not capital but punishable with imprisonment for a term of seven years upwards, shall be punishable with imprisonment for a term which shall not be less than six months but which may extend to seven years or upwards and with fine;

(iii) commits mischief by fire or any explosive substance intending to cause or knowing it to be likely that he will thereby cause damage to any property belonging to a member of a Scheduled Caste or a Scheduled Tribe shall be punishable with imprisonment for a term which shall not be less than six months but which may extend to seven years and with fine;

(iv) commits mischief by fire or any explosive substance intending to cause or knowing it to be likely that he will thereby cause destruction of any building which is ordinarily used as a place of worship or as a place for human dwelling or as a place for custody of the property by a member of a Scheduled Caste or a Scheduled Tribe, shall be punishable with imprisonment for life and with fine;

(v) commits any offence under the Indian Penal Code (45 of 1860) punishable with imprisonment for a term of ten years or more against a person or property on the ground that such person is a member of a Scheduled Caste or a Scheduled Tribe or such property belongs to such member, shall be punishable with imprisonment for life and with fine;

(vi) knowingly or having reason to believe that an offence has been committed under this Chapter, causes any evidence of the commission of that offence to disappear with the intention of screening the offender from legal punishment, or with that intention gives any information respecting the offence which he knows or believes to be false, shall be punishable with punishment provided for that offence; or

(vii) being a public servant, commits any offence under this section, shall be punishable with imprisonment for a term which shall not be less than one year but which may extend to the punishment provided for that offence.

NOTES

Section 3(i)(x) of the Act says that whoever, not being a member of a Scheduled Caste or Scheduled Tribe intentionally insults or intimidates with intent to humiliate a member of a Scheduled Caste or a Scheduled Tribe in any place within public view shall be punishable with imprisonment for a term which shall not be less than six months but which may be extend to five years and with fine. There is no legal infirmity in Sec. 3(i)(x) of the Act to hold that it is oppressive and unconstitutional.[2] In Chandra Poojari V. State of Kar.[3], it was held that unless it is made out that the petitioner was aware of the fact that the complainant belonged to that caste and with an intention to insult him, he used that word it cannot be said that there is *mens rea* on the part of this petitioner to insult him by calling him by that name. Therefore, none of the requirements in Section 3(i)(x) is satisfied.

Section 3 (i)(xi) of the Act says that whoever, not being a member of a Scheduled Caste or a Scheduled Tribe assaults or uses force to any woman belonging to a Scheduled Caste or a Scheduled Tribe with intent to dishonour or outrage her modesty shall be punishable with imprisonment for a term which shall not be less than six months but which shall extend to five years and with fine. Where victim is not a woman belonging to either Scheduled Caste or Scheduled tribe, it cannot be said that the accused has committed an offence as defined in Section 3(I)(xi) of the Act.

4. Punishment for Neglect of Duties

Whoever, being a public servant but not being a member of a Scheduled Caste or a Scheduled Tribe, willfully neglects his duties requires to be performed by him under this Act, shall be punishable with imprisonment for a term which shall not be less than six months but which shall extend to one year.

5. Enhanced Punishment for Subsequent Conviction

Whoever, having already been convicted for n offence under this Chapter is convicted for the second offence or any offence subsequent to the second offence, shall be punishable with imprisonment for a term which shall not be less than one year but which shall extend to the punishment provided for that offence.

6. Application of Certain Provisions of the Indian Penal Code

Subject to the other provisions of this Act, the provisions of Section 34, Chapter III, Chapter IV, Chapter V, Chapter V-A.

Section 149 and Chapter XXIII of the Indian Penal Code (45 of 1860), shall, so far as may be apply for the purposes of this Act as they apply for the purposes of the Indian Penal Code.

7. Forfeiture of Property of Certain Persons

(1) Where a person has been convicted of any offence punishable under this Chapter, the Special Court may, in addition to awarding any punishment, by order in writing, declare that any property, moveable or immovable or both belonging to the person, which has been used for the commission of that offence, shall stand forfeited to the Government.

(2) Where any person is accused of any offence under this Chapter, it shall be open to Special Court trying him to pass an order that all or any of the properties, moveable or immovable or both, belonging to him, shall, during the period of such trial, be attached, and where such trial ends in conviction, the property so attached shall be liable for forfeiture to the extent it is required for the purpose of realisation of fine imposed under this Chapter.

8. Presumption as to Offences

In a prosecution of an offence under this Chapter, if it is proved that:

(a) that accused rendered any financial assistance to a person accused of, or reasonably suspected of committing, an offence under this chapter, the Special Court shall assume, unless the contrary is proved, that such person has abetted the offence.

(b) a group of person committed an offence under this Chapter and if it is proved that the offence committed was a sequel to any existing dispute regarding land or any other matter, it shall be presumed to be presumed that the offence was committed in furtherance of the common interest or in prosecution of the common object.

9. Conferment of Powers

(1) Notwithstanding anything contained in the code or in any other provision of this Act, the State Government may, it if considers it necessary or expedient so to do;

(a) for the prevention of and for copying with any offence under this Act, or

(b) for any case or class or group of cases under this Act, in any district or part thereof, confer by notification in the official Gazette, on any officer of the State Government the power exercisable by a police officer under the Code in such district or part thereof or, as the case may be, for such case or class or group of cases, and in particular, the powers of arrest, investigation and prosecution of persons before any Special Court.

(2) All officers of police and all other officers of Government shall assist the officer referred to in sub section [1] in the execution of the provisions of this Act or any rule, scheme or order made under thereunder.

(3) The provisions of the code shall, so far as may be, apply to the exercise of the powers by an officer under sub-section (1).

CHAPTER - III

Externment

10. Removal of Person Likely to Commit Offence

(1) Where the Special court is satisfied, upon a complaint or a police report that a person is likely to commit an offence under Chapter ii of this Act in any area included in "Scheduled Areas" or "Tribes Areas" as referred to in Article 244 of the Constitution, it may, by order in writing, direct such person to remove himself beyond the limits of such area, by such route and within such time as may be specified in the order and not to return to that area form which he was directed to remove himself for such period, not exceeding two years, as may be specified in the order.

(2) The Special Court shall, along with the order under sub-section (1), communicative to the person directed and that sub-section the grounds on which such order has been made.

(3) The Special Court may revoke or modify the order made under sub-section (1) for the reason to be recorded in writing, on the representation made by the person against whom such order has been made or any other person on this behalf within thirty days from the date of the order.

11. Procedure on Failure of the Person to Remove Himself from the Area and enter thereon after Removal

(1) If a person to whom a direction has been issued under Sec. 10 to remove himself from any area;

(a) fails to remove himself as directed; or

(b) having so removed himself enters such area within the period specified in the order,

otherwise than with the permission in writing of the Special Court members sub-section (2), the Special Court may cause him to be arrested and removed in police custody to such place outside such areas the Special Court may specify.

(2) The Special Court may, by order in writing, permit any person in respect of whom an order under Sec. 10 has been made, to return to the area from which he was directed to remove himself for such temporary period and subject to such conditions as may be specified in such order and may require him to execute a bond with or without surety for the due observation of the condition imposed.

(3) The special Court may at any time revoke any such permission.

(4) Any person who, with such permission, returns to the area from which he was directed to remove himself shall observe the conditions imposed and at the expiry of the temporary period for which he was permitted to return or on the revocation of such permission before the expiry of such temporary period, shall remove himself outside such area an shall not return thereto within the unexpired portion specified under Section 10 without a fresh permission.

(5) If a person fails to observe any of the condition imposed or to remove himself accordingly or having so removed himself enters or returns to such area without fresh permission, the Special Court may cause him to be arrested and removed in police custody to such place outside such area as the Special Court may specify.

12. Taking Measurements and Photographs, etc., of Person Against whom Order under Section 10 is made

(1) Every person against whom an order has been made under Section 10 shall, if so required by the Special Court, allow his measurements and photographs to be taken by a police officer.

(2) If a person referred to in sub-section (1), when required to allow his measurements or photographs to be taken resists or refused to allow his taking of such measurements or photographs, it shall be lawful to use all necessary means to secure the taking thereof.

(3) Resistance to or refusal to allow the taking of measurement or photograph under sub-section (2) shall be deemed to be to an offence under section 186 of the Indian Penal Code (45 of 1860).

(4) Where an order under section 10 is revoked, all measurements and photographs (including negatives) taken under sub-section (2) shall

be destroyed or made over to the person against whom such order is made.

13. Penalty for Non-compliance with Order Under Sec. 10

Any person contravening an order of the Special Court made under the Section 10 shall be punishable with imprisonment for a term which may extend to one year and with fine.

CHAPTER - IV

Special Court

14. Special Court

For the process of providing for speedy trail, the State Government shall, with the concurrence of the Chief Justice of the High Court, by notification in the official Gazette, specify for each district a Court of session to be a Special Court to try the offences under this Act.

NOTES

The object of establishing the Special Court to try the offences under this Act is for the purpose of providing for speedy trial.[4] Sec. 14 of the Act specifies that the State government shall by notification in the official Gazette specified for each district a Court of session to be a Special Court to try the offence under this Act with the concurrence of the Chief Justice of the High Court.

Special Court constituted under Act 33 of 89 is a Court of the original criminal jurisdiction and it can try often under Indian Penal Code committed in the course of same transformation along with offence under Section 3 of the Act if conditions under Section 220 (1), (3) and (4) code of a Criminal Procedure are satisfied.[5] Special Court being a Court of an original jurisdiction shall have all the power's under Section 190 code of a Criminal Procedure to take cognizance of offence without a committal order.[6] It is not necessary to examine all the witnesses under Section 202 (2) proviso in as much as it is not applicable to special court bring a court of an original jurisdiction enjoying all powers which a criminal court of original jurisdiction enjoys.[7] Committal proceedings are not warranted in a case coming under the Act and triable by the Special Court.[8] Under the Provisions of the Atrocities Act it is the Special Court only, which has been empowered to try the cases, which includes the power of the inquiry also. *State of H.P. V. V.S. Balak Ram and four others.*[9]

15. Special Public Prosecutor

For every Special Court, the State Government shall, by notification in the official Gazette, specify a Public Prosecutor or appoint an advocate who has been in practice as an advocate for not less than seven years, as a Special Public Prosecutor for the process of cases in that Court.

CHAPTER - V

Miscellaneous

16. Power of State Government to Impose Collective Fine

The provision of Section 10-A of the Protection of Civil Rights Act, 1955 (22 of 1955) shall so far as may be, apply for the process of the imposition and realisation of the collective fine and four all other matters connected therewith under this Act.

17. Preventive Action to be Taken by the Law and Order Machinery

(1) A District Magistrate or a Sub-Divisional Magistrate or any order Executive Magistrate or any police officer not below the rank of a Deputy Superintendent of Police may, on receiving information and after such inquiry as he may think necessary, has reason to believe that a person or group of person not belonging to the Scheduled Castes or the Scheduled Tribes, residing in or frequenting any place within the local limits of his jurisdiction is likely to commit an offence or has threatened to commit any offence under this Act and is of the opinion that there is sufficient ground for proceeding, declare such an area to be prone to be an area of atrocities and take necessary actions for keeping the peace and good behaviour and maintenance of public order and tranquility and may take preventive measures.

(2) The provisions of Chapters VIII, X and XI of the Code shall, so far as may be, apply for the purposes of sub-section (1).

(3) The State Government may, by notification in the official Gazette, make one or more schemes specifying the manner in which the officers referred to in sub-section (1) shall take appropriate action in such specified scheme or schemes to prevent atrocities and to restore the feeling of security amongst the members of the Scheduled Castes and the Scheduled Tribes.

18. Section 438 of the Code not to Apply to Persons Committing an Offence under the Act

Nothing in the Section 438 of the Code shall apply in relation to any case involving the arrest of any person on accusation of having committed an offence under this Act.

NOTES

Section 18 of the Act 33 of 89 provides that Section 438 Code of Criminal Procedure will not apply to persons committing an offence under this

Act. The Act is not hit by Article 21 of the Constitution on the ground that Sec 18 of the Act excludes the application section 438 Code of Criminal Procedure.[10]

Sec. 18 of Act 33 of 89 does not unexceptionally bar grant of anticipatory bail when the offence punishable under the Act is alleged in the complaint.[11]

Where the injuries sustained by the complainant side were simple in nature and the incident took place because of some dispute relating to agricultural land belonging to different caste can be enlarged on bail.[12]

Where a case was registered under the Section 3 of the Act 33 of 89 and anticipatory bail was filed on the ground that he is a juvenile, such application need not be allowed in view of Section 18 of the Act.[13] Where the delay of three days of lodging FIR explained, it cannot be a ground for granting anticipatory bail.[14]

Where there is no evidence that after the release of the accused on bail, either he jumped bail or tampered with evidence and the grant of bail was not challenged by the State, court cannot direct cancellation of the bail in such circumstances.[15]

Where challan was not filed within ninety days from the date of arrest but Magistrate and Sessions Court rejected the bail application of accused and the accused again tried for bail wherein prosecutrix affidavit was found to manipulated and copies of challan were furnished after expiry of the statutory period it was held that the petitioners are entitled to be released on bail.[16] Sec. 18 of the Act specifying that provisions of Section 438 Code of Criminal Procedure cannot be invoked in case of offences under the Act, cannot be said to be violative of Article 14 and 21 of the Constitution.[17]

19. Section 360 of the code or the provisions of the Probation of Offenders Act not to apply to persons guilty of an offence under the Act

The provisions of Section 360 of the Code and the provisions of the Probation of Offenders Act, 1958 (20 of 1958) shall not apply to any person above the age of eighteen years who is found guilty of having committed an offence under this Act.

20. Duty of Government to ensure effective implementation of the Act

(1) Subject to such rules as the Central Government may make in this behalf, the State Government shall take such measures as may be necessary for the effective implementation of this Act.

(2) In particular, and without prejudice to the generality of the foregoing provisions, such measures may include;

(i) the provision for adequate facilities, including legal aid, to the persons subjected to atrocities to enable them to avail themselves of justice;

(ii) the provision for travelling and maintenance expenses to witness, including the victims of the atrocities, during investigation and trial of offences under this Act;

(iii) the provision for the economic social rehabilitation of the victims of the atrocities;

(iv) the appointment of officers for initiating or exercising supervision over the prosecutions for the contravention of the provisions of this Act;

(v) the setting up of committees at such appropriate levels as the State Government may think fit to assist that Government in formulation or implementation of such measures;

(vi) provision for a period survey of the working of the provisions of this Act with a view to suggesting methods for the better implementation of the provisions of this Act;

(vii) the identification of the areas where the members of the Scheduled Castes and the Scheduled Tribes are likely to be subjected to atrocities and adoption of such measures so as to ensure safety to such members.

(3) The Central Government shall take steps as may be necessary to co-ordinate the measures taken by the State Government under sub-section (1).

(4) The Central Government shall, every year, place on the table of each House of Parliament a report on the measures taken by itself and by the State Government in pursuance of the provisions of this section.

22. Protection of Action Taken in Good Faith

No suit, other prosecution of other legal proceedings shall lie against the Central Government or against the State Government or any officer or authority of Government or any other person or anything which is in good faith done or intended to be done under this Act.

23. Power to Make Rules

(1) The Central Government may, by notification of the official Gazette, make rules for carrying out the purposes of this Act.

(2) Every rule made under this act shall be laid, as soon as may be after it is made, before each House of Parliament, while it is in session for a total period of thirty days which may be comprised in one session or in two or more successive sessions, and if, before the expiry of the

session immediately following the session or the successive sessions aforesaid, both houses agree in making any modification in the rule, or both Houses agree the rule should not be made, the rule shall thereafter have effect only in such modified form or be of no effect, as the case may be; so, however, that nay such modification or annulment shall be without prejudice to the validity of anything previously done under that rule.

APPENDIX – II

THE [18]SCHEDULED CASTES AND THE SCHEDULED TRIBES (PREVENTION OF ATROCITIES) RULES, 1989

Ministry of Welfare, G.S.R. 316 (E), New Delhi, the 31-03-1995.

NOTIFICATION

In exercise of the Powers Conferred by sub-section (1) of Section 23 of the Scheduled Castes and the Scheduled Tribes (Prevention of Atrocities) Act, 1989 (33 of 1989), the Central Government hereby makes the following rules, namely: -

1. Short title and Commencement

(1) These rules may be called the Scheduled Castes and the Scheduled Tribes (Prevention of Atrocities) Rules, 1995.

(2) They shall come into force on the date of their publication in the Official Gazette.

2. Definitions

In these rules, unless the context otherwise requires:

(a) *"Act"* means the Scheduled Castes and the Scheduled Tribes (Prevention of Atrocities) Act, 1989 (33 of 1989);

(b) *"Dependent"*, with its grammatical variations and cognate expressions, includes wife, children, whether married or unmarried, dependent parents, widowed sister, widow and children of the pre-deceased son of the victims of atrocity;

(c) *"Identified area"* means such area where State Government has reason to believe that atrocity may take place, or there is an apprehension of reoccurrence of an offence under the Act or an area prone to victim of atrocity;

(d) *"Non-Government Organisation"* means a voluntary organisation engaged in the welfare activities relating to the Scheduled Castes and the Scheduled Tribes and registered under the Societies Registration Act, 1860 (21 of 1866) or under any law for the registration of the documents of such organisation for the time being in force;

(e) *"Schedule"* means the Schedule annexed to the Act;

(f) *"Section"* means section of the Act'

(g) *"State Government"* in relation to a Union Territory, means the Administrator of that union territory appointed by the President under Article 239 of the Constitution;

(h) words and expressions used herein and not defined but defined in the Act shall have the meanings respectively assigned to them in the Act.

3. Precautionary and Preventive Measures

(1) With a view to prevent atrocities on the Scheduled Castes and the Scheduled tribe, the State Government shall:

(i) identify the area where it has reason to believe that atrocities may take place or there is an apprehension of reoccurrence of an offence under the Act;

(ii) order the District Magistrate and Superintendent of Police or any other officer to visit the identified are and review the law and order situation;

(iii) if deem necessary, in the identified area cancel the arms licenses of the persons, not being member of the Scheduled Castes and the Scheduled Tribes, their near relations, servants or employees and family friends and get such arms deposited in the Government armory;

(iv) seize all illegal fire arms and prohibit any illegal manufacture of fire arms;

(v) with a view to ensure safety of a person and property, if deem necessary provide arms licenses to the members of the Scheduled Castes and the Scheduled Tribes;

(vi) constitute a high power State level committee, district and divisional level committees or such number of other committees as deem proper and necessary for assisting the Government in implementation of the provisions of the Act;

(vii) set up a vigilance and monitoring committee to suggest effective measures to implement the provisions of the Act;

(viii) set up Awareness Centres and organise Workshops in the identified are or at some other place to educate the persons belonging to the Scheduled Castes and the Scheduled Tribes about their rights and protections available to them under the provisions of various Central and State enactments or rules, regulations and schemes framed thereunder;

(ix) encourage Non-Government Organisations for establishing and maintaining Awareness Centres and organising Workshops and provide them necessary financial and other sort of assistance;

(x) deploy special police force in the identified area;

(xi) by the end of every quarter, review the law and order situation, functioning of different committees, performance of Special Public Prosecutors, Investigating Officers and other Officers responsible for implementing the provision of the Act and the cases registered under the Act.

4. Supervision of Prosecution and Submission of Report

(1) The State Government on the recommendation of the District Magistrate shall prepare for each district a panel of such number of eminent senior advocates who have been in practice not less than seven years, as it may deem necessary for conducting cases in the Special Courts. Similarly, in consultation with the Director Prosecutor incharge of the prosecution, a panel of such number of Public Prosecutions as it may deem necessary for conducting cases in the Special Courts, shall also be specified. Both these panels shall be notified in the Official Gazette of the State and shall remain in force for a period of three years.

(2) The District Magistrate and the Director of Prosecution incharge of the prosecution shall review at least twice in a calendar year, in the month of January and July, performance of Special Public Prosecutors so specified or appointed and submit a report to the State Government.

(3) If the State Government is satisfied or has reasons to believe that a Special Public Prosecution so appointed on specified has not conducted the case to the best of his ability and with due care and caution, his name may be, for reasons to be recorded in writing, denotified.

(4) The District magistrate and the Officer-in-charge of the prosecution at the District level, shall review the position of the cases registered under the Act and submit a monthly report on or before 20th day of each subsequent month to the Director of Prosecution and the State Government. This report shall specify the actions taken / proposed to be taken in respect of investigation and prosecution of each case.

(5) Notwithstanding anything contained in the sub rule (1), the District Magistrate or the Sub-Divisional Magistrate may, if deem necessary or if so desired by the victims of the atrocity, engage an eminent Senior Advocate for conducting cases in the Special Courts on such payment of fees as he may consider appropriate.

(6) Payment of fees to the Special Public Prosecutor shall be fixed by the State Government on a scale higher than the other panel advocates in the State.

5. Information to Police Officer-in-chare of a Station

(1) Every information relating to the commission of an offence under the Act, if given orally or an officer-in-charge of a police station shall be reduced to writing by him under his direction, and be read over to the informant, and every such information, whether given in writing or reduced to writings as aforesaid, shall be signed by the persons giving it, and the substance thereof shall be entered in a book to be maintained by that police station.

(2) A copy of the information as so recorded under sub-rule (1) above shall be given forthwith, free of cost, to the informant.

(3) Any person aggrieved by a refusal on the part of an officer-in-charge f a police station to record the information referred to in sub-rule (1) may send the substance of such information, in writing and by post, to the Superintendent of Police concerned who after investigation either by himself or by a police officer not below the rank of Deputy Superintendent of Police, shall make an order in writing to the officer-in-charge of the concerned police station to enter the substance of that information to be entered in the book maintained by that police station.

6. Spot Inspection by Officers

(1) Whenever the District Magistrate or the Sub-Divisional Magistrate or any other executive Magistrate or any police officer not below the rank of Deputy Superintendent of Police receives an information from any person or upon his own knowledge that an atrocity has been committed on the members of the Scheduled Castes or the Scheduled Tribes within his jurisdiction, he shall immediately himself visit the place of occurrence to assess the extent of atrocity, loss of life, loss and damage to the property and submit a report forthwith to the State Government.

(2) The District Magistrate or the Sub-Divisional Magistrate or any other Executive Magistrate or the Superintendent of Police, Deputy Superintendent of Police after inspecting the place or the area shall on the spot:

(i) draw a list of victims, their family members and dependents entitled for relief;

(ii) prepare a detailed report of the extent of atrocity loss and damage to the property of the victims;

(iii) order for intensive police patrolling in the area;

(iv) take effective and necessary steps to provide protection to the witnesses and other sympathisers of the victims;

(v) provide immediate relief to the victims.

7. Investigating Officer

(1) An offence committed under the Act shall be investigated by a police officer not below the rank of a Deputy Superintendent of Police. The investigating officer shall be appointed by the State Government and the director General of Police, Superintendent of Police after taking into account his past experience, sense of ability and justice to perceive the implications of the case and investigate it along with right lines within the shortest possible time.

(2) The investigating officer so appointed under sub-rule (1) shall complete the investigation on top priority within thirty days and submit the report to the Superintendent of Police who in turn will immediately forward the report to the Director General of Police of the State Government.

(3) The Home Secretary and the Social Welfare Secretary to the State Government, Director of Prosecution, the Officer-in-charge of Prosecution and the Director General of Police shall review by the end of every quarter the position of all investigations cone by the investigating officer.

8. Setting up of the Scheduled Castes and the Scheduled Tribes Protection Cell

(1) The State Government shall set up a Scheduled Caste and the Scheduled Tribe Protection Cell at the State headquarters under the charge of the Director of Police Inspector General of Police. The Cell shall be responsible for:

(i) conducting survey of the identified area;

(ii) maintaining public order and tranquility in the identified area;

(iii) recommending to the State Government for deployment of special police force or establishment of special police post in the identified area;

(iv) making investigations about the probable causes leading to an offence under the Act;

(v) restoring the feeling of security amongst the members of the Scheduled Castes and the Scheduled Tribes;

(vi) informing the nodal officer and special officer about he law and order situation in the identified area;

(vii) making enquiries about the investigation and spot inspections conducted by various officers;

(viii) making enquiries about the action taken by the Superintendent of Police in the cases where an offence in charge of the police station has refused to enter an information in a book to be maintained by that police station under the sub-rule (3) of the Rule 5;

(ix) making enquiries about the willful negligence by the public servant;

(x) reviewing the position of cases registered under the Act; and

(xi) submitting a monthly report on or before 20th day of each subsequent month to the State Government nodal officer about the action taken or proposed to be taken in respect of the above.

9. Nomination of Nodal Officer

The State Government shall nominate a nodal officer of the level of a Secretary to the Government preferably belonging to the Scheduled Castes or the Scheduled Tribes for coordinating the functioning of the District Magistrates and Superintendent of Police or other officers authorised by the investigating officer and other officers responsible for implementing the provisions of the Act. By the end of every quarter, the nodal officer shall review:

(i) the reports received by the State Government under sub-rule (2) and (4) of Rule 4, Rule 6, Clause (xi) of Rule 8;

(ii) the position of cases registered under the Act;

(iii) law and order situation in the identified area;

(iv) various kinds of measures adopted for providing immediate relief in cash or kind or both to the victims of atrocity or his or her dependent;

(v) adequacy of immediate facilities like rationing, clothing, shelter, legal aid, traveling allowance, daily allowance and transport facilities provided to the victims of atrocity or his or her dependents;

(vi) performance of Non-Governmental Organisations, the Scheduled Castes and the Scheduled Tribes Protection Cell, various committees and the public servants responsible for implementing the provisions of the Act.

10. Appointment of a Special Officer

In the identified area, a Special Officer not below the rank of an Additional District Magistrate shall be appointed to coordinate with the District Magistrate, Superintendent of Police or other officers responsible for implementing the provisions of the Act, various committees and the Scheduled Castes and the Scheduled Tribes Protection Cell.

The Special Officer shall be responsible for:

(i) providing immediate relief and other facilities to the victims of the atrocity and initiate necessary measures to prevent or avoid reoccurrence of atrocity;

(ii) setting an awareness centre and organising workshop in the identified area or at the district headquarters to educate the persons belonging to the Scheduled Caste and the Scheduled Tribe about their rights and the protection available to them under the provisions of various Central and State enactments or rules and schemes etc., framed therein;

(iii) coordinating with the Non-Governmental Organisations and providing necessary facilities and financial and other type of assistance to non-Governmental Organisation for maintaining centres or organising workshop;

11. Traveling Allowance, Daily Allowance, Maintenance Expenses and Transport Facilities to the victim of Atrocity, his or her Dependent and Witnesses

(1) Every victim of atrocity or his/her dependent and witnesses shall be paid to and fro rail fare by second class in express/mail/passenger train or actual bus or taxi fare from his/her place of residence or place of stay to the place of investigation or hearing of trial of an offence under the Act.

(2) The District Magistrate or Sub-Divisional Magistrate or any other Executive Magistrate shall make necessary arrangements for providing transport facilities or reimbursement of full payment thereof to the victims of atrocity and witnesses for visiting the investigation officer, Superintendent of Police/Deputy Superintendent of Police, District Magistrate or any other Executive Magistrate.

(3) Every women witness, the victim of atrocity or her dependent being a woman or a minor, or a person more than sixty years of age and a person having 40% or more disability shall be entitled to be accompanied by an attendant of his/her choice. The attendant shall also be paid traveling ad maintenance expenses as applicable to the witness or the victim of atrocity when called upon during hearing, investigation and trial of an offence under the Act.

(4) The witness, the victim of atrocity or his/her dependent and the attendant shall be paid daily maintenance expenses for the days he/she is away from the place of his/her residence or stay during investigation, hearing or trial of an offence, at such rates but not less than the minimum wages, as may be fixed by the State Government for the agricultural labourers.

(5) In addition to daily maintenance expenses the witness, the victim of atrocity [or his/her dependent] and the attendant shall also be paid diet expenses at such as may be fixed by the State Government form time to time.

(6) The payment of traveling allowance, daily allowance, maintenance expenses and reimbursement of transport facilities shall be made immediately or not later than three days by the District Magistrate or the Sub-Divisional Magistrate or any other Executive Magistrate to the victims, their dependents/attendant and witnesses for the days they visit the investigating officer or in-charge police station or hospital authorities or Superintendent of Police, Deputy Superintendent of Police or District Magistrate or any other Executive Magistrate or any other officer concerned or the Special Court.

(7) When an offence has been committed under Section 3 of the Act, the District Magistrate or the Sub-Divisional Magistrate or any other Executive Magistrate shall reimburse the payment of medicines, special medical consultation, blood transfusion, replacement of essential clothing, meals and fruits provided to the victim(s) of atrocity.

12. Measures to be taken by the District Administration

(1) The District Magistrate and the Superintendent of Police shall visit the place or area where the atrocity has been committed to assess the loss of life and damage to the property and draw a list of victims, their family members and dependents entitled for relief.

(2) Superintendent of Police shall ensure that the first information report is registered in the book of the concerned police station in the area and take such other preventive measures, as he may deem proper and necessary.

(3) The Superintendent of Police, after spot inspection, shall immediately appoint an investigation officer and deploy such police force in the area and take such other preventive measures as he may deem proper and necessary.

(4) The District Magistrate or the Sub-Divisional Magistrate or any other Executive Magistrate shall make arrangements fro providing immediate relief in cash or in kind or both to the victims of atrocity,

their family members and dependents according to the scale as in the schedule annexed to these Rules (Annexure–I read with Annexure–II). Such immediate relief shall also include food, water, clothing, shelter, medical aid, transport facilities and essential items necessary for human beings.

(5) The relief provided to the victim of the atrocity or his/her dependent under sub-rule (4) in respect of injury to or death of, or damage to property shall be in addition to any other right to claim compensation in respect thereof under any other law fro the time being in force.

(6) The relief and rehabilitation facilities mentioned in the sub-rule (4) above shall be provided by the District Magistrate or the Sub-Divisional Magistrate or any other Executive Magistrate in accordance to the scales provided in the schedule annexed to these rules.

(7) A report of the relief and the rehabilitation facilities provided to the victims shall also be forwarded to the Special Court by the District Magistrate or the Sub-Divisional Magistrate or the Executive Magistrate or the superintendent of Police. In case the Special is satisfied that the payment of relief was not made to the victim or his/her dependent in time or amount or relief or compensation was not sufficient or only a part of payment of relief or compensation was made, it may order for making in full or part the payment of relief or any other kind of assistance.

13. Selection of Officers and other State Members for Completing the Work Relating to Atrocity

(1) The State Government shall ensure that the administrative officers and other staff members to be appointed in an area prone to atrocity shall have the right aptitude and understanding of the problems of the Scheduled Castes and the Scheduled Tribes.

(2) It shall also be ensured by the State Government that persons from the Scheduled Castes and the Scheduled Tribes are adequately represented in the administration and in the police force at all levels, particularly at the level of police posts and police station.

14. Specific Responsibility of the State Government

The State Government shall make necessary provisions in its annual budget for providing relief and rehabilitation facilities to the victims of atrocity. It shall review atleast twice in a calendar year, in the month of January and July, the performance of the Special Public Prosecution specified or appointed under section 15 of the Act, various report received, investigations made and preventive measures taken by the District Magistrate, Sub-Divisional Magistrate and Superintendent of Police, relief and rehabilitation facilities provided to the victims and the reports in respect of lapses on behalf of the concerned officers.

15. Contingency Plan by the State Government

(1) State Government shall prepare a model contingency plan for implementing the provisions of the Act and notify the same in the Official Gazette of the State Government. It should specify the role and responsibility of various departments and their officers at different levels, the role and responsibility r Rural/Urban Local Bodies and Non-Government Organisations, *inter alia* this plan shall contain a package of relief measures including the following;

(i) scheme to provide immediate relief in cash or in kind or both;

(ii) allotment of agricultural land and house-sites;

(iii) the rehabilitation package;

(iv) scheme for employment in Government or Government undertaking to the dependent or one of the family members of the victim;

(v) pension schemes for widows, dependent children of the deceased, handicapped or old-age victims of atrocity;

(vi) mandatory compensation for the victims;

(vii) scheme for strengthening the socio-economic condition of the victim;

(viii)provisions for providing brick/stone masonry house to the victims;

(ix) such other elements as health care, supply of essential commodities, electrification, adequate drinking water facility, burial/cremation ground and link roads to the Scheduled Castes and the Scheduled Tribes habitats.

(2) The State government shall forward a copy of the contingency plan or a summary thereof and a copy of the scheme, as soon as may be, to the Central Government in the Ministry of Welfare and to all District Magistrates, Sub-Divisional Magistrates, Inspectors General of Police and Superintendents of Police.

16. Constitution of State level Vigilance and Monitoring Committee

(1) The State Government shall constitute a high power vigilance and monitoring committee of not more than 25 members consisting of the following;

(i) Chief Minister/Administrator-Chairman (in case of a State under President's rule Governor-Chairman).

(ii) home Minister, Finance Minister and Welfare Minister-Members (in case of a State under the President's rule Advisors Members).

(iii) all elected Members of Parliament and State Legislative Assembly and legislative Council from the stage belonging to the Scheduled Castes and the Scheduled Tribes-members.

(iv) Chief Secretary, the Home Secretary, the Director General of Police, Director/Deputy Director, National Commission for Scheduled Castes and the Scheduled Tribes-Members.

(v) The Secretary-in-charge of the welfare and development of the Scheduled Castes and the Scheduled Tribes-convenor.

(2) The high power vigilance and monitoring committee shall meet atleast twice in a calendar year, in the month of January and July to review the implementation of the provisions of the Act, relief and rehabilitation facilities provided to the victims and other matters connected therewith, prosecution of cases under the Act, rule of different officers/agencies responsible for implementing the provisions of the Act and various reports received by the State Government.

17. Constitution of District Level Vigilance and Monitoring Committee

(1) In each district within the State, the District Magistrate shall set up a vigilance and monitoring committee in his district to review the implementation of the provisions of the Act, relief and rehabilitation facilities provided to the victims and other matters connected therewith, prosecution of cases under the Act, role of different officers/agencies responsible for implementing the provisions of the Act and various reports received by the district Administration.

(2) The District level vigilance and monitoring committee shall consist of the elected Members of the Parliament and State Legislative Assembly and Legislative Council, Superintendent of Police, three group "A" Officers, Gazetted Officers of the State Government belonging to the Scheduled Castes and the Scheduled Tribes not more than not more than 5 non-official members belonging to the Scheduled Castes and the Scheduled Tribes and not more than 3 members from the categories other than the Scheduled Castes and the Scheduled Tribes having association with Non-Government Organisations. The District Magistrate and the District social Welfare Officer shall be Chairman and member-Secretary respectively.

(3) The District level Committee shall meet atleast once in three months.

18. Material for Annual Report

The State Government shall, every year before the 31st of March, forward the report to the Central Government about the measures taken for implementing provisions of the Act and various schemes / plans framed by it during the previous calendar year.

APPENDIX – III

THE PROTECTION OF CIVIL RIGHTS ACT, 1995

(Act No. 22 of 1955)

[8th May, 1955]

An Act to prescribe punishment for the [19][presiding and practice of "Untouchability"] for the enforcement of any disability arising therefrom and for matters connected therewith.

Be it enacted by Parliament in the Sixth Year of the Republic of India as follows;

1. Short Title Extent and Commencement

(1) This Act may be called [20][the Protection of Civil Rights Act], 1955.

(2) It extends[21] to the whole of India.

(3) It shall come into force on such date[22] as the Central Government may, by notification in the official Gazette, appoint.

2. Definitions

In this Act, unless the context otherwise requires,

[23][(a) *"civil rights"* means any right accruing to a person by reason of the abolition of Untouchability by Article 17 of the Constitution].

[24][(aa) *"hotel"* includes a refreshment room, a boarding house, a lodging house, a coffee house and a café;].

[25][(b) *"place"* includes a house, building and other structure ad premises, and also includes a tent, vehicle and vessel;].

[(c) *"place of public entertainment"* includes any place to which the public are admitted and in which an entertainment is provided or held;].

Explanation: - "Entertainment" includes any exhibition, performance, game, sport and may other form of amusement;

[(d) *"place of worship"* means a place by whatever name known, which is used as a place of public religions worship or which is dedicated generally to, or is used generally by persons professing any religion or belonging to any religious denomination or any section or for offering prayers therein[26][and includes] –

(i) all lands and subsidiary shrines appurtenant or attached to any such place;

(ii) a privately owned place of worship which is, in fact allowed by the owner thereof to be used as a place of public worship; and

(iii) such land or subsidiary shrine appurtenant to such privately owned place of worship as is allowed by the owner thereof to be used as a place of public religious worship]]

[27][(da) *"prescribed"* means prescribes by rules made under this Act;]

[(db) *"Scheduled Castes"* has the meaning assigned to it in Clauses (24) of Article 366 of the Constitution;]

[(e) *"shop"* means any premises where goods are sold either wholesale or by retail or both wholesale and by retail [and includes –

(i) any place from where goods are sold by a hawker or vendor or from a mobile van or cart;

(ii) a laundry and a hair-cutting saloon;

(iii) any other place where services are rendered to customers]].

3. Punishment for Enforcing Religious Disabilities

Whoever on the ground of "Untouchability" prevents any person –

(a) from entering any place of public worship which is open to other persons professing the same religion[28] of any section thereof as such person; or

(b) from worshipping or offering prayers or performing any religious service in any place of public worship, or bathing in, or using the waters of, any sacred tank, well, spring or water-course[29][river or lake or bathing at any ghat of such tank, water-course, river or lake] in the same manner and to the same extent as is permissible to the other persons professing the same religions or any section thereof, as such person;

[30][shall be punishable with imprisonment for a term of not less than one month and not more than six months and also with fine which shall be not less than one hundred rupees and not more then five hundred rupees].

Explanation: - For the purposes of this section and Section 4 persons professing the Buddhist, Sikh and Jain religion or persons professing the Hindu religion in any of its forms or development including Virashaivas,

Lingayats, Adivasis, followers of Brahmi, Prarthana, Arya Samaj and Swaminarayan Sampradaya shall be deemed to be Hindus.

4. Punishment for Enforcing Social Disabilities

Whoever on the ground of "Untouchability" enforces against any persons any disability with regard to –

(i) access to any shop, public restaurant, hotel or place of public entertainment; or

(ii) the use of any utensils; and other articles kept in any public restaurant, hotel dharmashala sarai or musafirkhana for the use of the general public or of [31][any section thereof]; or

(iii) the practice of any profession or the carrying on of any occupation, trade or business[32] [or employment in any job]; or

(iv) the use of, or access to, any river, stream, spring, well, tank, cisten, water-tap, or other watering place, or any bathing ghat, burial or cremation ground, any other place of public resort which other members of the public, or[33] [any section thereof], have right to use or have access to; or

(v) the use of or access to, any place used for a charitable or a public purpose maintained wholly or partly out of State funds or dedicated to the use of the general public or[34] [any section thereof]; or

(vi) the enjoyment of any benefit under a charitable trust created for the benefit of the general public or of[35] [any section thereof]; or

(vii) the use of, or access to, any public conveyance; or

(viii) the construction, acquisition, or occupation of any residential premises in any locality, whatsoever; or

(ix) the use of any dharmashala, sarai or musafirkhana which is open to the general public; or to[36] [any section thereof]; or

(x) the observance of any social or religious custom, usage or ceremony or[37] [taking part in, or taking out, any religious, social or cultural processing]; or

(xi) the use of jewelry and finery.

[38][shall be punishable with imprisonment for a term of not less than one month and not more than six months and also with fine which shall be not less than one hundred rupees and not more than five hundred rupees].

[39][*Explanation:* - For the purposes of this section "enforcement of any disability" includes any discrimination on the ground of "Untouchability".]

5. Punishment for Refusing to Admit Persons to Hospitals etc.

Whoever on the ground of "Untouchability":

(a) refuses, admission to any person to any hospital, dispensary, educational institution or any hostel [40][x x x x], if such hospital, dispensary, educational institution or hostel is established or maintained for the benefit of the general public or any section thereof; or

(b) does any act which discriminates against any such person after admission to any of the aforesaid institutions;

[41][shall be punishable with imprisonment for a term of not less than one month and not more than six months and also with fine which shall be not less than one hundred rupees and more than five hundred rupees].

6. Punishable for Refusing to Sell goods or Render Services

Whoever on the ground of "Untouchability" refuses to sell any goods or refuses to render any service to any person at the same time and place and on the same terms and conditions at/on which such goods are sold or services are rendered to other persons in the ordinary course of business [42][shall be punishable with imprisonment for a term not less one month and not more than six months and also with fine which shall not be less than one hundred rupees and not more than five hundred rupees].

7. Punishable for other offences arising out of "Untouchability"

(1) Whoever

(a) prevents any person from exercising any right accruing to him by reason of the abolition of "Untouchability" under Article 17 of the Constitution; or

(b) molests, injures, annoys, obstructs r causes or attempts to cause obstruction to any person in the exercise of any such right or molests, injures, annoys or boycotts any person by reason of his having exercised any such right; or

(c) by words, either spoken or written, or by signs or by visible representation or otherwise, incites or encourages any person or class of persons or the public generally to practice "Untouchability" in any form whatsoever, [43][or]

[44][(d) insults or attempts to insult, on the ground of "Untouchability" a member of a Scheduled Castes].

[45][shall be punishable with imprisonment for a term of not less than one month and not more than six months and also with fine which shall not be less than one hundred rupees and not more than five hundred rupees.]

[46]*[Explanation 1]*: - A person shall be deemed to boycott another person who –

(a) refuses to let such other person or refuses to permit such other person, to use or occupy, any house or land or refuses to deal with, work for, hire for, or do business with, such other person or to render to him receive from him any customary service, or refuses to do any of the said things on the terms on which such things would be commonly done in the ordinary course of business; or

(b) abstains from such social, professional, or business relations as he would ordinarily maintain with such other person.

[47]*[Explanation:* - For the purpose of clause (c) a person shall be deemed to include or encourage the practice of "Untouchability" –

(i) if he, directly or indirectly, preaches "Untouchability" or it practice in any form; or

(ii) if he justifies, whether on historical, philosophical or religious grounds or on the ground of any trading of the caste system or on any other ground, the practice of "Untouchability" in any form.]

[48][1-A] Whoever commits any offence against the person or property of any individual as a reprisal or revenge for his having exercised any right accruing to him by reason of the abolition of "Untouchability" under Article 17 of the Constitution, shall, where the offence is punishable with imprisonment for a term exceeding two years, be punishable with imprisonment for a term which shall not be less than two years and also with fine.]

2. Whoever

(i) denies to any person belonging to his community or any section thereof any right or privilege to which such person would be entitled as a member of such community or section; or

(ii) takes any part in the ex-communication of such person, on the ground that such person has refused to practice "Untouchability" that such person has dine any act in furtherance of the object of this Act.

[49][shall be punishable with imprisonment for a term not less than one month and less than six months, and also with fine which shall be not less than one hundred rupees and not more than five hundred rupees.]

NOTES

Where P.W. 1 P.W.2. and respondent , accused belong to one and the same group, shown in the list of S.C., these cannot be any practicing of Untouchability.[51] Where a minimum sentence is prescribed under Section 7 (1) (d) of the Protection of Civil rights Act, it will not be proper to invoke the provisions of Probation of offenders Act.

[51][7-A. Unlawful Compulsory Labour when to be Deemed to be A Practice of "Untouchability"

(1) whoever compels any person, on the ground of "Untouchability", to do any scavenging or sweeping or sweeping or to remove any carcass or to flay any animal, or to remove the umbilical cord or to do any other job of a similar nature shall be deemed to have enforced a disability arising out of "Untouchability".

(2) Whoever is deemed under sub-section (1) to have enforced a disability arising out of "Untouchability" shall be punishable with imprisonment for a term which shall not be less than three months and not more than six months and also with fine which shall not be less than one hundred rupees and not more than five hundred rupees.

Explanation: - For the purposes of the section, "compulsion" includes a threat of social or economic boycott.]

8. Cancellation or Suspension of Licenses in Certain Cases

When a person who is convicted of an offence under Section 6 holds any licence under any law for the time being in force in respect of any trade, profession, calling or employment in relation to which the offence is committed, the Court trying the offence may, without prejudice to any other penalty to which such person any be liable under that section, direct that the licence shall stand cancelled or to be suspended for such period, as the Court may deem fit, and every order of the Court so canceling or suspending a licence shall have effect as if it had been passed by the authority competent to cancel or suspend the licence under any such law;

Explanation:-In this section, "licence" includes a permit or a permission.

9. Resumption or Suspension of Grants made by the Government

Where the manager or trustee of a place of public worship[52] [or any educational institution or hostel] which is in respect of a grant of land or money from the Government is convicted of an offence under this Act and such conviction is not reversed or quashed in any appeal or revision, the Government may, if in its opinion the circumstances of the case warrant such a course, direct the suspension or resumption of the whole or any part of such grant.

Section 9 of the Act deals with resumption or suspension of grants made by the Government.

10. Abetment of offence

Whoever abets any offence, under this Act, shall be punishable with the punishment provided for the offence.

[Explanation: - A public servant, who willfully neglects the investigation of any offence punishable under this Act, shall be deemed to be have abetted an offence punishable under this Act.]

[53][10-A. Power of State Government to Impose Collective Cine

(1) IF after an inquiry in the prescribed manner, the State Government is satisfied that the inhabitants of an area are concerned in, or abetting the commission of, any offence punishable under this Act, or harbouring person concerned in the commission of such offence or failing to render all the assistance in their power to discover or apprehend the offender or offenders or suppressing material evidence of the commission of such offence, the State Government, may, by notification in the Official Gazette, impose a collective fine on such inhabitants and apportion such fine amongst the inhabitants who are liable collectively to pay it, and such apportionment shall be made according to the State Government's judgement if the respective means of such inhabitants an din making any such apportionment the State Government may assign a portion of such fine to a Hindu undivided family to be payable by it;

Provided that the fine apportioned to an inhabitant shall not be realised until the petition, if any, filed by him under sub-section (3) is disposed of.

(2) The notification made under sub-section (1) shall be proclaimed in the area by beat of drum or in such other manner as the State Government may think best in the circumstances to bring the imposition of the collective fine to the notice of the inhabitants of the said area.

(3) (a) A person aggrieved by the imposition of the collective fine under sub-section (1) or by the order of apportionment, may, within the prescribed period, file a petition before the State Government or such other authority as that Government may specify in this behalf for being exempted from such fine or for modification of the order of apportionment;

Provided that no fee shall be charged for filing such petition,

(b) The State Government or the authority specified by it shall, after giving to the petitioner a reasonable opportunity or being heard, pass such order as it may think fit.

Provided that the amount of the fine exempted or reduced under this section shall not be realisable from any person, and the total fine imposed on the inhabitants of an area under sub-section (1) shall be deemed to have been reduced to that extent.

(4) Notwithstanding anything contained in sub-section (4), the State Government may exempt the victims of any offence punishable

under this Act or any person who does not, in its opinion, fail within the category of persons specified in sub-section (1), from the liability to pay the collective fine imposed under sub-section (1), or any portion thereof.

(5) The portion of collective fine payable by any person [including a Hindu undivided family] may be recovered in the manner provided by the Code of Criminal Procedure, 1973 (2 of 1974), for the recovery of fines imposed by a Court as if such portion were a fine imposed by a Magistrate.]

11. Enhanced Penalty on Subsequent Conviction

Whoever having already been convicted of an offence under this Act or of an abetment of such offence is again convicted of any such offence or abetment,[54] [shall, on conviction, be punishable –

(a) for the second offence, with imprisonment for a term of not less than six months and not more than one year and also with fine which shall be not less than two hundred rupees and not more than five hundred rupees;

(b) for the third offence or any offence subsequent to the third offence with imprisonment for a term of not less than one year and not more than two years and also with fine which shall be not less than five hundred rupees and not more than one thousand rupees.]

12. Presumption by Courts in Certain Cases

Where any act constituting an offence under this Act is committed in relation to a member of a Scheduled Caste[55] (xx), the Court shall presume, unless the contrary is proved, that such act was committed on the ground of "Untouchability".

13. Limitation of Jurisdiction of Civil Courts

(1) No Civil Court shall entertain or continue any suit or proceeding or shall pass any decree or order or executive wholly or partially any decree or order of the claim involved in such suit or proceeding or if the passing of such decree or order or if such execution would, in any way, be contrary to the provisions of this Act.

14. Offences by Companies

(1) If the person committing an offence under this Act is a company, every person who at the time the offence was committed was in-charge of, and was responsible to, the company for the conduct of the business of the company, shall be deemed to be guilty of the offence and shall be liable to be proceeded against and punished accordingly;

Provided that nothing contained in this sub-section shall render any such person liable to any punishment, if he proves that the offence was committed without his knowledge or that he exercised all due diligence to prevent the commission of such offence.

(2) Notwithstanding anything contained in sub-section (1), where and offence under this Act has been committed with consent of any Director or Manager, Secretary or other Officers of the company, such Director, Manager, Secretary or other Officers shall also be deemed to be guilty of that offence and shall be liable to be proceeded against and punished accordingly.

Explanation: - For the purpose of this section –

(a) *"company"* means anybody corporate and include a firm or other association of individuals; and

(b) *"director"* in relation to a firm means a partner in the firm.

[56][14-A. Protection of Action Taken in Good Faith

(1) No suit, prosecution **or** other legal proceeding shall lie against the Central Government or a State Government for anything which is in good faith done or intended to be done under this Act.

(2) No suit or other legal proceeding shall lie against the Central Government or a State Government for any damage caused or likely to be caused by anything which is in good faith done or intended to be done under this Act.]

[57][15. Offence to be Cognizable or Triable Summarily

(1) Notwithstanding anything contained in the Code of Criminal Procedure, 1973 (2 of 1974), every offence punishable under this Act shall be cognizable and every such offence, except where it is punishable with imprisonment for a minimum term exceeding three months, may be tried summarily by a Judicial Magistrate of the first class or in a Metropolitan area by a Metropolitan Magistrate in accordance with the procedure specified in the said Code.

(2) Notwithstanding anything contained in the Code of criminal Procedure, 1973 (2 of 1974), when any public servant is alleged to have committed the offence of abetment of an offence punishable under this Act, while acting or purporting to act in the discharge of his official duty, no Court shall take cognizance of such offence of abetment except with the purpose sanction –

(a) of the Central Government, in the case of a person employed in connection with the affairs of the Union; and

(b) of the State Government, in the case of a person employed in connection with the affairs of a State.

15-A.Duty of State Government to ensure that the rights accruing from the abolition of "Untouchability" may be availed of by the concerned persons

(1) Subject to such rules as the Central Government may make in this behalf, the State Government shall take such measure as may be necessary for ensuring that the rights arising from the abolition of "Untouchability" or made available to, and are availed of by, the person subjected to any disability arising out of 'Untouchability".

(2) In particular, and without prejudice to the generality of the provisions of sub-section (1), such measure may include: -

  (i) to provision to adequate facilities, including legal aid, to the person subjected to any disability arising out of "Untouchability" to enable them to avail themselves of such rights,

  (ii) the appointment of officers for initiating or exercising supervision over prosecution for the contravention of the provisions of this Act;

  (iii) the setting up of a Special Court for the trial of offence under this Act;

  (iv) the setting up of committees at such appropriate levels as the State Government may think fit to assist the State Government in formulating or implementing such measures;

  (v) provision for periodic survey of the working of the provision of this act with a view of suggesting measures for the better implementation of the provisions of this Act;

  (vi) the identification of the areas where persons are under any disability, arising out of "Untouchability" and adoption of such measures as would ensure the removal of such disability from such area.

(3) The Central Government shall take such steps as may be necessary to coordinate the measures taken by the State Government under sub-section (1).

(4) The Central Government shall, every year, place on the table of each Houses of Parliament, a report on the measures taken by itself and by the State Government in pursuance of the provisions of this Section.

16. Act to Override other Laws

Save as otherwise expressly provided in this Act, the provisions of this Act shall have effect notwithstanding anything inconsistent therewith contained in any other law for the time being in force, or any custom or usage or any instrument having effect by virtue of any such law or any decree or order or any Court or other authority.

[58][16-A. Probation of Offenders Act, 1958, not to apply to persons above the age of fourteen years

The provisions of the Probation of Offenders Act, 1958, (20 of 1958) shall not apply to any person above the age of fourteen years who is found guilty of having committed of any offence punishable under this Act.

16-B. Power to make Rules

(1) The Central Government may be notification in the Official Gazette, make rules to carry out the provisions of this Act.

(2) Every rule made by the Central Government under this Act shall be laid, as soon as may be after it is made, before each House of Parliament while it is in the Session for a total period of thirty days, which may be comprised in one session or in two or more successive sessions, and if, before the expiry of the session immediately following the session of the successive sessions aforesaid, both Houses agree making any modification in the rule or both Houses agree that rule should not be made, the rule shall thereafter have effect only in such modified form or to be of no effect, as the case may be;-so however, that any such modification or annulment shall be without prejudice to the validity of anything previously done under that rule.]

17. Repeal

The enactments specified in the Schedule are hereby repealed to the extent to which they are any of the provisions contained therein correspond or are repugnant to this Act or to any of the provision contained therein.

Section 17 of the Act deals with repeal.

APPENDIX – IV

THE PROTECTION OF CIVIL RIGHTS RULES, 1977

S.O. 3006 – Dated 15th September, 1977

In exercise of the powers conferred by section 16 –B of the protection of Civil Rights Act, 1955 (22 of 1955), the central Government hereby makes the following rules namely:

1. Short Title and Commencement

(1) These rules may be called the Protection of Civil Rights Rules, 1977.

(2) They shall come into force on the date of their publication in the Official Gazette.

2. Definition

In these rules, unless the context otherwise requires –

(a) *"Act"* means the Protection of Civil Rights Act, 1955 (22 of 1955);

(b) *"Section"* means a Section of the Act.

3. Manner of Inquiry Under sub-section (1) of the Section 10-A

(1) The State Government may appoint an officer not below the rank of a Sub-Divisional Magistrate for the purpose of making an inquiry referred to in sub-section (1) of Section 10-A.

(2) The officer appointed under sub-rule (1) (hereinafter in this rule referred to as the inquiry officer) shall issue a public notice specifying the date, time, place and the purpose of the inquiry and calling upon all the residents of the area in respect of which the inquiry is to be held to furnish such information and material s including documents in their positions, as may be relevant for the purpose of the Enquiry, or

(3) The public notice referred to in sub-rule (2) shall be in the local language or language of the area and the same shall be,

(i) published on the notice board of the office of the District Magistrate, the Superintendent of Police, the Village Panchayat or the Municipal Committee of the area and such other place of the inquiry officer deems fit and atleast in one daily newspaper circulating in the area; and

(ii) Proclaimed in the area by beat of drum in such other manner as inquiry officer may think best in the circumstance to bring the contents of the public notice to the notice of the inhabitants of the area.

(4) The inquiry officer, while making such inquiry shall follow as nearly as practicable, the procedure for summary trials including the recording of evidence as laid down in Chapter XXI of Code of criminal Procedure, 1973, (2 of 1974).

(5) The inquiry officer shall complete the inquiry as expeditiously as possible and submit his report to the State Government within such period, not exceeding six weeks as may be specified by the State Government in the order appointing the inquiry officer.

Provided that the State government may having regard to the nature of the inquiry, extend the period of submission of the report by such period not exceeding two months in total as it may considered necessary.

4. Period for Filling a Petition under sub-section (3) of Section 10-A

Any person aggrieved by the imposition of the collective fine under sub-section (1) of Section 10-A or by the order of apportionment, may within a period of thirty days from the date of proclamation of the notification under sub-section (2) of that Section file a petition before the State Government or the authority specified by it:

Provided that where the State Government or the authority, as the case may be, may entertain the petition after the expiry of the said period, if it is satisfied that the petitioner was prevented by sufficient cause from filing the petition in the time.

(2) The state Government or the authority before which the petition is filed shall dispose off the petition as expeditiously as possible.

5. Report by the Government

Every State Government shall, for the purpose of enabling the Central Government, place the report referred to in sub-section (4) of Section 15-A on the Table of each House of Parliament, furnish to the Government before the 15th day of February, each year, a summary of the measures taken by it under sub-section (1) and (2) of that section during the preceding calendar year and shall also furnish such other information as may be required by the Central Government from to time.

APPENDIX – V

TEXT OF THE POONA PACT

1. There shall be seats reserved for the Depressed Classes out of general electorate seats in the Provincial Legislatures as follows;

   Madras 30, Bombay with Sind 15; Punjab 8; Bihar and Orissa 18; Central Provinces 20; Assam 7; Bengal 30; United Provinces 20; Total 148.

   These figures are based on the total strength of the Provincial Councils, announced in the Prime Minister's decision.

2. Election to these seats shall be by joint electorate subject, however, to the following procedure:

   All the members of the Depressed Classes, registered in the general electoral roll in a constituency, will form an electoral college, which will elect a panel of four candidates belonging to the Depressed Classes for each of such reserved seats, by the method of the single vote; the four persons getting the highest number of votes in such primary election shall be candidates for election by the general electorate.

3. Representation of the Depressed Classes in the Central Legislature shall likewise be on the principle of joint electorates and reserved seats by the method of primary election in the manner provided for

in the Clause 2 above, for their representation in the Provincial Legislatures.

4. In the Central Legislatures, eighteen percent, of the seats allotted to the general electorate for British India in the said legislature shall be reserved for the Depressed Classes.
5. The system of primary election to a panel of candidates for election to the Central and Provincial Legislatures, as here-in before mentioned, shall come to an end after the first ten years, unless terminated sooner by mutual agreement under the provision of Clause 6 below.
6. The system of representation of the Depressed Classes by reserved seats in the Provincial Central Legislatures as provided for in Clauses 1 and 4 shall continue until determined by mutual agreement between the communities concerned in the statement.
7. Franchise for the Central and Provincial Legislatures for the Depressed Classes shall be as indicated in the Lothian Committee Report.
8. There shall be no disabilities attaching to anyone on the ground of his being a member of the Depressed Classes in regard to any elections to local bodies or appointment to the Public Services. Every endeavour shall be made to secure fair representation of the Depressed Classes in these respects, subject to such educational qualifications as may be laid down for appointment to the Public Services.
9. In every province, out of the educational grant, an adequate sum shall be earmarked for providing educational facilities to the members of the Depressed Classes.

APPENDIX – VI

TEXT OF THE EVIDENCE PLACED BY DR. AMBEDKAR BEFORETHE SIMON COMMISSION (INDIAN STATUTORY COMMISSION)

1. The first thing I should like to say is this, the figures of the different Provinces, and the computations, are given on page 39 of my memorandum under the heading "Population of the Depressed Classes in India", and show the figures for different Provinces, giving the population of the depressed classes in each. In fact, if the conference will refer to the remarks of the Director of Census of India, who goes on to say "This, however, must be taken as a low and conservative estimate since it does not include (1) the full strength of the castes and tribes concerned, and (2) the tribal aborigines most

recently absorbed in Hinduism, many of whom are considered impure. We may confidently place the numbers of the depressed classes, all of whom are considered impure, at something between 55 and 60 millions in India proper". Then he gives the figures for each province.

2. I should, therefore, like to point out to the Conference that the provincial figures do not include certain castes, which are, as a matter of fact, Untouchable castes.

3. I do not think that is so in this place, because the figures I have given seem to have reference to the depressed classes as distinct form the hill tribes ad the criminal tribes.

4. The total population classes according to these lists as depressed amounted to 31 million persons or 19% of the Hindu and tribal population of British India. That remark would appear to exclude the tribal people from the depressed classes.

5. One point I wish to mention is this, that the figures from the provincial figures are computed are in the table which deals only with the principle Indian castes. It is not an exhaustive table.

6. I am not accepting altogether he fact that the figure, which I have given in my memorandum, covers the aborigines and the hill tribes.

7. The criminal tribes have so little social intercourse with the rest of the Hindus that there is no basis for any definite opinion on that point, but if they did have such intercourse I think they would be regarded as Untouchables.

8. My point is this, that with respect to the criminal tribes we have no data for forming an opinion as to whether they are Untouchable or not, because there is very little intercourse between the main body of Hindus and the criminal tribes.

9. The first thing I would like to submit is that we claim that must be treated as a distinct minority, separate form the Hindu community. Our minority character has been hitherto concealed by our inclusion in the Hindu community, but as a matter of fact there is really no link between the depressed classes and the Hindu community. Therefore, I would stress before the Conference is that we must be regarded as a distinct and independent minority needs far greater political protection than any other minority in British India. For the simple reason that it is economically poor, and socially enslaved. We claim reserved seats if accompanied by adult franchise.

10. Then we would ask for separate electorates. Further, we would like to have certain safeguards either in the Constitution. If it is possible, or else in the way of advice in the instrument to the Governor

regarding the education of the depressed classes and their entry into the public services.

11. The authority gave two different figures on two different pages. On one page they gave the smaller figure, and they took that up, and as soon as the Report of the Southborough Committee was published we protested against this estimate to the Government of Bombay.
12. I happened to defend a depressed class man in one of the courts, and, to my great surprise, I found that the man had to stand outside the court behind a little window, outside the wall, and he would not come in simply because, he said, "It is all right so far as you are concerned, but after you have left there will be terrible social ostracism if I enter the court".
13. The social ostracism would be that if he went back to the village there would be the boycott of the shopkeepers; nobody would sell him grain. The villagers would stop his dues as a village servant. He would not be allowed to come into the village, not in the centre or in the midst.
14. I do not quite accept the principle or representation of minorities according to population of the legislature as though it was a museum in which we have only to keep so many specimens of so many communities. A Legislative Council is more than a museum, it is a place where, for instance, social battles have to be fought, privileges have to be destroyed, and rights have to be won. Now, of that s the conception of a Legislative Council, I do not think it at all in the fitness of things to confine the minority to proportional representation according to population, that means you are condemning a minority to be perpetually a minority without the power necessary to influence the actions in the minority.
15. Well, I would really insist upon adult suffrage. The lower the franchise the better, on that principle I would accept an lowering, but I certainly would not say I would be content with that.
16. My feeling is that every man is intelligent enough to understand exactly what he wants. Literacy has not much bearing on this point; a man may be illiterate, none the less he may be very intelligent.
17. Even assuming it dies lead to tension I do not see how you can get rid of it. Whether it does lead to tension is questionable, I do not see in any case how you can get rid of it, having regard to the fact that society is divided into classes and communities.
18. As a result of communal representation, the leaders of the communities are less prone to compromise than they would otherwise be. That is my feeling but I do not think it leads to communal riots, which are due, I think, to something very different.

19. The depressed class men are all labourers. I am talking of industry. You have members of the depressed classed who work in villages, for the most part in certain occupations. But are there large numbers of the depressed classes engaged in industry?
20. If minorities put together make up a majority there is no majority ad the question does not arise. There may be class distinctions among the minorities. I can quite conceive the Mohammedans in the Bombay presidency being divided into two groups, one favouring the capitalists and one labourers.
21. The depressed classes as such, of course, are not very much interested in Constitutional questions; they are more interested in obtaining the guarantees and protection they require, under whatever form of Government that may come to be. Therefore, I do not think that the depressed classes as such have any definite views to form of Provincial Government or the form of the Central Government; but, of course, I have my own individual views of the depressed classes themselves. It is on that account that something is said about the Constitution in my memorandum.
22. I think there might be some safeguards with regard to the transfer of law and order. It is not that I object to the transfer; but still I should like some safeguard. I am not certain today what it should be, but there might be with advantage some safeguard in that respect.
23. Speaking only on behalf of the depressed classes, I emphatically maintain that the depressed classes will exercise their vote in a most intelligent manner, speaking for the Bombay Presidency. Having regard to the fact that the cancer of Untouchability is before their minds every minute of their lives, and having regard to their being alive to the fact that political power is the only solvent of this difficulty, I emphatically maintain that the depressed class voter would be an intelligent voter.
24. The depressed classes have been dubbed to be unfit for association because of certain unclean habits. That is the allegation of the upper classes. That is to say, they eat the meat of the dead animals and they are not clean, and so on. In this Presidency during the last two years I started a campaign to purify the depressed classes, so to say, and to persuade them to give up some of their dirty habits. But, to my great misfortune, I found the whole caste- Hindu population up against me when in a manner like this I expected the utmost co-operation from them. But when I began to analyse the basis of their opposition I found that they insisted upon the depressed classes doing the unclean things because giving up doing these things meant that the depressed classes were exceeding their social status and rivaling the upper class. Every sort of pressure, social and economic,

has been brought to bear upon the depressed classes in order to compel them to resume their dirty habits. The officials, who are all caste-Hindus, give no protection to the depressed classes, whose condition has really become pitiable, and all this because they sought to give up their dirty habits. Instead of getting co-operation I find that the members of the upper classes are up against me, and they say "these evil habits of the depressed classes are all insignia of their inferiority and they must remain".

FOOTNOTES

1. Came into force from 30.1.1990 (Vide S.O. 106(E), dt. 29.11.1990). Published in Gazette of India (Ext.) Part II Section– 3 (ii) 29.1.1990.
2. Ravindran Pillai V. Union of India, 1997 (1) ALT (Cri.) 843. See also 1996 (2) ALT (Cri.) 55 Chandramohan V. S.I. of Police.
3. II (1998) CCR 129.
4. 1981 Cr.LJ 876, R. Raju V. State of A.P. AIR 1967 SC 1599, Premnath V. State of Raj.
5. 1993 (1) ALT (Cri.) 52, Inre S.C.S.T. (Prevention of Atrocities Act, 1989.
6. 1996 Cr. LJ 3271 = 1996 (1) ALD (Cri.) 645 D. Reddy V. State of A.P. See 1996 Cr. LJ 3596.
7. 1996 (1) ALT (Cri.) 452 Madhava Reddy V. State of A.P.
8. 1996 (1) ALT (Cri.) 162 Hagendran V. Sarada 1992 (2) KLT 748.
9. II (1998) CCR 591 (DB).
10. AIR 1993 Raj. 177, Jai Singh V. Union of India.
11. 1992 (1) Crimes 1122, Pankaj V. State of Gujarat.
12. 1992 (3) Crimes 478, Mangalram V. State of Raj.
13. 1992 (2) Crimes 934, Prakash V. State of Raj.
14. 1993 (2) Crimes 839, Gordhanbai V. State Gujarat.
15. 1993 (2) Crimes 403, Babaldas V. State of Gujarat.
16. 1993 (2) Crimes 172, Atik Mohd. V. State of M.P.
17. 1995 (3) SCC 221 = 1995 (3) ALT (DN) State of M.P> V> Ram Kishna Balotia See also 1996 Cr.LJ 1613; 1996 Cr.LJ 2743.
18. Gazette of India (Ext.) Part II Section 3(1), dated 31-3-1995 at p. 24.
19. Subs, by Act 106 of 1976, Sec. 2, for 'Practice of Untouchability' (w.e.f. 19-11-1976).
20. Subs, by section 3, Act 106 of 1976, for "the Untouchability (Offences) Act" (w.e.f. 19-11-1976).
21. Extended to Goa, Diu and Daman with modification by Regulation 12 of 1962, Section 3 and Schedule; to Dadra and Nagar Haveli by regulation 6 of 1963, Section 2 and Schedule 1 (w.e.f. 1st July, 1965) and to Pondicherry by Regulation 7 of 1963, Section 3 and Schedule 1 (w.e.f. 1st October, 1963).
22. 1st June 1955, vide Notification No. S.R.O., 1109, dated the 23rd May 1955, Gazette of India 1995, Extraordinary, part II, Section 3, Page 1971.

23. Ins. By Act 106 of 1976, Section 4 (w.e.f. 19-11-1976).
24. Clause (a) was re-lettered as clause (aa) by Section 4, Ibid. (w.e.f. 19-11-1976).
25. Subs. by Section4, Ibid. for clause (b) (w.e.f. 19-11-1976).
26. Subs. by Act 106 of 1976, Section 4 for certain words (w.e.f. 19-11-1976).
27. Ins. By Act of 1976, Section 4 (w.e.f. 19-11-1976).
28. The words "or belonging to the same religious denomination" omitted by section Ibid., (w.e.f. 19-11-1976).
29. Ins. By Section 5, Ibid., (w.e.f. 19-11-1976).
30. Subs. by Section 5, Ibid., for certain words (w.e.f. 19-11-1976).
31. Subs. by Act 106 of 1976, (w.e.f. 19-11-1976).
32. Ins. by Section 6, Ibid., (w.e.f. 19-11-1976).
33. Subs. by Act 106 of 1976, (w.e.f. 19-11-1976).
34. Refer the above citation.
35. Refer the above citation.
36. Refer the above citation.
37. Subs. by Sec. 6, Ibid., for "taking part in any religious procession" (w.e.f. 19-11-1976).
38. Subs. by Section 7, Ibid., for certain words (w.e.f. 19-11-1976).
39. Ins. by Act 106 of 1976, Section 6, (w.e.f. 19-11-1976).
40. The words "attached thereto" omitted by Section 7, Ibid., (w.e.f. 19-1-1976).
41. Subs. by Act 106 of 1976, (w.e.f. 19-11-1976).
42. Subs. by Section 8 Ibid., for certain words (w.e.f. 19-11-1976).
43. Subs. by Act 106 of 1976 (w.e.f. 19-11-1976).
44. Ins. by Section 9, Ibid., (w.e.f. 19-11-1976).
45. Subs, by Section 9, Ibid., for certain words (w.e.f. 19-11-1976).
46. Renumbered by Act 106 of 1976, Section 9, (w.e.f. 1976).
47. Ins. by Act 106 of 1976, Section 9, (w.e.f. 19-11-1976).
48. Refer to the above citation.
49. Subs. by Section 9, Ibid., for certain words (w.e.f. 19-11-1976).
50. 1997 (III) C.C.R. 144 state of Kar. V. Shantappa, See also 1983 (2) Crimes 531. At 533 S.H.O. CID Pondicherry V. Ponnuvel alias Manivelu.
51. Ins. by Section 10, Ibid., (w.e.f. 19-11-1976).
52. Ins. By Act 106 of 1976, Section 11 (w.e.f. 19-11-1976).
53. Ins. By Section 12, Ibid., (w.e.f. 19-11-1976).
54. Subs. by Act 106 of 1976, Section 14 for certain words (w.e.f. 19-11-1976).
55. Words "as defined in clause (24) of Articles 366 of the Constitution" omitted by Section 15, Ibid., (w.e.f. 19-11-1976).
56. Ins. By Act 106 of 1976, Section 16 (w.e.f. 19-11-1976).
57. Subs. by Section 17, Act 106 of 1976 Section 15 (w.e.f. 19-11-1976).
58. Ins. By Act 106 of 1976, Section 18 (w.e.f. 19-11-1976).

TABLE OF CASES

1. A.K. Gopalan V State of Madras, AIR 1950 SC 27.
2. Ahmedabad Municipal Corporation V Nawab Khan Gulab Khan, (1997) 11 SCC 121.
3. Akhil Bharathiya Shoshit Karamchari Sangh [Rly] V. Union of India, AIR 1981 SC.
4. All India Sainik Schools Employees Association V Sainik School Society, AIR 1989 SC 88.
5. Ananti V State of Tamil Nadu, AIR 1995 SC 2114.
6. Anil Yadav V State of Bihar, AIR 1982 SC 1008.
7. Appa Balu Ingale V State of Karnataka, AIR 1993 SC.
8. B. Shah V Labour Court, Coimbatore, AIR 1978 SC 12.
9. Bandhu Mukti Morcha V Union of India, AIR 1984 SC 802 : (1984) 3 SCC 161.
10. Berubari Union & Exchange of Enclaves, R, (AIR 1960 SC 845, 856).
11. Centre of Legal Research V State of Kerala, AIR 1986 SC 1322 : (1986) 2 SCC 708.
12. Chameli Singh V State of Uttar Pradesh, (1996) 2 SCC 549.
13. Consumer Education and Research Centre V Union of India, (1995) 3 SCC 42.
14. Daily Rated Casual Labour V Union of India, (1988) 1 SCC 122.
15. Delhi Water Supply and Sewage Disposal Undertaking V State of Haryana, AIR 1996 SC 2992 : (1996) 2 SCC 572.
16. Dr. Chakradhar Paswan V State of Bihar, AIR 1988 SC 959 : (1988) 2 SCC 214.
17. Express Newspapers (Pvt.) Ltd. V Union of India, AIR 1958 SC 578.
18. Federation of All India Customs and Central Excise Stenographers V Union of India, (1988) 3 SCC 91.
19. Francis Coralie V Union Territory of Delhi, AIR 1981 SC 746.
20. General Manager, S. Rly. V Rangachari, AIR 1962 SC.
21. Hussainara Khatoon V State of Bihar, AIR 1979 SC 1369.
22. Indra Sawhney V Union of India, 1992 Supp (3) SCC; AIR 1993 SC 477.
23. Jagwant Kaur V State of Bombay, AIR 1952, Bombay.
24. Jaipal V State of Haryana, (1988) 1 SCC 354.
25. K.C. Vasanth Kumar V State of Karnataka, 1985 Supp SCC 714.
26. K.S. Jayashree V State of Kerala, AIR 1976 SC 2381: (1976) 3 SCC 736.
27. Khatri V State of Bihar, AIR 1981 SC 928 : (1981) 2 SCR 408.
28. Kendra Pahadiya V State of Bihar, AIR 1981 SC 939.
29. Keshavananda Bharathi V State of Kerala, (1973) 4 SCC 225.

30. Kharak Singh V state of Uttar Pradesh, AIR 1963 SC 1295.
31. Kirloskar Brothers Ltd. V Employees State Insurance Corporation, (1996) 2 SCC 682.
32. Life Insurance Corporation V Consumer Education and Research Centre, (1995) 5 SCC 482.
33. M.C. Mehta V Union of India, (1987) 4 SCC 463.
34. M.R. Balaji V State of Mysore, AIR 1963 SC 649.
35. Madhav V Union of India, AIR 1997 SCW 3113: [1997] 2 SCC 332.
36. Menaka Gandhi V Union of India.
37. Mohini Jain V. State of Karnataka, AIR 1992 SC 1858: (1992) 3 SCC 666.
38. Neeraja Chaudhury V State of Madhya Pradesh, AIR 1984 SC 1099: (1984) 3 SCC 243.
39. P. Rajendran V State of Madras, AIR 1968 SC 1012.
40. Paschim Banga Khet Mazdoor Samiti V State of West Bengal, (1996) 4 SCC 37.
41. Paramananda Katara V Union of India, AIR 1989 SC 2039 : (1989) 4 SCC 286.
42. People's Union for Democratic Rights V Union of India, AIR 1982 SC 1473: (1982) 3 SCC 235.
43. Post–Graduate Institute of Medical Education & Research, Chandigarh V Faculty Association, AIR 1998 SC 1767.
44. R. Chitralekha V State of Mysore, AIR 1964 SC 1823.
45. Rural Litigation and Entitlement Kendra, Dehradoon V State of Uttar Pradesh, AIR 1985 SC 652.
46. S.R. Bommai V Union of India, [1994] 3 SCC 1.
47. Sanjit Roy V State of Rajasthan, AIR 1983 SC 328.
48. Sheela Barse V State of Maharashtra, AIR 1983 SC 378.
49. Standard Vacuum Refining Co. of India V Workmen, AIR 1961 SC 895.
50. State of Andhra Pradesh V Balram, AIR 1972 SC 1875.
51. State of Andhra Pradesh V P. Sagar, AIR 1968 SC 1379.
52. State of Kerala V N.M. Thomas, AIR 1976 SC.
53. State of Madras V Champakam Dorairajan, AIR 1951 SC 226.
54. Sunil Batra V Delhi Administration, AIR 1978 SC 1675.
55. T. Devadasan V Union of India, AIR 1964 SC 179.
56. Umed Ram V State of Himachal Pradesh, AIR 1986 SC 847 : (1986) 2 SCC 68.
57. Unni Krishnan V. State of Andhra Pradesh, (1993) 1 SCC 645.
58. Volga Tellis V Bombay Municipal Corporation, AIR 1986 SC 180: (1985) 3 SCC 545.

INDEX